MOPAR B-Body PERFORMANCE UPGRADES 1962-1979

Andy Finkbeiner

CarTech®

CarTech®

CarTech®, Inc.
39966 Grand Avenue
North Branch, MN 55056
Phone: 651-277-1200 or 800-551-4754
Fax: 651-277-1203
www.cartechbooks.com

© 2012 by Andy Finkbeiner

All rights reserved. No part of this publication may be reproduced or utilized in any form or by any means, electronic or mechanical, including photocopying, recording, or by any information storage and retrieval system, without prior permission from the Publisher. All text, photographs, and artwork are the property of the Author unless otherwise noted or credited.

The information in this work is true and complete to the best of our knowledge. However, all information is presented without any guarantee on the part of the Author or Publisher, who also disclaim any liability incurred in connection with the use of the information and any implied warranties of merchantability or fitness for a particular purpose. Readers are responsible for taking suitable and appropriate safety measures when performing any of the operations or activities described in this work.

All trademarks, trade names, model names and numbers, and other product designations referred to herein are the property of their respective owners and are used solely for identification purposes. This work is a publication of CarTech, Inc., and has not been licensed, approved, sponsored, or endorsed by any other person or entity. The Publisher is not associated with any product, service, or vendor mentioned in this book, and does not endorse the products or services of any vendor mentioned in this book.

Edit by Paul Johnson
Layout by Monica Seiberlich

ISBN 978-1-61325-250-5
Item No. SA191P

Library of Congress Cataloging-in-Publication Data

Finkbeiner, Andrew.
  Mopar B-Body performance upgrades / by Andy Finkbeiner.
    p. cm.
  ISBN 978-1-934709-30-6
  1. Chrysler automobile–Motors–Modification. 2. Chrysler automobile–Performance. I. Title.

TL215.C55F566 2012
629.28'72–dc23

2011026111

Printed in U.S.A.

Front Cover:
A 1970 Dodge Super Bee is fitted with high-performance Baer disc brakes and steel-braided brake lines, and as a result, brake performance for this car improved immensely. This stand-out Mopar B-Body car was photographed at Vintage Autohause & Imports in Amarillo, Texas. Thanks to sales representative Mark Childs who helped stage the shoot. (Photo Courtesy Jerry Heasley)

Title Page:
This 505-inch stroker big-block has been dyno tested and is now ready to be installed. On the dyno, this engine produced 615 hp at 5,800 rpm, which is enough to push a B-Body car well into the 11s a the drag strip. The Edelbrock dual carb intake delivers ample air and fuel for a big motor like this.

Back Cover Photos

Top Left:
A stroker kit typically consists of the crankshaft, connecting rods, and pistons. Some kits also include the rings, piston pins, and bearings to make a complete drop-in assembly. Kits may also be purchased fully balanced and ready to assemble from some vendors.

Top Right:
Keisler Engineering also offers various 5-speed kits, including several based on the Tremec TKO transmission. Keisler offers 5-speed kits for 1962–1974 B-Body cars. (Photo Courtesy Keisler Engineering)

Middle Left:
It's important to have steering/suspension component and wheel clearance. One possible problem with a dropped knuckle is that the lower ball joint is moved up into a location where it can interfere with the rim. Here, a 17-inch wheel has been mounted on the Magnum Force dropped knuckle and the outer tie rod end is very close to the lip of the rim.

Middle Right:
Magnum Force Racing offers coil-over-suspension kits for the 1973–1974 B-Body cars. The Magnum Force suspension eliminates the torsion bars and converts the steering system to a forward-located rack and pinion. (Photo Courtesy Magnum Force Racing)

Bottom Left:
A big brake kit, such as this one, can be built from scratch. Porsche calipers and Baer rotors were used to build this custom brake system. A local machine shop fabricated the hubs and brackets.

Bottom Right:
A slightly different version of the CAP K-frame has motor mounts as well as triangular bracing. Also notice the tow loops, which are welded to the front crossbeam. (Photo Courtesy QA1 Performance Products)

CONTENTS

Acknowledgments 5
About the Author 6
Preface 6
Introduction 7

Chapter 1: Aluminum Cylinder Heads 8
    Lighter Weight 8
    Porting 9
    Conversion Complications 10
    Small-Block Heads 12
    Big-Block Heads 12
    Hemi Engines 13
    Project: Installing Aluminum Cylinder Heads 13

Chapter 2: Upgrade to a Roller Camshaft 15
    Alignment 16
    End Play 17
    Oil Pressure Control 18
    Valvetrain Components 18
    Gear Compatibility 20
    Project: Installing Roller Cams 21

Chapter 3: Engine Stroking or Swapping 23
    Small-Blocks 24
    Big-Blocks 25
    Aftermarket Blocks 26
    Drivetrain Considerations 27
    Matching Top End 27
    Project: Building a 427-ci Small-Block 28
    Engine Swap Guide 30
        1962 to 1965 30
        1966 to 1972 31
        1973 to 1978 32
    Support Systems for Engine Swaps 32
    Modern Engine Swaps 33

Chapter 4: Engine System Upgrades 35
    Performance Intake Manifolds 35
    Carburetor Choices 37
    Wide-Band Essentials 38
    Cooling System Fundamentals 39
    Oiling System Modifications 44
    Oil Coolers and Remote Filters 45
    Oil Pump Pickups 47
    Windage Trays and Scrapers 47
    Steering Linkage Clearance 48

    Dry Sump Systems 48
    Electrical System 49

Chapter 5: Brake System Fundamentals 51
    Master Cylinder Bore Size 52
    Caliper Design, Fixed or Floating 52
    Rotor Size 52
    Piston Area 53
    Matching Brake System Parts 53
    Bias 54
    Proportioning Valves 55

Chapter 6: Brake Upgrades with Factory Parts ..56
    Factory Brake System 56
    Knuckle Interchange 57
    Calipers 59
    Master Cylinders 59
    Brake Pads 60
    Rotors 61
    Stainless Steel Brake Hoses 61
    Power vs. Manual Brakes 62
    Summary 62

Chapter 7: Aftermarket Brake Systems 63
    Street Kits 63
    Drag Racing Kits 64
    Caliper Upgrades for Factory Rotors 64
    Big Brakes for High Speed and Road Racing 65
    Building a Custom Brake Kit 70
    Project: Installing a Custom Brake Kit 74
    Baer Builder Series 75

Chapter 8: Rear Disc Brakes 76
    Design Considerations 76
    Axle Shaft Bearings 76
    Bias 77
    Tuning a Rear Disc Brake System 77
    Master Cylinder Selection 78
    Drag Race Kits 78
    Road Race Kits 79
    Street Driving 79
    Project: Installing a Rear Disc on a Track Car ..80

Chapter 9: Front Suspension Upgrades 82
    Torsion Bars 82
    Shock Absorbers 83

    Ride Height 84
    Upper Control Arms 84
    Lower Control Arms 85
    Strut Rods 86
    Sway Bars 86
    Frame Isolators for Late B-Body Cars 89
    Coil-Over Front Suspensions 89
    Rack-and-Pinion Steering 90

Chapter 10: Rear Suspension Upgrades 91
    Leaf Springs 91
    Shock Absorbers 94
    Sway Bars 95
    Advanced Modifications 96

Chapter 11: Performance Steering Systems 98
    Power Steering 98
    Manual Steering 99
    Quick-Ratio Pitman Arm 100
    Factory Steering System Upgrades 100

Chapter 12: Unibody Chassis Upgrades 103
    Frame Connectors 103
    Torque Boxes 104
    Bracing Systems 104
    Seam Welding 106
    Roll Cages 106
    Race Car Techniques 106
    K-member Modifications 108

Chapter 13: Weight Reduction and Distribution 111
    Front End Weight Reduction 111
    Drivetrain Weight Reduction 113
    Interior Weight Reduction 115
    Weight Distribution 115

Chapter 14: Ride Height, Wheels and Tires 118
    Ride Height 118
    Wheels 121
    Retrofitting Modern Wheels 125
    Tire Considerations 128

Chapter 15: Drivetrain Upgrades 130
    Flywheels 130
    Clutches 131
    Driveshafts 134
    Rear Ends 135

Chapter 16: Automatic and Manual Transmission Swaps 136
    5-Speed Options 136
    6-Speed Options 139
    Gear Vendors Overdrive 141
    Automatic Overdrives 142

Source Guide 143

ACKNOWLEDGMENTS

This book is a continuation of a lifetime of reading about and working on Mopar vehicles. I remember staying up late at night poring over *Mopar Performance*, written by Larry Schrieb and Larry Atherton, as well as *How to Make Your Car Handle*, *Brake Handbook*, and *Mopar Suspensions*. Many of these books are now out of print, and the information is dated, but the approach and the method that those authors used are still something that I follow.

I need to thank several magazine editors who took a chance on me and provided guidance and opportunities to me over the years. Scott Parkhurst at *Popular Hot Rodding* was the first to give me a shot at a magazine article. From there, I was fortunate to work with Rick Ehrenberg at *Mopar Action*, Randy Bolig at *Mopar Muscle*, and Johnny Hunkins at *Popular Hot Rodding*. I'm still working with these same editors today on various projects as we all continue to modify cars and write about our experiences.

I am fortunate to be able to access hundreds of other Mopar enthusiasts at any time of the day or night, on websites such as www.moparts.com, www.slantsix.org, and www.bigblockdart.com. I highly encourage the readers of this book to get involved in the online community. It is an excellent place to connect with other enthusiasts and to ask for help. In addition to asking questions, please share the knowledge that you have learned along the way with others. The online community is a great way for everyone to share knowledge and to help others with their projects.

Tim Werner, with his red 1968 Valiant, was a major help during this entire project. Even though his Plymouth is an A-Body car, I was able to use it as a test bed for many parts, and Tim and I spent a lot of hours out in the shop twisting wrenches. It has been a great experience to go to the track with Tim and watch his Valiant blast down the track at 150 mph. His driving ability was invaluable while we were testing various suspension and brake systems.

I also need to acknowledge the tremendous amount of help that this project received from those listed in the Source Guide. Representatives of these companies were willing to answer questions, provide parts for testing, send pictures, and provide information. Without their help, I would not have been able to cover this subject matter in nearly as much detail.

And, of course, I could not have ever finished a major task like this without the support of my wife, Tami, and our two children, Joshua and Ally. A book requires a lot of time, so there was some family time that went missing while I was busy in the shop or on the computer.

About the Author

Andy Finkbeiner used his paper route money to buy a 1956 Ford F-100 when he was 14 years old. That F-100 pickup was immediately treated to a number of modifications, including the installation of a 351C engine when Andy was 16. Within a few years, he traded the F-100 for a Dodge Coronet with a Max Wedge engine and has been working on Mopars ever since. Andy still has his 1965 Dodge Coronet, but these days it has a 512-ci big-block, a 5-speed transmission, and Viper disc brakes.

Andy has a BSME from the University of Idaho, an MBA from the University of Portland, and a JD from Northwestern School of Law. He owns AR Engineering, which is a company devoted to the design and manufacturing of parts for muscle car era Mopars. He is married and lives with his wife and two children in the Pacific Northwest.

Preface

The intent of this book is to showcase and illustrate a group of performance modifications that the average person can make to his or her B-Body Mopar. The modifications shown in this book are based on an overall goal of modernizing the performance and handling of a street-driven B-Body Mopar. The modifications in this book fall into an area generally described as pro-touring or restomod. The basic concept is to combine the classic looks of a B-Body Mopar with modern technology to have the best of both worlds. This book is not a restoration guide, nor is it about building race cars. Rather, the focus is on combining the power and performance of a newer muscle car with classic B-Body styling.

INTRODUCTION

B-Body models were mid-size Dodge and Plymouth cars produced from 1962 to 1979. The B-Body cars include popular models, such as Road Runner, GTX, Charger, Super Bee, Coronet, and Satellite. The factory made minor changes to the B-Body platform each model year, with major generational changes occurring in both 1966 and 1973. To save space throughout the book, I use the notation "early B-Body" or "B1" for the 1962 to 1965 cars, "B2" for the 1966 to 1972 cars, and "B3" for the 1973 to 1979 cars.

Working with B-Body vehicles can be a little confusing until you become familiar with each generation of the platform. The 1966 to 1972 cars were different from the early B-Body cars in many ways, but a majority of the suspension parts do interchange across these first two generations. The design changes for 1973 were more significant for the B-Body in terms of suspension and brakes. The year 1973 was when the B-Body car moved to a totally different front suspension design with longer torsion bars, taller steering knuckles, and an isolated subframe. These changes substantially limit the number of parts that interchange between the later B-Body cars and the vehicles from the two earlier generations.

Although this book focuses on B-Body vehicles, all of the general principles, and some of the specific content, also applies to the A-Body and E-Body vehicles. The E-Body borrowed heavily from the B-Body for chassis, suspension, and brake components, so many parts interchange between these two vehicle families. Starting in 1973, some A-Body parts, such as disc brakes, also interchange with parts on various B-Body vehicles. FMJ vehicles, such as the Volare, Diplomat, and Aspen, can also share some components with the B-Body vehicles. The FMJ front suspension is unique with its transverse torsion bars, but the steering knuckles are the same as on the B3 units. Therefore, most of the disc brake kits sold for B-Body vehicles actually swap over to the FMJ vehicles, even if they are not marketed in that manner.

There is an excellent list of makes and models in the Mopar Performance catalog that shows which nameplates correspond to which body style by year. Other helpful reference items are the complete selection of Mopar Performance "bibles," including the engine books, *Mopar Performance Parts Chassis Manual*, and *Mopar Crate Motor Installation Manual*. And, of course, the correct service manual for the make and model of the vehicle that you are working on is an absolute necessity.

CHAPTER 1

ALUMINUM CYLINDER HEADS

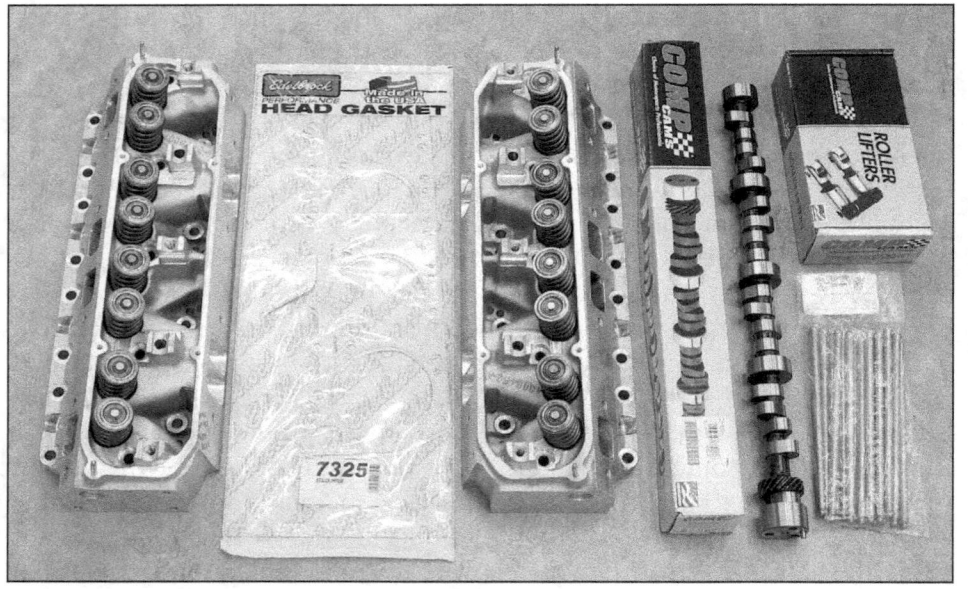
Installing a set of ported aluminum heads and a matching roller cam is a great way to increase the performance of any Mopar engine.

One advantage of aluminum cylinder heads is that they are much easier to repair than cast-iron heads. Welding and machining can repair the severe damage on this aluminum head.

Aluminum cylinder heads were never a production option for the small-block or big-block Mopar engines, but they were used on the race Hemi in 1965. Fortunately, the aftermarket has stepped up to provide several aluminum cylinder head choices for Mopar V-8 engines. Besides the obvious weight savings, aluminum cylinder heads are easier to port than cast-iron heads, and they are easier to repair and modify. Originally, there were concerns about the durability of aluminum cylinder heads, but the alloys used today are quite durable, so these concerns have dissipated.

Lighter Weight

Aluminum has about one-third the density of cast iron, so the weight savings from a set of aluminum cylinder heads is usually quite significant. Typically, aluminum heads are made with thicker walls to compensate for aluminum's lower strength. The thick wall sections reduce the weight savings to some degree, but they can still be significant. Aluminum heads can save up to 50 pounds on a small-block or big-block motor and even more on a Hemi. As discussed in Chapter 13, the weight reduction from a set of cylinder heads is very important because the heads are located above and in front of the center of gravity.

Porting

Although any cylinder head can be ported for additional flow, aluminum cylinder heads are generally much easier to work with than cast-iron heads. Not only does the aluminum material cut easier and faster than iron, but the shavings are not nearly as nasty to deal with. The lighter weight of the aluminum heads reduces shipping cost if your porter isn't local, and the lighter weight requires less effort when wrestling with the heads on the bench. Aluminum cylinder heads are especially well suited for CNC porting because aluminum is much easier to machine than cast iron. The reduction in machining time for aluminum heads reduces the porting cost of what the equivalent port work on a set of cast-iron heads would be.

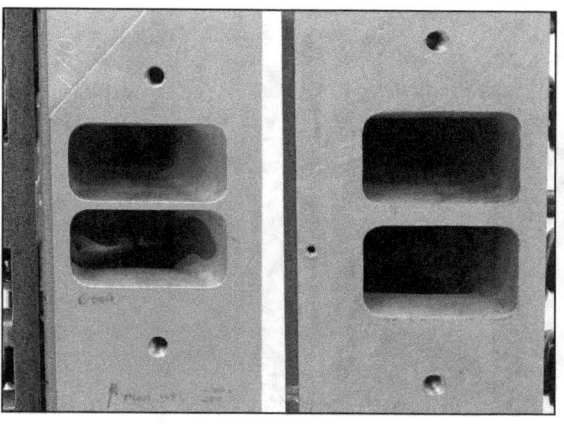

Different port sizes are available when buying Mopar aluminum heads. The ports in the B1 head on the right are much larger than the Max Wedge ports on the left. Large-port heads are generally better suited for high-RPM racing applications, and smaller-port heads produce better performance for low- to mid-RPM street performance.

Port Size Implications

One key element of engine building is to properly match the components, so they all work together to meet the engine's requirements. Picking the proper port size is one part of this exercise. Ports that are too large have poor performance at lower speeds, and ports that are too small limit the power output of the engine. A simple equation, called the McFarland formula, provides some help in picking the proper port size. This formula is based on research conducted on engines, and the research showed that the induction system works best when the air velocity is kept below a critical point.

The McFarland formula calculates where the torque peak for the engine is, based on the displacement of the engine and the cross section area of the port size in the head:

RPM for peak torque = (cross section area x 88,200) ÷ cylinder volume

In this formula, cross-section area is in square inches, and cylinder volume is in cubic inches. The formula, as written, assumes an eight-cylinder engine. The McFarland formula is fairly accurate as long as the rest of the engine components are properly matched. Obviously, a camshaft or a carburetor that is too small can restrict the engine enough to change the engine speed at which peak torque occurs.

The engine in a street car spends a lot of time operating at less than 3,000 rpm, so you should select cylinder heads with ports that are much smaller than those used in a comparable racing head. You might give up some bragging rights about peak horsepower numbers when using the small-port heads, but the odds are that you will be happier with the performance on the street. For racing purposes, the peak RPM point is an important consideration because it needs to be matched with the proper converter stall and the rear-end gear for maximum acceleration. Therefore, the port size of the heads needs to be properly matched with the rest of the engine components as well as the chassis for best results.

Aluminum cylinder heads are easier to port than cast-iron heads, and most vendors offer porting as an option. These Edelbrock Performer RPM heads have been treated to the Stage III CNC porting package from Hughes Engines.

Aftermarket cylinder heads often have a different appearance than original heads. The flat front surface on these Edelbrock heads is attractive, but it can interfere with some alternators. Sometimes, an aftermarket alternator is required to provide adequate clearance.

Aftermarket aluminum heads often have the spark plugs relocated for better combustion. Angled spark plugs on big-block heads increase performance, but they cause interference with some exhaust headers. Therefore, in many cases, you need to consult the header manufacturer to select compatible headers.

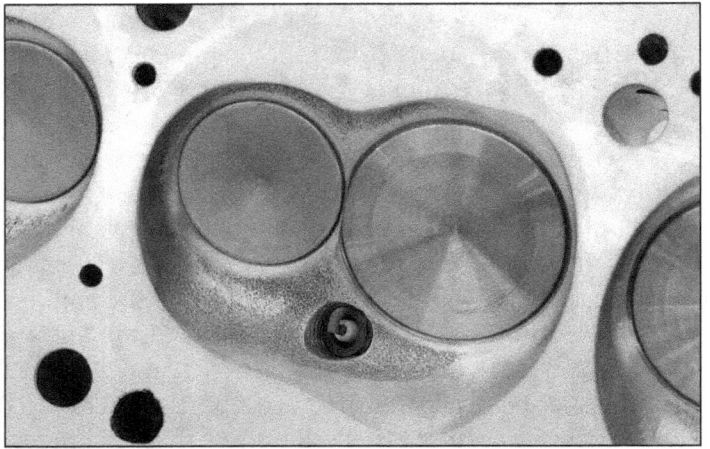

Spark plug fit should always be checked before installing new cylinder heads. Exposed threads in the combustion chamber can cause hot spots and pre-ignition.

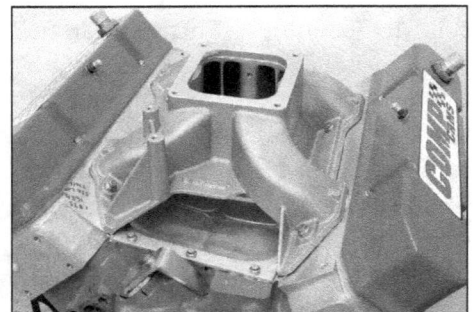

Replacement-type aluminum heads accept original parts, such as the pan-style intake gasket and stock-width intake manifolds.

Conversion Complications

Converting from cast-iron cylinder heads to aluminum heads is a fairly easy process, but it is a little more complex than just replacing one with the other. Most aluminum cylinder heads have slight design differences, which the engine builder must prepare for before starting the conversion. For starters, aluminum cylinder heads almost always use a long .750-inch-reach spark plug, and big-block cast-iron heads use a shorter .375-inch-reach spark plug. More significantly, many big-block aluminum cylinder heads have angled spark plugs, and the OEM heads use straight spark plugs. These angled spark plugs can cause clearance issues between the exhaust headers and the spark plug wires.

Aluminum cylinder heads often have redesigned combustion chambers, which can change the compression ratio of the engine. The different chamber designs can also cause engine damage when used with incompatible piston designs. For example, domed pistons designed for original, open-chambered, cast-iron cylinder heads might not work with newer aluminum cylinder heads. Some aluminum cylinder heads have the valve sizes, valve locations, and maybe even the valve angles changed from the stock locations. If the valve locations have been changed, the

The spark plugs on these Mopar Performance aluminum heads are straight rather than angled. Straight plugs provide additional clearance for factory high-performance exhaust manifolds.

pistons need to be replaced, or else severe engine damage will result.

Port Location

High-performance aluminum cylinder heads can also have the intake and exhaust ports relocated for better airflow. Indy Cylinder Heads, Koffel, Mopar Performance, and Edelbrock, as well as others, offer cylinder heads with raised port locations. Some of these cylinder heads require special intake manifolds; others have been designed in such a way that the original intakes still bolt on.

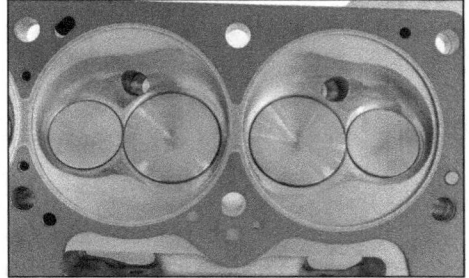

When switching to aluminum cylinder heads, be sure to use a head gasket that is designed for aluminum heads. Verify that the cylinder head surface fully supports the head gasket, and that no portion of the gasket hangs into the combustion chamber.

Exhaust ports on a B1 cylinder head are located quite a bit higher than those in the stock location. Higher ports usually mean better airflow, but finding headers that fit the chassis can be a challenge when the ports are raised this much.

Relocated exhaust ports can mean that special headers are required. Some exhaust vendors, such as TTi Performance Exhaust, have headers that fit the more popular raised-port heads, but other cylinder heads require full-custom exhaust systems. As is always the case, a little research up front can save a lot of expense down the road.

Head Gasket Failure

Aluminum cylinder heads expand much more with temperature than cast-iron heads, so the heads move back and forth on the block each time the engine is run. Cast-iron cylinder heads expand at the same rate as the cast-iron engine block, so the heads basically stay fixed to the block during operation. This lack of relative motion between the heads and the block allowed the factory to use very inexpensive steel shim head gaskets with cast-iron heads. When the OEMs began to produce engines with aluminum cylinder heads, they quickly ran into problems with head gasket failures.

Some multi-layer head gaskets use rivets to hold the gasket together. If the rivets are allowed to catch between the block and the cylinder head, the gasket does not properly seal. When using gaskets like this, you need to perform a careful examination for proper clearance during trial assembly. If this situation isn't corrected, the engine leaks water and may be damaged.

Eventually, the OEM suppliers developed the multi-layer steel (MLS) head gasket, which solved the problem. MLS gaskets are available for both small-block and big-block engines and are highly recommended when installing aluminum cylinder heads on a cast-iron block.

Some racers still use steel shim or inexpensive composition gaskets with aluminum heads, but those solutions are not recommended for any engine that will see extended duty. Just because something works for a few runs down the quarter-mile doesn't mean it will stay together for 10,000-plus miles on the street.

Combustion Chamber Size and Shape

Not only does the type of head gasket matter when changing over to aluminum cylinder heads, but so does the shape of the combustion chamber. Some aftermarket cylinder heads use a stock-type combustion chamber that accepts a replacement-type head gasket, but this isn't always the case. Many cylinder head designers choose to improve the shape of

This engine required a head gasket with an extra-large bore size to properly clear the CNC-ported combustion chambers. The large bore size reduces the compression ratio and leaves a dead space around the top of the piston, but a smaller-bore-size gasket would not have worked with the heads chosen for this engine.

the combustion chamber to produce more power or increase compression.

Any time the combustion chamber size and shape are changed, you must be very careful to double-check the fit of the head gaskets. It is important that the head gaskets do not overhang the chambers because that can lead to rapid failure and possible engine damage. Experienced engine builders usually keep a small selection of used head gaskets on hand so that they can verify the fitment of a gasket before ordering new parts for the engine build. If the combustion chambers in the cylinder head have been modified during the porting process, it is very important to verify that the head gasket fits properly. Often, the combustion chambers are enlarged during porting, and a standard head gasket overhangs into the chamber.

Corrosion

Aluminum is great for reducing weight, but one potential downside is the possibility of increased corrosion within the cooling system due to a chemical reaction between the coolant and the aluminum material. This chemical reaction is called galvanic corrosion, and it occurs any time that aluminum and cast iron come in contact with each other.

The potential for corrosion can be greatly reduced by using high-quality antifreeze and changing it on a regular basis. Modern antifreeze solutions are designed to protect aluminum cylinder heads in automotive applications and should work fine for any street-driven vehicle. Some race tracks prohibit the use of antifreeze because it leaves a slick film if leaked or dumped onto the pavement, so race vehicles need to find another solution to the corrosion problem. If

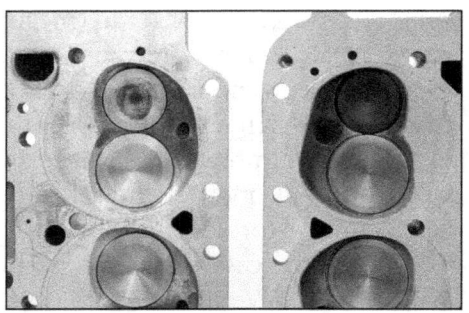
Aluminum cylinder heads are available with different combustion chamber shapes and sizes. Smaller chambers increase the compression ratio significantly. Both of these big-block heads have closed chambers, but the head on the right has a larger quench pad and a smaller chamber than the head on the left.

you cannot use antifreeze, an additive, such as WaterWetter, can reduce corrosion.

Another option is to drain the coolant after each race and store the engine dry, but that is a lot of extra maintenance work.

Small-Block Heads

There is a wide selection of aluminum heads available for the small-block Mopar engine. Edelbrock produces high-quality replacement cylinder heads in aluminum for both the LA and the Magnum motors. Mopar Performance also offers a wide selection of aluminum heads for the small-block, but many of its heads are fairly exotic W-series heads designed for drag racing or circle track use. Indy Cylinder Heads has several heads available for the small-block ranging from its version of the Edelbrock head on up to heads designed for maximum-power-output drag race motors.

Small-block cylinder heads are available for both the production

CNC porting of the combustion chambers is a fairly quick process that equalizes the chambers. If the porting is done correctly, it improves the flame travel and produces more power.

59-degree lifter angle blocks and the more race-orientated 48-degree lifter angle blocks. When choosing an aluminum head for a small-block motor, it is important to consider the size of the ports and combustion chamber as well as rocker arm compatibility. What might seem like a killer deal at a swap meet can turn into a money pit if you have to buy custom pistons, rocker arms, and headers to make the heads work.

Big-Block Heads

Production engines were only available with cast-iron cylinder heads, but the aftermarket has aggressively produced a wide selection of aluminum heads for the big-block. The available choices range from stock replacement heads with standard-sized ports all the way to exotic racing heads with oval-shaped ports that have been raised and spread.

Big-block heads are available in either a standard-port version, where the intake port is roughly the same size as that on a standard factory head,

ALUMINUM CYLINDER HEADS

or a larger Max Wedge–size version. Typically, the Max Wedge–size ports are used for racing, although they work on the street when matched with a 500-ci-or-larger short-block.

Some cylinder heads with very large intake runners, such as the B1 and Predator, are also available for the big-block. These super-large intake ports are designed for use on very large engines and/or engines that are operating at high rotational speeds. Hence, they are not optimized for lower engine speeds, and as a result, they wouldn't perform well for most street applications.

Hemi Engines

The Hemi is the one engine that the factory produced aluminum cylinder heads for during the muscle car years. Aluminum heads were part of the A990 Race Hemi package back in 1965. Those particular aluminum heads didn't stay in production long, but other aluminum Hemi heads were available from Direct Connection for a number of years.

Today, a wide selection of aluminum heads is available for the Hemi engine. Vendors, such as Indy Cylinder Heads, Mopar Performance, and Stage V, have heads that cover the range from stock replacement to 1,000-plus-hp racing heads.

As you can imagine, the weight difference between cast-iron heads and aluminum heads is very significant on a Hemi engine!

Edelbrock's Victor big-block head is a very high-performance design. The intake and exhaust ports in the Victor head are raised significantly to improve airflow. The intake valve size is larger than stock at 2.200 inches.

Project: Installing Aluminum Cylinder Heads

Aftermarket cylinder heads often require special-length head bolts for proper assembly. This stud kit from ARP is designed to fit Indy cylinder heads. ARP also has kits for Edelbrock and B1 heads.

1 Head studs should be lightly lubricated with engine oil and installed finger tight into the engine block. Do not torque the studs into the block, as that can cause damage when the cylinder head is tightened down.

2 The head gasket is slipped into place over the head studs and installed onto the dowel pins. According to the instructions, these MLS gaskets are installed dry. Some engine builders smear a little RTV around the water passages, but Cometic recommends that the gaskets be installed dry.

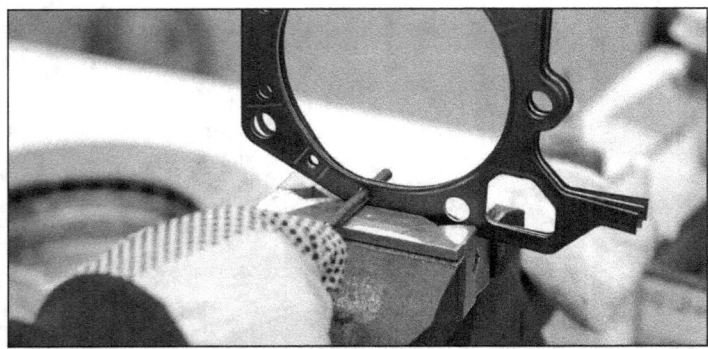

3 Our head gasket could not be installed because the dowel pin holes had not been properly punched. The gasket had to be removed so that the dowel pin holes could be opened up with a file. After enlarging the holes, the gasket was carefully cleaned and then re-installed on the engine.

4 Once the head gasket is in place, the cylinder head can be lowered into place.

5 One item to check before torquing the head stud nuts is the clearance between the header flange and the head stud. On a big-block motor, head studs that are too long interfere with the header flange. The head stud on the right is the correct length and should clear the header flange. The stud on the left is too long and causes interference problems with most headers.

6 The nuts on the head studs must be tightened in the correct sequence specified in the service manual. Head stud nuts are brought to the final torque value in three or four steps. MLS gaskets should not need to be re-torqued.

With the new aluminum cylinder heads bolted in place, this big-block motor is ready for final assembly.

CHAPTER 2

UPGRADE TO A ROLLER CAMSHAFT

The hydraulic roller camshaft is the result of years of passenger car engine evolution. Solid lifters were used originally due to their simplicity, but over time the preference shifted to hydraulic flat-tappets, which were quieter and required very little maintenance. Solid-roller lifters were developed for use in heavy-duty engines but were slow to displace the hydraulic flat-tappets in passenger car engine because of the extra noise and maintenance requirements. Eventually, technology was developed to produce a hydraulic roller lifter, and the car companies began to adopt this technology. Chrysler converted the 318-ci motor to hydraulic rollers in 1988, and then the 360 motor was converted in 1989. Production of the big-block and Hemi engines had been discontinued well before 1988, so they never did receive roller lifters from the factory.

The hydraulic roller lifter offers the power benefits from extra valve lift, quiet operation, and low maintenance that people expect from their production engine. This combination of power potential and low maintenance is desirable to most muscle car owners, so the aftermarket has led the way in designing parts that can be retrofitted to any of the Mopar V-8 engines.

Roller cams typically have an oval-shaped lobe, and flat-tappet cams have a lobe with a more pointed nose. The lobes on the hydraulic roller camshaft on the left have a significantly different shape, even though these two camshafts have similar seat durations.

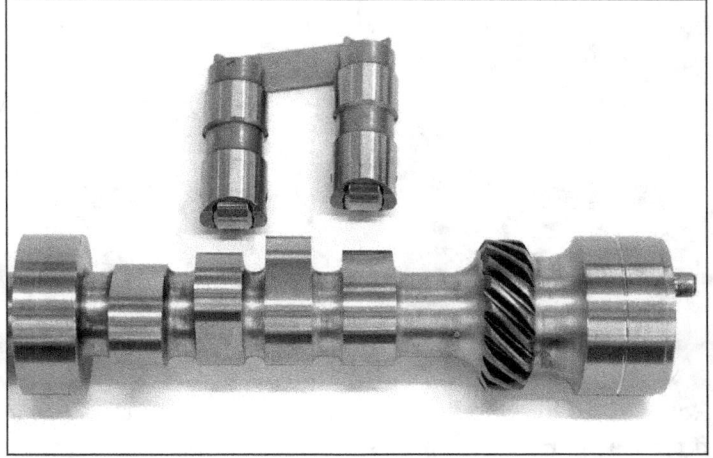

Hydraulic roller cams can be made from either cast material or billet steel. This hydraulic roller camshaft was custom ground from steel billet. The copper coating between the lobes is from the heat-treating process. This race camshaft does not have a fuel pump lobe.

CHAPTER 2

Alignment

The key difference when using a roller lifter is that the roller on the lifter must be kept in alignment with the cam lobe at all times. If the lifter is allowed to rotate even a small amount, the roller wheel gets sideways to the lobe on the camshaft and quickly destroys itself. Another difference between a roller lifter and a flat-tappet lifter is that the roller lifter is longer length and that extra length requires extra room for the roller mechanism. Although it is fairly easy for an engine designer to take these two issues into account when designing a new engine block, it is another issue to resolve these problems when installing roller lifters into an engine block that wasn't designed for them.

Tie Bars

A tie bar links a pair of roller lifters together so that they are kept in proper alignment during operation. The tie bar allows the lifters to move vertically but prevents them from rotating in the lifter bores. This solution works just fine in many cases, but on some engine blocks the tie bar interferes with either the block or with the pushrods. Some of these interference issues can be resolved with a minor amount of grinding, but in other situations certain lifters cannot be used in certain engine blocks.

For example, it is fairly common to have interference issues with the Hemi engines because the taller roller lifters change the angle of the pushrods. Also, the taller lifter bores in most aftermarket blocks can cause interference with the tie bars if the lifters are not designed for the extra height. Another known issue is with the 59-degree small-block race blocks. These Mopar race blocks are cast with extra head bolt provisions in the lifter valley that get in the way of any tie bar. Even with the extra head bolt bosses ground away, there is still material in the valley that interferes with the tie bars. Mopar Performance says that the R3 blocks cannot be used with roller lifters, although a few brave engine builders have gone ahead and ground on the blocks until the tie bars clear. However, grinding that much material away is very risky because you can puncture the water jacket and ruin the engine block if you grind too much.

Comp Cams recently introduced new roller lifters for the small-block that have a redesigned tie bar. This new tie-bar design provides more clearance for the valley wall than earlier designs. Preliminary tests show that these new lifters work just fine in the R3 blocks once the extra head bolt bosses have been removed.

One other option that can be made to work with the race blocks is to use roller lifters that use a keyway in the lifter bores for alignment rather than a tie bar. Jesel makes a keyway type of solid lifter. The keyway lifters are very expensive and are usually only used in higher-end race motors.

Offset Lifters

Several vendors now produce solid-roller lifters with the pushrod cup off center in the lifter. Moving the pushrod cup over to the side helps to provide additional clearance for an oversize intake runner in the cylinder head. The combination of offset rocker arms and offset lifters works to move the pushrods away from the intake runners. By offsetting rocker arms and lifters, the pushrod angle can be reduced and the valvetrain becomes more efficient. If a standard lifter is used with

Roller lifters need to be held in the proper alignment during operation. The lifter pair on the left uses a tie bar to hold the rollers in line with the camshaft lobes, while the Magnum lifters on the right use a "dog bone" bracket for alignment.

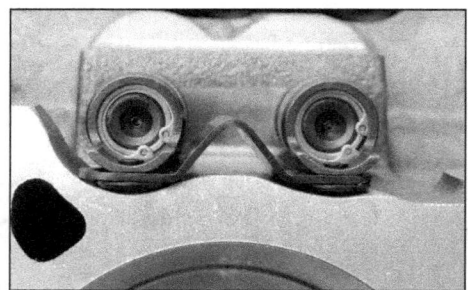

The tie bars can interfere with the cylinder block on some engines. This picture illustrates the difficulty of installing hydraulic roller lifters into a Mopar R3 race block. There is significant interference between the block and the tie bar in this case.

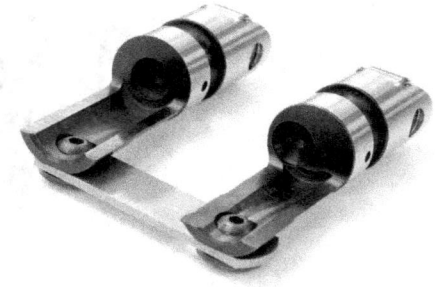

Some roller lifters have the option of offsetting the pushrod cup. Moving the pushrod over slightly, like this, can provide extra clearance for a larger intake runner.

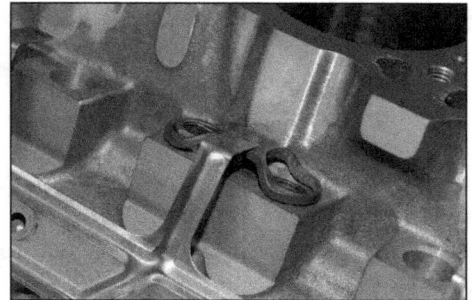

The production Magnum-type lifters can be fitted to the R3 race block once a little bit of machine work is performed on the block. The dog bone doesn't require as much room as the tie bar, so it is less work to adapt the Magnum lifter into these blocks.

Any time a roller camshaft is used in an engine block, there must be some method for controlling the end play of the camshaft. On this big-block engine, a roller button was installed in the timing chain gear. A small gap is set between the roller button and the timing chain cover.

Small-block engines have a thrust plate that controls the camshaft's end play. The thickness of the thrust plate determines the end play.

a highly offset rocker arm, the pushrod has to operate at a steep angle. The valvetrain parts are under tremendous loads in a racing engine, so it is better to keep the rocker lined up directly over the lifter, if possible, rather than have the pushrod operating at an extreme angle.

Magnum Lifters

One option that hasn't been fully developed yet is the use of factory Magnum roller lifters in non-Magnum engines. The Magnum lifters only cost $125 a set, while aftermarket hydraulic roller lifters are usually $400 to $500 per set. With that much of a price difference, it is easy to see why people would like to use the Magnum lifters, if possible. The Magnum lifters require tall lifter bores to work properly, but most aftermarket blocks are designed with taller lifter bores these days. The Magnum lifters use an external dog bone bracket to maintain alignment, rather than a series of link bars. The stamped-steel dog bone can be modified slightly to work with an R3 race block, if you are willing to spend a little time. The engine block also needs to be modified in the valley area to accommodate the dog bones and the valley spider.

Some simple measurements show that the Magnum lifters might also work in the big-block casting produced by World Products. The lifter bores in the big-block engine were not designed for the Magnum lifters, but it appears that there is enough material there to make it work. Some development work would be required because a special dog bone and spider bolt-in solution would need to be created for the big-block.

A dial indicator mounted directly on the end of the camshaft measures camshaft end play on this big-block. This special timing chain cover from Mancini Racing has an access panel for the dial indicator.

End Play

The ability to control end play is another important difference between roller and flat-tappet camshafts. The lobes on a flat-tappet camshaft are ground with a slight taper on them. The force of the valve spring acts on this taper and pulls the timing gear back against the engine block. But the lobes on a roller cam cannot be ground with a taper, because that would quickly destroy the bearings in the roller lifter. Without any taper on the lobes, you can

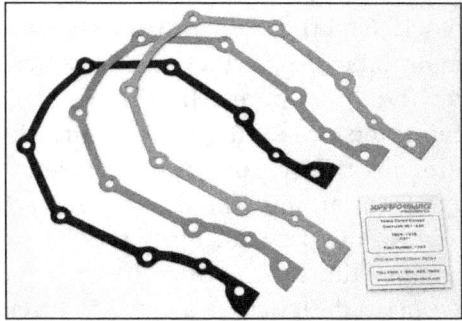

The thickness of the timing chain cover gasket influences the end play of the camshaft on a big-block motor. Superformance makes timing chain cover gaskets in three different thicknesses, if adjustment is required.

use another method to control the end play of the camshaft.

On a small-block engine, a cam retainer plate at the front of the block prevents the camshaft from moving forward, but the big-block and Hemi motors do not have such a feature.

On a big-block or Hemi motor, a small button is installed in the center of the timing gear to act as a stop against the timing chain cover. The button must be precisely machined in order to control the end play to a range of .005 to .010 inch. One complicating factor with the big-block design is that the thickness of the timing chain cover gasket is part of the end-play calculation. Once the end play has been set, replace the gasket with another one made of the same material and thickness, or else the end play changes. Timing chain cover gaskets are available as thin as .022 inch or as thick as .062 inch, so there is a wide range of options available.

Oil Pressure Control

One issue to pay attention to is how the design of the roller lifter works with the oil galleries in the engine block. The Mopar engine blocks feed the main bearings from a main oil gallery, which is intersected by the lifter bores. In this design, the lifters are sitting partially inside the oil gallery, and excessive leakage from around the lifters can lead to low oil pressure and immediate engine failure. Any roller lifter that is properly designed as a retro-fit lifter should work just fine in a production block, but you always need to be concerned with any lifter design that you haven't verified.

There are still several solid-roller lifter designs on the market that result in low oil pressure and possible engine damage when used in a production block. Typically, the race-type roller lifters are intended for a block that has been modified with lifter bushings. Those lifters work fine when used with bushings but do not work in a block that has not been bushed. This concern usually only applies to solid-roller lifters, but you should always verify that the lifter to be used operates throughout the entire range of lift without exposing the main oil gallery.

Pushrod and Roller Oiling

Pushrod oiling is more of a rocker arm issue than a camshaft issue, but the lifter choice is part of the overall solution for effective oiling. Some engine builders prefer to oil the rocker arms through the pushrods, just as Magnum engines do. Using the correct lifters accomplishes this, but you need to be very careful to select the proper parts. Some pushrod oiling lifters are designed to only work with bushed lifter bores, and do not work with the stock lifter bores.

A number of new lifter designs have appeared in the past several years that provide extra oil for the

Pushrod quality also needs to be upgraded when using high-lift roller cams and stiff valvesprings. These 3/8-inch-diameter pushrods from Smith Brothers fit the bill nicely for a street roller camshaft.

roller lifter and/or the camshaft lobe. Several lifter designs now have internal passages that direct pressurized oil into the roller wheel itself. These lifters are designed for various situations, such as street motors that don't have enough splash lubrication to keep the wheels lubricated.

The pressurized oil feed can also be useful in modern race engines equipped with either a vacuum pump or a dry sump system. In that type of motor, there may not be enough of an "oil cloud" floating in the crankcase to keep the roller lifters well lubricated. Using lifters that direct oil to the rollers and to the pushrods reduces oil pressure slightly, due to the extra "leaks" in the oil system. It is normal to see a 5-psi drop in oil pressure when switching over to these lifters. If that reduction in oil pressure causes an issue, the pressure relief spring in the oil pump can be shimmed slightly.

Valvetrain Components

High-performance engines equipped with aggressive high-lift cams simply place too high of a load on stock valvetrain parts, and as a result, high-quality aftermarket valvetrain parts are required for top performance and reliability.

Valvesprings

The extra valve lift and the increased acceleration required to achieve that lift puts extra stress on all of the valvetrain parts, including the valvesprings. Valvesprings rated for use with either solid-roller or hydraulic roller lifters tend to have more seat pressure than flat-tappet springs and usually have a slightly higher spring rate. Valvespring selection is best left to the experts at the

UPGRADE TO A ROLLER CAMSHAFT

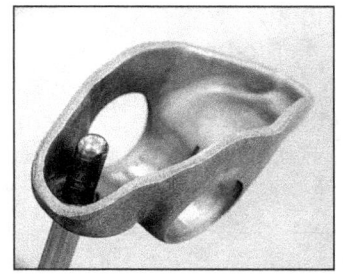

The use of stock rocker arms with a roller camshaft can quickly lead to parts failure. This big-block rocker arm failed fairly quickly after the engine was upgraded with a performance camshaft.

cam company, so be sure to get a valvespring recommendation when you order the roller camshaft.

Over the past decade, there has been a significant shift toward beehive valvesprings, especially for flat-tappet and hydraulic roller applications. The beehive springs are lighter, and their shape gives them additional rocker arm clearance. The beehive shape and the oval wire used to make the springs provide another benefit—reduced valve surge or other such spring behavior—which can cause damage to the valvetrain.

It is fairly common now to use a set of beehive valvesprings as a way to add extra engine speed capability to a hydraulic roller-equipped engine. Where a conventional dual spring might start to float at 6,000 rpm, the beehive spring might continue to operate up to 6,500 rpm. I've had personal experience with beehive-equipped engines where hydraulic flat-tappet cams have worked well past 7,000 rpm. The roller lifters are heavier, so the engine speed limit is usually lower, but beehive springs can still help the situation.

Pushrods

The stiffer valvesprings required to control heavy roller lifters increase the loads on the pushrods. The factory usually used a 5/16-inch-diameter pushrod, but there is typically enough room for a 3/8-inch-diameter pushrod. You need to carefully check over this area during the mockup phase of the engine build, because it is almost impossible to enlarge pushrod clearance once the engine is built without getting metal chips into the engine.

Aftermarket vendors such as Trend, Smith Brothers, and Manton, are pushrod experts that can provide any parts required. A 3/8-inch-diameter pushrod with a .080-inch-thick wall should be strong enough for the majority of street roller camshaft profiles.

A racing engine with high valve lift and extra-strong valvesprings benefits from 7/16- or even 1/2-inch-diameter pushrods. The use of large-diameter pushrods is one of those "speed secrets" that is well documented, but not really well adopted. Amateur engine builders are often surprised at how much of a power increase is possible with stiffer pushrods.

A performance roller camshaft puts additional stress on the valvetrain and requires an upgrade in the components. This small-block valvetrain is upgraded with high-quality beehive springs and stainless steel rocker arms from PRW. These PRW rocker arms are 1.60:1 ratio for a little additional valve lift. Talk to the tech line to be sure your camshaft will work with high-ratio rocker arms.

Rocker Arms

The rocker arms become more important when stepping up to the higher loads and stresses associated with a roller cam, but that doesn't mean that you need the latest trick of the week. The vast majority of OEM V-8 engines sold these days are equipped with roller lifters, and production rocker arms are definitely not "super trick." Nodular-iron rocker arms, such as the ones used on the factory Max Wedge or 340 TA engines, are perfectly adequate for any hydraulic roller combination and should work fine for a mild solid-lifter street roller. Aluminum rocker arms work fine for drag racing, but they can have durability issues on the street with roller camshaft valvespring pressures. For street use, a rocker arm with a bronze or polymer bushing seems to work best.

A roller tip isn't really required with low-lift camshafts, but it is a nice feature when the lift is more than .550 inch. Rocker arms are a poor place to use cheap parts, but super-expensive parts aren't always required, either. Look at the solutions that the OEMs are using, and shop wisely for your application.

Cast rocker arms from Rocker Arm Specialist are an excellent choice for a roller-cam-equipped big-block. These rocker arms are bronze-bushed and have a well-designed oiling system.

CHAPTER 2

A wide selection of rocker arms is available for Mopar engines. These big-block rocker arms range from stock stamped rockers to exotic multi-shaft rocker arms systems. There should be something here to fit the needs of any motor. From top to the bottom, Jesel aluminum, Hughes aluminum, Comp Cams steel, Crane Nodular iron, and stock rocker arm shafts are shown.

Gear Compatibility

Camshafts can be made from a variety of materials including cast iron, austempered ductile iron, or billet steel. Flat-tappet camshafts are typically made from cast iron, and solid-roller camshafts are most likely made from billet steel. Hydraulic roller camshafts are sometimes billet and sometimes a cast material, so it is best to verify with the cam company when ordering. The camshaft material is important because the oil pump driveshaft gear must be made from a compatible material to prevent premature gear wear and possible engine failure.

The gear material used on the production oil pump drives is compatible with camshafts made from a cast material. The stock gear works just fine with aftermarket camshafts that are also made from cast material, but does not work with steel billet camshafts. By looking at the camshaft, you can determine the material it's made of. A cast core shows a parting line, while a billet cam has a smooth finish.

As spring pressures increase, the cam material needs to be stronger, so most solid-roller camshafts are made from billet steel. Some hydraulic roller camshafts are made from cast iron because the spring pressure is less than what is used on a solid-roller camshaft. When the camshaft is made from steel billet, the oil pump driveshaft needs a bronze gear. A composite gear can also be used with a billet camshaft, if such an option is available.

Mopar Performance and Milodon both sell oil pump driveshaft gears for the big-block and small-block motors with bronze gears. Chrysler engineering changed the oil pump gear material on the small-block oil pump driveshaft for the Magnum motors to be compatible with the material used by the OEM hydraulic roller camshafts. That new gear material was also retrofitted to the Mopar Performance oil pump driveshaft assembly (PN P3690715). Therefore, the Mopar Performance drive gear assembly is compatible with aftermarket hydraulic roller camshafts made from ductile-iron material.

The aftermarket has developed composite distributor drive gears for Chevy and Ford motors, but at the present time, this is not an option for the Mopar engines. A trick that is used for some Chevy and Ford motors is to press an iron drive gear onto a billet camshaft. This two-piece assembly provides the strength needed for the roller lifters while still providing a compatible material for the drive gear. At one time Crane made roller cam cores for Chrysler small-block engines using a pressed-on iron gear so it might be possible to still find two-part cores.

Some people report fairly short life expectancy of the bronze oil pump gears, such as only one year of use. Others have reported being able to use the same gear for several years with no wear noticed. With these undocumented examples, so many factors are unknown, such as the number of miles people were driving, the kind of conditions they drove in, and what type of oil they were using. It does seem wise that if a bronze gear is being used on a street engine, it should be inspected on an annual basis to check for wear.

The material of the oil pump drive gear must be compatible with the camshaft material. This hydraulic roller small-block camshaft is a cast material, so it works just fine with a production-style oil pump driveshaft.

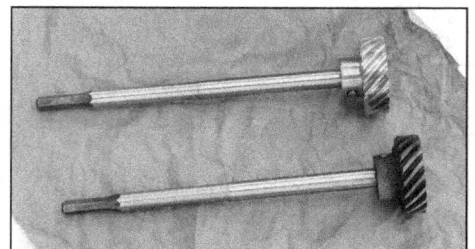

Roller camshafts made from billet steel material require a bronze-type oil pump gear, such as the one shown at the top. The lower gear is made from a production-type cast material and is designed to work with camshafts made from cast material.

Project: Installing Roller Cams, Small-Block and Big-Block

1 Storing roller lifters in oil keeps the bearings lubricated and prevents corrosion.

2 Always verify that the tie bar clears the block. The lifter bores in this Mopar race block are taller than the production block's lifter bores and require extra-tall roller lifters. The tie bar on these roller lifters hangs up on the top of the lifter bores and prevents the roller from contacting the camshaft lobe.

3 A high-quality timing chain is essential with the increased stress of a high-lift roller cam. This Pro Gear chain set from Hughes Engines has seven adjustment locations for cam timing. The Pro Gear timing chain set is well-made and is an excellent design.

4 Once the timing chain has been installed, the camshaft end play needs to be checked. Mount a dial indicator securely to the engine block and position the plunger on the camshaft nose. The camshaft can then be moved back and forth with a small pry bar while the end play is noted on the dial indicator.

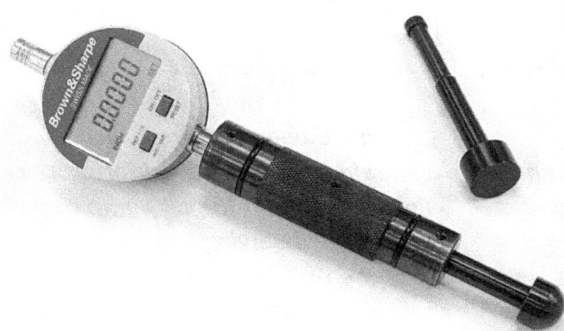

5 Comp Cams makes this simple tool for checking lobe lift. The tool sits in the lifter bore and allows the dial indicator to directly measure the camshaft lobe.

6 With the dial indicator in place in the lifter bore and the degree wheel properly installed, it is a fairly straightforward process to determine the camshaft centerline. The cam card typically provides a recommended centerline for the camshaft.

Installing Roller Cams, Small-Block and Big-Block CONTINUED

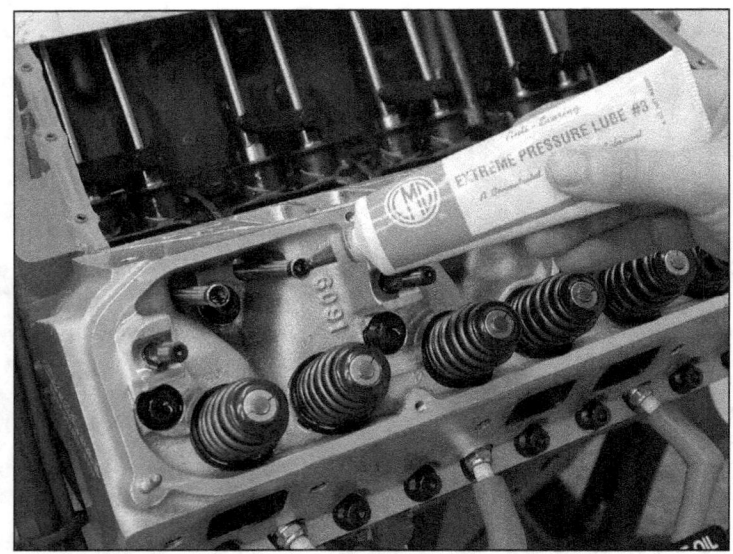

7 Once the camshaft and lifters have been properly installed, the pushrods can be installed. A little bit of high-pressure lube is applied to the pushrod cups to keep the parts lubricated during initial start-up of the engine. Many engine builders use Extreme Pressure Lube #3 for this task.

8 The rocker shafts should always be mounted with studs, rather than bolts, in a performance application. This is especially important with aluminum heads, because bolts can pull the threads out of the cylinder heads. Hughes Engines supplied this small-block stud kit. ARP offers a similar kit for big-block engines.

9 The rocker shaft hold-downs need to be tightened in sequence to prevent the rocker shaft from bending. Once the shaft has bottomed out in all five saddles, a torque wrench should be used to properly tighten the fasteners. Once the rocker shaft has been torqued to specification, the lash can be set.

10 Actual valve lift should always be verified before the engine is started. Carefully inspect the valvetrain operation through the entire cycle for any problems. Common issues with high-lift cams are interference between the pushrods and the head and interference between the rocker arms and the valvespring retainers. Always verify proper clearance at full lift between the retainer and the oil seal, and check for any coil bind issues.

11 Once all mechanical issues have been resolved, the valvetrain can be checked for proper oiling. Slowly turn the oil pump by hand while observing the flow of oil out of the rocker shafts. Each rocker arm should flow an equal amount of oil onto both the valvestem and the pushrod. Proper oil flow is essential. Without adequate oil flow, the valvetrain quickly overheats and seizes up.

CHAPTER 3

ENGINE STROKING OR SWAPPING

As the old saying goes, "There is no replacement for displacement." When working with a B-Body vehicle, there are two choices for more engine displacement. Either the existing engine can be swapped out for a larger engine, or the existing engine can be made larger by boring and stroking.

Increasing the displacement of the engine appeals to some Mopar owners because the engine's appearance can remain perfectly original. The modifications are all internal to the engine block, and therefore, a stealth appearance can be maintained. Of course, the use of aftermarket parts, such as aluminum cylinder heads, high-rise intake manifolds, and exhaust headers, can yield additional performance gains, but those modifications are not required in order to obtain excellent performance.

The small-block and big-block motors have really benefited over the past several years from a large increase in the number of stroker kit options. Both the small-block and the big-block motors have tall deck heights, which make them ideal candidates for additional displacement from a longer stroke. Kits are available that increase the small-block motor from 360 to 426 ci, and the big-block motors can be bumped up from 440 to well over 500 ci without breaking the bank.

If an original engine is in need of a rebuild, you might want to seriously consider the use of a stroker kit when rebuilding the engine. In many cases, the only additional part that needs to be purchased is the crankshaft. Typically, a performance rebuild requires new pistons, rings, and bearings anyway, so there is no additional cost for those parts when building a stroker motor. Many muscle car owners have come to the conclusion that if they are going to

This 505-ci stroker big-block has been dyno-tested and is now ready to be installed. On the dyno, this engine produced 615 hp at 5,800 rpm, which is enough to push a B-Body car well into the 11s at the drag strip. The Edelbrock dual-carb intake delivers ample air and fuel for a big motor like this.

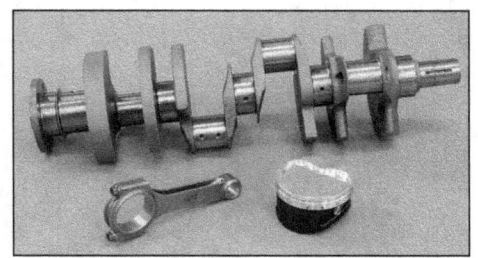

A stroker kit typically consists of the crankshaft, connecting rods, and pistons. Some kits also include the rings, piston pins, and bearings to make a complete drop-in assembly. Kits may also be purchased fully balanced and ready to assemble from some of the vendors.

rebuild the motor anyway, it makes sense to just go ahead and stroke it at the same time. A typical rebuild can easily cost more than $5,000, so the extra $500 for a stroker crankshaft adds only 10 percent to the cost.

Small-Blocks

The small-block Mopar engine, with its tall deck height and raised camshaft position, is ideally suited as a foundation for a stroker motor. The aftermarket has recognized this potential, and over the past several years a number of stroker kits have been released. The 408-ci small-block stroker engine is now quite common, with larger sizes, such as 427, 440, and 454 ci, also becoming available.

There are a number of lower-priced kits available for the small-block Mopar engine using cast crankshafts. The use of a 4.000-inch-stroke crankshaft with a bore size of 4.030 inches creates a 408-ci engine. These 408-ci engines have become very popular lately, due to the very economical price of the crankshafts. A cast crankshaft is not quite as strong as a forged crank, and it might require the use of an externally balanced dampener and flywheel, but these are not significant disadvantages for a street engine.

For higher-performance applications, a forged crankshaft is recommended, and the engine should be internally balanced. Small-block stroker motors with strokes up to 4.125 inches can be balanced internally without any issues. Once the stroke gets longer than 4.125 inches, internal balancing may require Mallory metal. A number of forged crankshafts are available for the small-block motor, including strokes of 4.000, 4.125, 4.180, and 4.250 inches. Small-block stroker crankshafts were originally designed for the smaller 340 main bearing size, but stroker cranks for the larger 360 mains are now readily available.

Connecting Rod Options

When ordering a stroker crankshaft for a new small-block engine, you should carefully consider the type of connecting rod to use. Although inexperienced engine builders often use a Mopar connecting rod in a Mopar engine, the more experienced shops tend to use Chevy connecting rods. The Chevy connecting rods use either a 2.100- or 2.000-inch rod journal and a .927-inch-diameter piston pin. Chevy connecting rods are available in a wide variety of lengths, beam styles, weights, and price points, which provides more choices for the engine builder. The Chevy connecting rods also provide a much wider selection of rod bearings to pick from. The Chevy rod is slightly wider than the Mopar connecting rod, so the crankshaft has to be matched to the type of connecting rod that will be used. Most of the crankshaft vendors these days offer crankshafts with the rod pins sized for Chevy connecting rods.

Block Options

Production 360 engine blocks are still fairly easy to find in salvage yards, and these make an excellent base for stroker engines up to 550 hp. The early-production 360 blocks have thick cylinder walls and make an excellent starting point for a stroker motor. The late-model Magnum engines are also fairly easy to find and respond very favorably to increased displacement. The Magnum engine design is superior to the LA engine in many ways, but aftermarket support isn't quite as extensive, so there are some tradeoffs to consider when going with a Magnum engine.

The original 340 engine blocks are quite difficult to find in useable shape anymore, but Mopar Performance does offer a reproduction 340

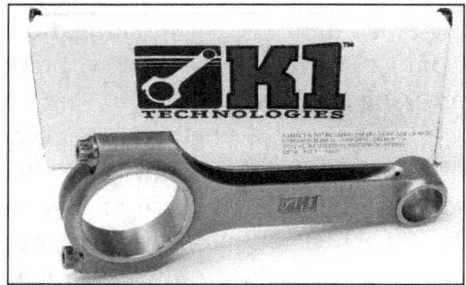

Chevy connecting rods are the way to go when building a small-block stroker. The Chevy rods are readily available in multiple lengths, with a wide selection of rod bearings. These 6.200-inch-long rods from K1 are going into a 427-ci small-block Mopar.

A big-inch stroker needs a good block to stay alive. This heavy-duty 340 restoration block from Mopar Performance handles whatever you can throw at it. This block has massive four-bolt mains and extra-thick cylinder walls, but all of that cast iron is heavy. This scale reads 212 pounds, which is the same weight as a stock 440 block.

block. These 340 restoration blocks can be purchased from your local Dodge dealer ready to use. They come with 4.040-inch bores and have the cam bearings and freeze plugs already installed. The 340 restoration blocks weigh about 210 pounds, which is 50 pounds heavier than the original blocks. Much of this weight is in the thicker cylinder walls, the thick deck surface, and the heavily reinforced bottom end. The combination of a 340 restoration block with a set of aftermarket aluminum cylinder heads tips the scales at approximately the same weight as an original 340 engine, but the performance potential is much greater. By using a long-stroke crankshaft you can build up a 426- or 440-ci small-block that looks almost identical to an original 340.

Mopar Performance also has a variety of other blocks available for the small-block engine, including racing blocks with 18 head bolts, blocks with a 48-degree tappet angle, and blocks with short deck heights. About the only thing that isn't currently available is a lightweight aluminum block.

Big-Blocks

The big-block engine design also makes an excellent foundation for a stroker motor. The tall deck height of the 440 block provides plenty of room for both a stable piston design and a long connecting rod, even with the additional travel of a stroker crankshaft. The 440 came from the factory with a 3.750-inch stroke, which seems quite dainty compared to crankshafts currently on the market. The most popular stroker kit currently available uses a 4.250-inch-stroke crankshaft, but 4.150- or 4.375-inch cranks also work just fine.

Combining a 4.250-inch-stroke crankshaft in a 440 block with a .030-inch overbore creates a healthy 505-ci engine. Some engine builders go ahead and bore the block to 4.375 inches, which is a popular size for piston rings. At this larger bore size, the 4.250-inch stroke makes a 511-ci engine. The 4.250-inch stroke combination has become very popular because it is a very simple combination to build, and it has excellent power capability.

Connecting Rod Options

As with small-block engines, the big-block engine builder needs to consider which connecting rods work best with the stroker crankshaft. The current trend is to use the Chevy rod with the 2.200-inch journal on Mopar stroker crankshafts as a way to reduce weight and bearing speed.

Another benefit to using the Chevy journal size is that connecting rods and connecting rod bearings are easier to source, and generally the prices are lower than Mopar equivalents. There is plenty of room in a 440 block to use a 7.100-inch-long connecting rod with a 4.250-inch-stroke

Chevy rods are the way to go with a big-block stroker, just as with the small-block. This 6.800-inch-long rod from Compstar is going into a 514-ci big-block motor. This is a standard Chevy big-block connecting rod with a 2.200-inch rod journal and a .990-inch piston pin.

crankshaft. Even with the long rod and the additional 1/2 inch of stroke, the compression height of the piston is still almost 1.500 inches. This piston height provides plenty of room for a conservative ring pack and a stable skirt design.

The increased displacement of the stroker engine raises the static compression ratio of the engine, so countermeasures must be taken for a street engine. A 4.375- x 4.250-inch engine with flat-top pistons and 75-cc cylinder heads has almost 13:1 compression. Although this is an excellent compression ratio for a bracket drag race motor, it is way too high for a pump-gas-friendly motor. Fortunately, most of the piston vendors offer dished pistons for street-performance applications. Engine builders typically specify a compression ratio of 10:1 when building a street-driven/pump-gas combination, but certain variables, such as combustion chamber design, altitude of operation, and vehicle weight, can also come into play.

Block Options

The low-deck motors, such as the 383 and 400, are also candidates for stroking, but do have some

One big advantage of using the slightly smaller Chevy big-block rods is that they provide extra clearance around the oil pickup boss. The Chevy rods are also lighter and less expensive than Mopar connecting rods.

limitations due to the shorter deck height. One very popular combination for the 400 block is to use a 3.750-inch-stroke crankshaft for a final displacement of 451 ci. Another good combination is the 470-ci motor, which is built with a 400 block and a 3.900-inch-stroke crankshaft. The low-deck block uses a smaller 2.625-inch-diameter main bearing, which complicates matters a bit. There isn't a wide selection of main bearings in this smaller size, so sometimes the engine builder has to work a little harder to achieve the correct main bearing clearances. One advantage of the low-deck stroker is that the engine is physically a little smaller, so there is a little more room in the engine compartment for the intake manifold and the exhaust headers.

Aftermarket Blocks

Although the supply of production engine blocks hasn't dried up yet, it is getting a little tougher to find a clean 440 block these days. Even if a nice clean production block can be found, it is very unlikely that it has good sonic numbers in all eight cylinders. And even if you were able to find such a block, the production two-bolt main cap design just can't handle more than 650 hp before it starts to fail.

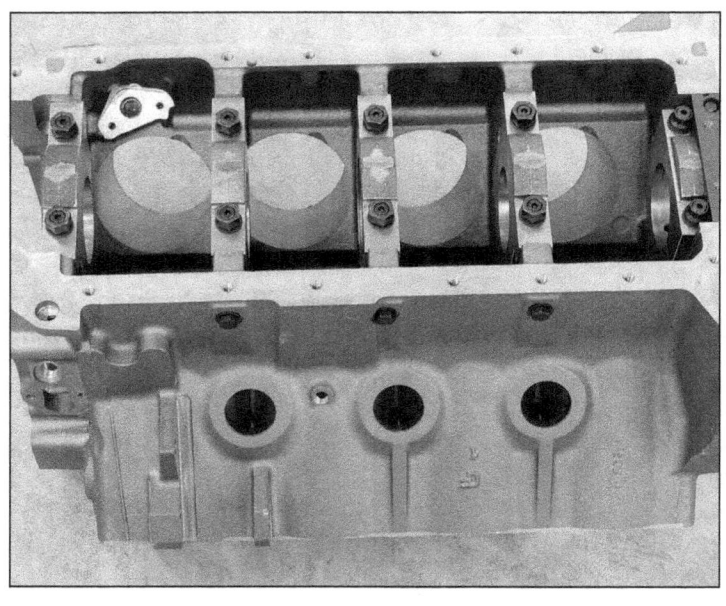

Mopar Performance sells this heavy-duty block. This block has cross-bolted main caps, thick cylinder walls, and an extra-thick deck surface. World Products and Koleno Performance also offer their own heavy-duty, big-block castings.

Aluminum blocks are available from Keith Black, Indy, and World Products. These aluminum blocks can handle a lot of power, and they reduce the weight on the front of the car by a significant amount.

Common failure points for a production block are the main caps and the main webs. Typically, the caps begin to chatter or bounce in the block at high-power levels. Main cap chatter can lead to broken main caps or cracks in the main webs. If the main webs become distorted during use, the oiling system can become compromised, leading to spun bearings and engine failure.

Fortunately for us, Mopar Performance has tooled up a nice selection of heavy-duty cast-iron blocks for the RB wedge engines. These blocks all use the Hemi cross-bolt design on the main webs, and they have extra material in the deck area and around the cylinder bores. World Performance sells a race version of the Mopar block with bushed lifter bores and a dual-pattern bolt pattern for the bellhousing. Koleno Performance sells a very heavy-duty cast-iron block, and Indy Cylinder Heads and Keith Black sell aluminum versions. Given all these choices, there are plenty of blocks to choose from if you need a heavy-duty block for a stroker build.

ENGINE STROKING OR SWAPPING

Drivetrain Considerations

Increasing the displacement of the engine raises the torque output of the engine by a proportional amount. This is true even if the cylinder heads, camshaft, and intake manifold remain original. If the breathing capability of the heads and intake are improved at the same time, the engine output can, and most often does, increase dramatically. Combining a set of properly ported heads, a hydraulic roller camshaft, and a 500-ci short-block easily produces well in excess of 600 hp. This is a level of power that very few production vehicles have ever seen, and it is well beyond what any of the B-Body vehicles were designed to handle.

A muscle car owner quickly realizes that it is much easier to build a 600-hp engine than it is to use that power. The stock drivetrain quickly fails when transferring 600 hp to the ground, especially if slicks are used. Throughout the rest of this book, I cover possible upgrades to the chassis, drivetrain, and suspension of the B-Body in question. Performance upgrades, such as the ones detailed in this book, are required to properly handle a high-output stroker motor.

Matching Top End

As you can imagine, the increased displacement of the stroker motor places additional demands on the cylinder heads and the exhaust system. In general, you can assume that if the engine size is increased by a significant amount, the induction system should also be increased by that amount. This linear relationship is mostly true, but additional considerations can come into play. For example, if the engine builder desires a very smooth engine with tremendous low-speed torque, cylinder heads with standard port sizes should be used. On the other hand, an engine builder who is aiming for dramatic increases in power will install cylinder heads with extra-large intake ports for increased power at higher engine speeds.

The McFarland formula, discussed in Chapter 1, provides a quick way of determining where the torque peak is for a combination of engine size and cross-section area in the cylinder heads. For a high-performance street engine, it is usually best to keep the torque peak below 4,000 rpm. This provides excellent performance and manners on the street while still providing adequate performance at the drag strip. A race motor, on the other hand, uses larger cylinder head ports to raise the power peak as high as the budget allows.

A good rule of thumb is to use standard-port heads for any motor primarily driven on the street, regardless of the size of the engine. For engines significantly larger than stock, a larger port size, such as the Max Wedge port, can be used, but there will be some loss of low-end torque. Of course, these are just general recommendations, and people disagree on which setup is streetable and which isn't.

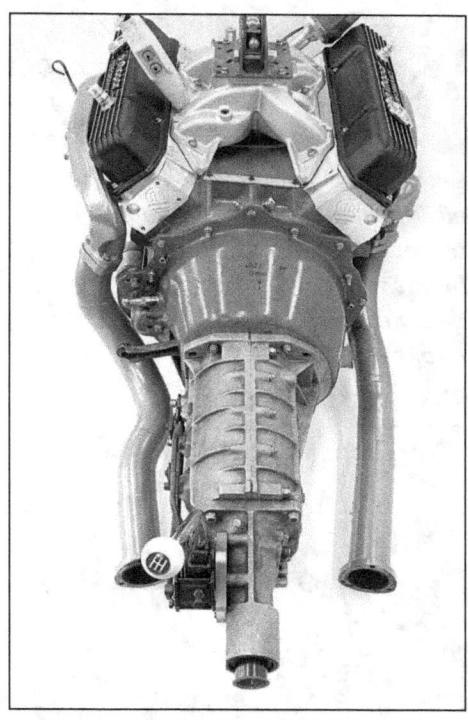

Once the clutch has been upgraded, the next weak link behind a big stroker big-block is the transmission. The Doug Nash 5-speed transmission is an old-school way to handle the power. Modern solutions include the Tremec TKO or the T-56.

Large stroker motors need more air in order to make more power. One typical upgrade is to use a roller camshaft and high-quality valvetrain components. Large-displacement engines require more lift and duration than a stock-sized engine.

Bigger engines also require more airflow from the cylinder heads. The power difference between stock heads and fully ported heads can easily exceed 100 hp on a large stroker engine.

A big-inch stroker engine can make full use of a large carburetor, such as this Holley Dominator.

Adding a bunch of cubic inches is the perfect way to smooth out a racy intake system. The cross ram was a little peaky on 413- and 426-ci engines, but put it on top of a 500-ci-or-larger engine, and the torque curve smoothes right out.

Project: Building a 427-ci Small-Block

1 Our 427-ci stroker small-block project started with a Mopar Performance 340 block (PN P5007552AB). This block comes with extra-heavy-duty four-bolt main caps and very thick cylinder walls.

2 We mounted the Mopar 340 block into a machining center so that the unnecessary material could be machined away. This is a fairly complex process many shops cannot handle. Specialized engine builders, such as Shady Dell Speed Shop, are able to accommodate machine work like this.

3 Once the block is fully machined, we are ready to begin a trial assembly of the rotating parts. The first part to install is the K1 crankshaft. This crankshaft has a stroke of 4.125 inches, which is much greater than the original stroke of only 3.310 inches. The large increase in stroke means that we need to carefully check every aspect of the rotating assembly to verify clearance.

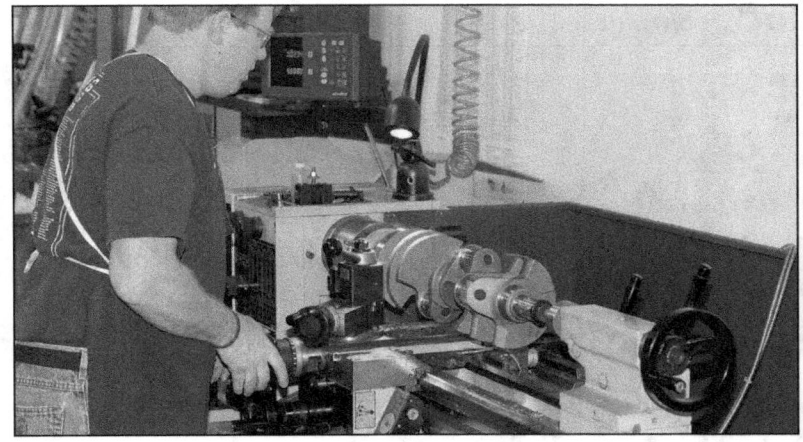

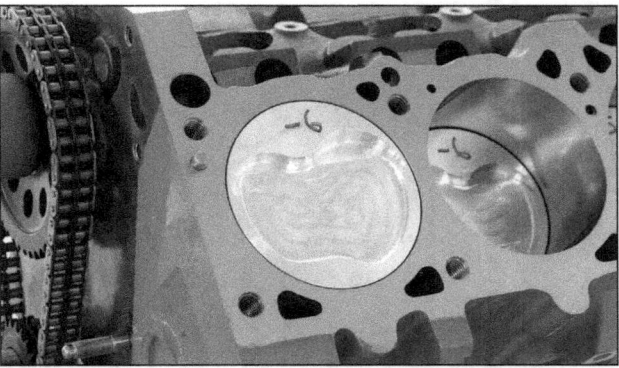

4 Our crankshaft was a little too heavy and could not be balanced properly without removing material. The best way to reduce the weight of a crankshaft is to have a machinist turn down the two end counterweights on a large engine lathe. Spinning a big heavy crankshaft in a lathe is not something to try at home. The rotating counterweights are dangerous to work around, and it can be difficult to machine the heat-treated 4340 material used in aftermarket crankshafts.

5 JE built us a trick set of pistons for this small-block motor. With a bore size of 4.060 inches and a stroke of 4.125 inches, the final displacement is exactly 427 ci. We needed a 20-cc dish in the piston to keep the compression at 10.5:1. We wanted a coated skirt to reduce friction, and we needed a short compression height to work with the extra-long stroke and the longer connecting rods. JE was able to quickly turn our specifications into a set of full custom pistons.

6 Given the extra-long stroke, the clearance between the connecting rods and the oil pump pickup becomes very tight. This rotating assembly with the small-journal Chevy connecting rods cleared the pickup, even with the 4.125-inch stroke. This is another good reason for using the Chevy connecting rods with the smaller journal size.

7 The long stroke pulls the piston through an additional .815 inch of travel in the cylinder bore. Therefore, the skirt-to-crankshaft clearance can become an issue at bottom dead center. We did not have an issue with this rotating assembly because the JE pistons are properly designed to work with the long-stroke crankshaft. Also, this crankshaft has cam-shaped counterweights, which provide extra clearance for the piston. Stroker kits that do not have these features require expensive modifications at the machine shop.

8 This 427-ci engine requires a lot of air, so we stepped up to the top rung with these CNC-ported Edelbrock heads. Hughes Engines prepared the heads with its Stage III porting, which included larger intake valves and full machine work. Also visible here are the shaft-mounted rocker arms from Comp Cams, as well as the beehive springs.

Project: Building a 427-ci Small-Block CONTINUED

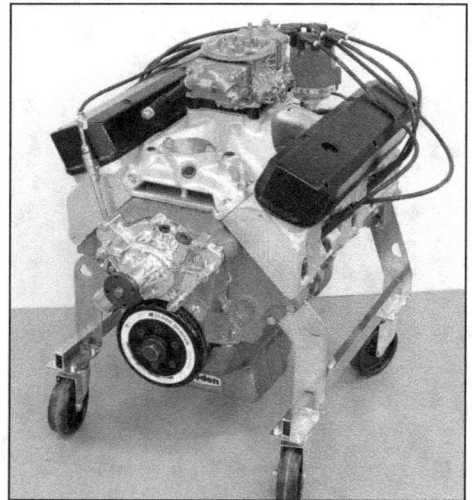

9 Our 427-ci small-block Mopar engine has been completed and is ready to take to the dyno. Finishing touches include a polished water pump and fabricated valve covers from PRW, a Victor 340 intake manifold from Edelbrock, an ATI dampener, and a custom carburetor from Bo Laws Performance. According to the stack of receipts, the total build cost for this engine was $18,700.

10 On the dyno, the 427-ci small-block pounded out 500 ft-lbs of torque at 4,000 rpm and 515 hp at 5,500 rpm. The idle was nice and smooth at 900 rpm, due to the well-calibrated BLP carburetor and the excellent MSD ignition system.

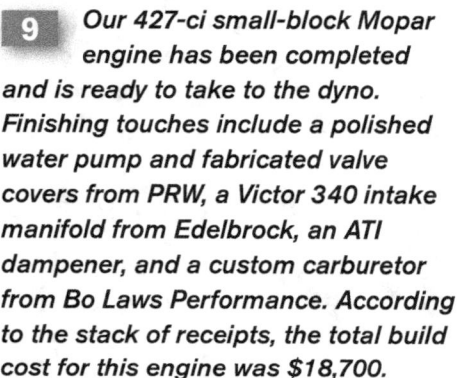

The complete engine was weighed on a scale before installation. Total weight, fully dressed, was only 450 pounds. A big-inch small-block engine like this can be the perfect way to improve performance in a B-Body car.

Engine Swap Guide

If stroking the existing engine does not provide enough of a performance increase, you might want to consider an engine swap. Swapping engines is certainly one of the older hot rodding traditions, and Mopar muscle cars have been recipients of engine swaps since the very beginning of the muscle car era. Original Hemi and 440 cars were usually too expensive for the average guy to purchase, so instead, a Slant-6 or a 318 car was procured and modified. Fortunately, B-Body cars are quite receptive to engine swaps.

There is quite a bit of engine swap information available, including the swap guide printed in the Mopar Performance *Chassis* bulletin. Additional information is available from Mopar Performance in the *Crate Motor Installation* book, as well as in various *Engine* bulletins written over the years. Even if some of that information is now outdated, these bulletins are still good references to have on hand. All of the Mopar Performance publications are available from a local Dodge dealer or from a Mopar parts specialist, such as Mancini Racing.

A booklet titled *Engine Swaps Simplified* is available from Schumacher Creative Services (SCS), a recognized expert on Mopar engine swaps. SCS manufactures and sells a very complete line of engine-swap-related parts, including conversion motor mounts, headers, oil pans, and other items. SCS should be the very first place to look when starting to investigate the possibility of swapping engines in your muscle car era Mopar. Another vendor whose products are very important to the success of many Mopar engine swaps is TTi. TTi sells a variety of engine swap headers and in many applications; it is the only vendor that offers an exhaust header.

1962 to 1965

The early B-Body cars were available with a wide range of engines,

ENGINE STROKING OR SWAPPING

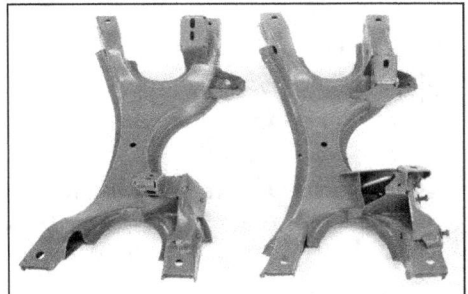

The early B-Body K-member (left) shows how the motor mounts are positioned slightly forward of the mount locations on the 1966 to 1972 K-member (right). The motor mount pads are also slightly different for the early B-Body. SCS makes both big-block and small-block mounts for the early B-Body K-member.

The forward placement of the engine in the early B-Body cars causes problems when trying to use a later-model clutch fan and radiator. The popular Mopar Performance clutch fan package usually does not fit in a big-block early B-Body car, unless the engine is moved back. The engine in this early B-Body has been moved back slightly, but fan clearance is still very tight.

including the Slant-6, small-block, and big-block.

The 1963 to 1965 V-8 K-members are all the same, so replacing a factory 318 with a 383 or 440 just requires a set of the correct engine brackets.

The 1962 K-member was slightly different, but Schumacher has a set of adapter brackets, which adapt the later-style engine mounts to the 1962 K-member.

These early B-Bodies used a rubber, sandwich type of motor mount, which is prone to failure, so the Poly-Loc replacement mounts from SCS might be a good investment. SCS also has the correct engine brackets to install a later-model 340 or 360 small-block engine into an early B-Body. Big-block engines were fairly common in the early B-Body cars, so there is a wide selection of aftermarket parts, such as oil pans and exhaust headers, available.

The Hemi engine was installed in the early B-Body chassis in 1964 and 1965, but only as a race option, so finding original parts for this swap is very unlikely. Schumacher offers a conversion mount kit that mates a Hemi engine to an existing early B-Body V-8 K-member. Headers are readily available due to the popularity of this combination, but some modifications, such as a modified passenger's-side shock tower, might be required to get the Hemi to fit. Modifications like this can be performed, given the correct skills and equipment, but the parts need to be fabricated from scratch.

The modifications also depend on which cylinder heads are used, as well as which intake manifold is used. Some of the aftermarket cylinder heads are taller and wider than original heads, and large intake manifolds, such as the cross ram, cause interference issues with the hood and maybe the firewall.

The K-members for the early B-Body cars locate the engine in a slightly more forward position than the 1966 to 1972 K-members. Swapping the K-member from a 1966 to 1972 car into an early B-Body is a good way to move the engine back, but beware of the other changes that have to be made to accommodate the new engine position. Moving the engine back improves the weight distribution and adds additional room for the fan and radiator, but the transmission mount, clutch linkage, and driveshaft all need to be modified.

1966 to 1972

These were the golden years for the B-Body vehicle, with the Slant-6, small-block, big-block, and Hemi engines all available as factory-installed options. Many parts can be interchanged on these cars, including suspension components, K-members, radiators, etc. A very large selection of aftermarket parts, such as headers, motor mounts, oil pans, etc., are available to assist engine swappers.

The small-block and big-block engines used the same K-member, so changing the motor mounts allows you to swap engines. The 1966 to 1972 B-Body chassis still used the failure-prone, rubber, sandwich type of motor-mount insulator. Schumacher sells reproduction motor mounts for these years, as well as the upgraded Poly-Loc type of insulator with the interlocking steel plates that prevent the insulator from coming apart.

For the more ambitious engine swapper, Schumacher sells conversion kits that allow V-8 engines to bolt onto Slant-6 K-members, as well as a kit that mounts a Hemi engine on a V-8 K-member. Another option for those interested in a Hemi engine swap is to purchase a reproduction Hemi K-member from Mega Parts. A reproduction K-member is more expensive than the conversion motor mounts, but it has the added benefit of looking original and using factory replacement parts.

CHAPTER 3

Engine torque tends to tear apart the biscuit-style engine isolators. To solve this problem, SCS has redesigned the original isolators with interlocking steel brackets. If the rubber mount fails on these brackets, the steel plates lock together and prevent the engine from moving out of place. (Photo Courtesy SCS)

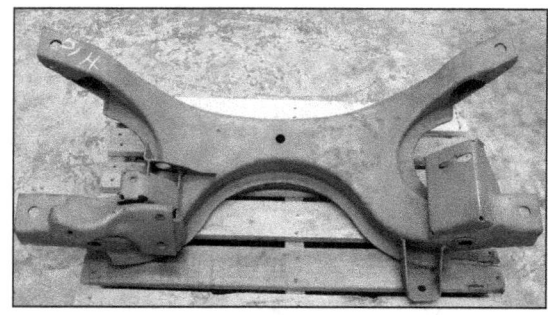

The Hemi K-member is a unique design with motor mount pads that are larger and relocated from the V-8 pad position. Original B-Body Hemi K-members are very desirable and are quite difficult to find these days.

The supply of original engine brackets has dried up over the years, making it difficult to perform even the most basic of engine swaps. Fortunately, vendors such as SCS have begun to reproduce the parts necessary to bolt a big-block engine into any B-Body chassis. (Photo Courtesy SCS)

SCS makes conversion brackets that allow a 426 Hemi to be bolted directly to the 1962 to 1972 K-members. These cleverly designed brackets use a spool-type design to reduce the chance of mount failure.

1973 to 1978

The late-model B-Body vehicles came at the end of the muscle car era, and they are much less popular than the earlier B1 and B2 vehicles. Given the lower popularity of vehicles from these years, less aftermarket support exists for these cars. The good news is that big-block versions of the late B-Body car were widely available, so it is possible to find the parts necessary for a big-block engine swap. Choices for aftermarket parts, such as headers and oil pans, are limited, but a few parts are available.

The late B-Body cars used the spool type of motor mount, which is an excellent design. They also used a different K-member for small-block and big-block vehicles. The use of different K-members for the different engines slightly complicates the engine swap process. If you have the proper tools available, the small-block mounts on the K-member can be cut off and re-located to properly position a big-block engine.

An even easier solution is to purchase conversion motor mounts from SCS; they allow a big-block to be bolted onto the small-block K-member.

Another option would be to replace the small-block K-member with a big-block K-member, but this is a chore, due to the size and complexity of the late-model K-members.

The Hemi was not an option for these vehicles, and nobody sells a conversion kit, but the engine bay is quite large in these cars, and determined hot rodders have successfully swapped Hemi engines into the late B-Body. Spool mount brackets are not available for the Hemi, so you would most likely cut the spool mount brackets off the K-member and convert it back to the pad style when swapping a Hemi into a B3 chassis.

Support Systems for Engine Swaps

Although stock parts can be used to complete most any Mopar engine swap, some engine swaps are performed primarily for racing purposes. For drag racing, stock parts, such as oil

ENGINE STROKING OR SWAPPING

pans, exhaust manifolds, and cylinder heads, are often replaced with specialized aftermarket parts. Fortunately, a B-Body car usually has space for a deep sump oil pan and large-tube headers.

Racers often decide to use motor plates, rather than motor mounts, for a variety of reasons. A motor plate allows more flexibility in locating the engine than the factory mounting system, and the motor plate eliminates the stress from the motor mounts on the side of the block. The motor plate can be used to tie together the front of the frame to add rigidity to the chassis, and it is a handy place to mount a variety of components.

Several vendors, such as Mancini Racing, sell motor plate kits, which are designed to properly mount a big-block or Hemi engine into a B-Body vehicle.

Modern Engine Swaps

Although the vast majority of engine swaps performed still focus on installing a big-block or Hemi engine in place of a Slant-6 or a small-block, swaps involving newer engines are gaining in popularity. A Magnum engine, for example, is an excellent choice to swap into any B-Body car.

Magnum

The Magnum design incorporates a number of design improvements over the LA engine, such as a roller camshaft, better gasket design, and improved cylinder heads. Magnum engines are very closely related to LA engines, so swapping one for the other is a fairly straightforward process.

Viper

The Viper engine has obvious power potential, but unfortunately it also has limited swap potential due

This small-block engine is being prepped to drop into a B-Body. The Doug's D453 headers and Milodon road race oil pan work just fine in any 1966 to 1972 B-Body chassis.

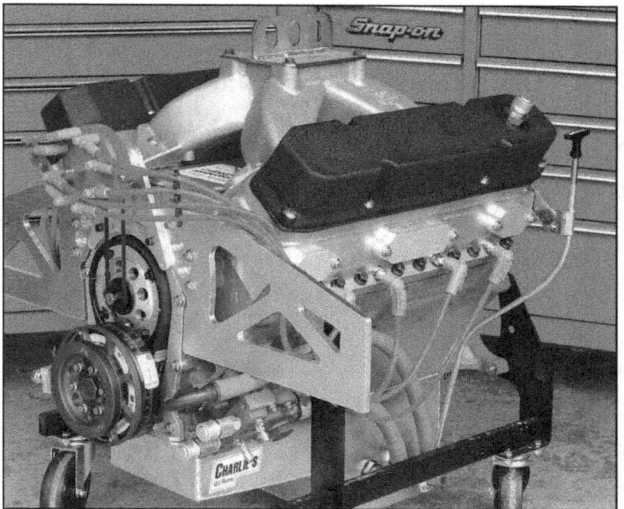

Racing engines often use a motor plate, rather than production-style motor mounts, to mount the engine to the vehicle. The motor plate provides a more universal way to mount an engine onto a frame, and it frees up some space on the sides for larger exhaust headers. This 505-ci race engine is fitted with one of Mancini Racing's CNC-machined motor plates.

The Magnum engine is an excellent candidate for swapping into B-Body cars, such as this 1962 Savoy. The 406-ci crate version from Mopar Performance is rated at 435 hp and 470 ft-lbs of torque, which should be more than adequate for street performance. (Photo Courtesy Richard Ehrenberg)

to its size and cost. Vipers are fairly rare, so salvage engines do not show up very often. The length and weight of the V-10 design also combine to make this swap a challenging process. Engine mounts, headers, and cooling system would all need to be custom-built for a Viper swap, and there would certainly be a number of challenges to overcome in the area of engine management, including the ignition and fuel-injection systems.

Third-Generation Hemi

One engine that is becoming more popular all the time is the third-generation, or 3G, Hemi. The 5.7L Hemi has been factory-installed in a large number of vehicles by now, so engine cores are starting to become fairly common in salvage yards. In fact, it is probably easier to find a complete 5.7 Hemi in a salvage yard today than a big-block.

A few vendors, such as TTi and XV Motorsports, are building components to support 3G swaps. TTi sells a variety of parts, such as motor mounts and headers, for the 3G swap, and Milodon has the necessary oil pans.

One potential issue with the 3G swap is the computer-controlled ignition and the fuel-injection system. There are a few ways to go, such as performing a complete computer swap from the donor vehicle, performing a conversion to an aftermarket computer system, or retrofitting the 3G Hemi with a standard distributor and carburetor. XV Motorsports and Mopar Performance have intake manifolds that convert the 3G to a carburetor, and vendors such as FAST sell standalone systems, which can drive the factory injectors without having to use the production computer.

A 3G engine swap is moderately more difficult than an old-school big-block swap, due to these complications. But, once those items are sorted out, the 3G Hemi is a powerful performer packed into a lightweight package. Over time, this will most likely become a very popular swap, due to the stunning power potential of the 3G platform. You would also expect to see a variety of 3G crate engines available in the future, as well as more complete swap kits.

Several vendors are now offering parts, such as these motor mounts, to support 3G Hemi-to-B-Body swaps. (Photo Courtesy TTi)

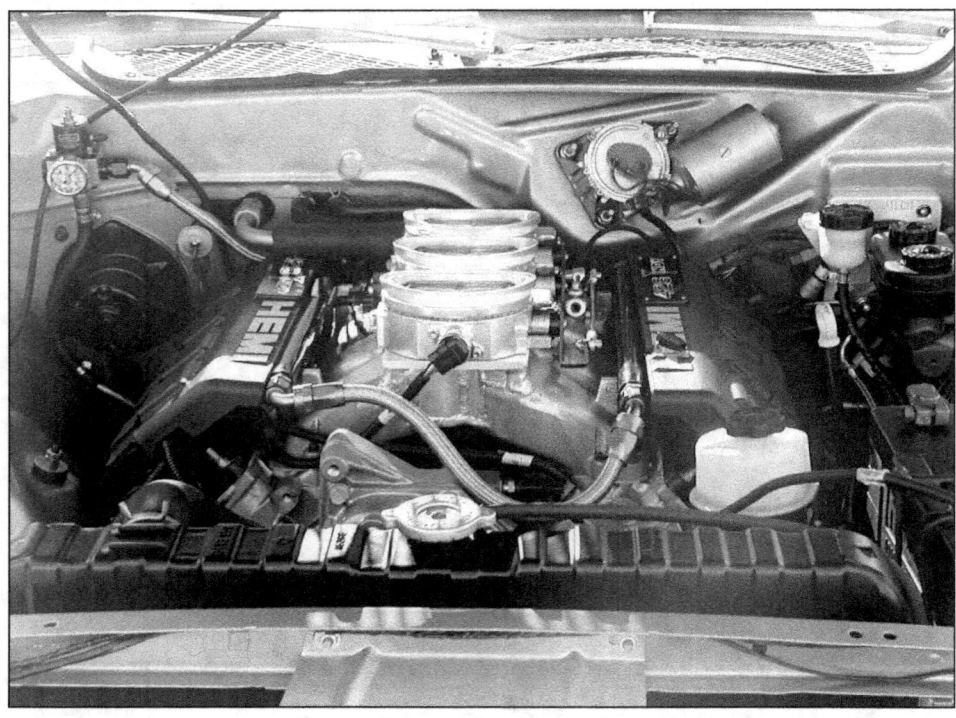

Third-generation Hemi swaps are becoming more popular. This 1971 Charger is updated with a 6.1L Hemi that was bored and stroked to 426 ci. (Photo Courtesy Gary Beineke)

TTi offers several different 3G Hemi headers for the 1962 to 1974 B-Body cars. Headers for 5.7L and 6.1L engines are available in a variety of tube sizes. (Photo Courtesy TTi)

CHAPTER 4

ENGINE SYSTEM UPGRADES

In the pursuit of higher performance, there's a wondrous variety of high-performance engine parts to choose from. But before you start buying parts you should do some homework, and this chapter will help you do that homework. Obviously, you need to determine how the car will be used–pro touring/track car, weekend cruiser, drag racer, and many other applications.

Once you've determined how the car will be used, you can figure out where in the RPM the power needs to be generated. A street car needs to get off the line quickly, and therefore the engine should produce a lot of low-end torque. A drag race or road race car operates at sustained high RPM, and as a result, peak horsepower is a high priority and low-end torque is a lesser concern.

Next, determine your performance target (400-, 500-, 600-hp or more), and your horsepower goals will largely depend on your budget. With this target defined, select a compatible engine component package, and the heads, valvetrain, cam and intake should function as an integrated system.

Performance Intake Manifolds

Installing an aftermarket intake manifold and carburetor is a classic performance upgrade. Although people have been performing this upgrade for many years, there are still a few little issues to watch out for when updating a Mopar engine.

Chrysler engineers typically attached the throttle bracket directly to the intake manifold on production vehicles. Although this is a very simple mounting method, the factory brackets were not designed to work with taller aftermarket intake manifolds. High-performance intake manifolds raise the carburetor in order to provide a more direct path for the airflow. Raising the carburetor improves performance, but the carb linkage then moves out of alignment with the factory throttle bracket. When you look at a number of Mopars at a car show, you see some creative and scary-looking home-built solutions to this problem, but fortunately, there are a number of aftermarket solutions for this problem.

Tall intake manifolds improve engine performance by providing a straighter path for the airflow, but the extra height prevents the stock throttle bracket from working properly. Fortunately, vendors such as Hughes Engines carry throttle brackets and throttle return kits for various high-rise intake manifolds.

CHAPTER 4

A variety of intake manifold designs is available for both small-block and big-block engines. This Edelbrock CH-28 is a dual-carb intake designed for big-block engines. Mancini Racing has the linkage kit, as well as other related parts needed for installation of the CH-28 into any B-Body.

Indy Cylinder Heads sells a number of intake manifolds for Mopar engines, including this Hemi intake designed for a single Holley Dominator. Indy also sells the matching throttle linkage and throttle return kit.

The classic Max Wedge intake manifold can be updated with Edelbrock carbs and a modern linkage kit with Heim ends. Mopar Performance sells reproduction cross ram intake manifolds.

Several vendors, such as Mancini Racing and Hughes Engines, carry taller throttle brackets that mount in the original location. These taller brackets are also adjustable, so they work with a variety of aftermarket intakes and carb spacers. There is a limit to the range of adjustability, so, in some cases, you must buy a special bracket when using a really tall intake, such as those from Indy Cylinder Heads.

Besides the issue of taller intake manifolds, there are also versions available that never had a factory linkage. For example, the CH-28 dual-quad intake manifold from Edelbrock is unique, as is the Mopar Performance single 4-barrel Hemi intake manifold. Once again, vendors, such as Mancini Racing, have developed various throttle linkage kits to connect these aftermarket intakes with a B-Body throttle cable.

Throttle Rod

The throttle rod, also known as the kick-down linkage, is the source of much frustration when upgrading to an aftermarket intake manifold. The factory throttle rod linkage is designed to signal to the transmission the need for additional line pressure as the throttle is opened. The throttle rod performs the simple task of pushing back on the throttle pressure lever on the transmission when the carburetor throttle is opened. The problem is that the original throttle rod linkage design does not have enough adjustability to properly fit the taller aftermarket intake manifolds.

Mancini Racing sells a new throttle rod, or kick-down, bracket that works with the popular Performer RPM intake manifold. This throttle rod bracket only works with the three-piece throttle rod assembly, and it relocates the pivot point high enough to align with the carburetor.

These brackets are only available for the B and RB engines. Later-model big-block engines came with a 1-piece throttle rod linkage, and there is not a throttle bracket available to accommodate that linkage with an aftermarket intake. It would be possible to cut and weld extensions into the existing production parts to achieve the proper alignment, if you have the necessary skill and tools to take on such a task.

One other option that is used by many people is a conversion to a cable kick-down type of arrangement.

There are no known solutions at this time for either the Hemi or the small-block engine other than converting to a cable type of kick-down when using aftermarket intakes that do not accept the factory brackets. There is the possibility of converting the transmission to a manual valve body, but typically this isn't desirable for a street-driven vehicle. A manual valve body certainly has merit for a drag race vehicle, but the higher line pressures, and constant shifting, gets old fairly quickly on a daily driver.

Return Bracket

The throttle return bracket is another issue that usually needs to be looked at when swapping on a taller intake manifold. The factory bracket-and-spring arrangement often does not work properly with a taller intake because the original spring is not long enough to reach the extra distance. There are various solutions to this problem available from vendors such as Mancini Racing and Hughes Engines.

Tall return spring brackets with dual springs are available for small-blocks, big-blocks, and Hemi engines. Other kits feature a return spring

ENGINE SYSTEM UPGRADES

Aftermarket carburetors need throttle lever extensions to work properly with the original kick-down linkage. These lever extensions fit Holley, Edelbrock, and Barry Grant carburetors.

The factory kick-down linkage can be made to work on the taller Performer RPM intake manifold by using this Mancini Racing throttle bracket.

that connects to a bracket and then attaches under the carburetor.

Manifold Height

The height of the intake manifold needs to be taken into account when choosing which hood to use. Some Mopar muscle cars came with fairly complex fresh-air induction systems. These factory air cleaner systems are designed to operate with the carb in a certain position, and they usually do not accept a taller intake manifold. There is room under a normal flat hood to raise the carburetor a small amount, especially if the stock air cleaner is removed and replaced with a lower-profile unit. And, of course, you can always add a hood scoop.

Many Mopars were equipped with hood scoops, starting with the Max Wedge dual scoop and including various Six-Pack scoops, as well as the wonderfully designed 340 T/A scoop. Any of these hood scoops provide several inches of additional clearance, which should work for everything except the tallest of intake manifolds.

Throttle Cables

When swapping engines, or changing to a high-rise intake manifold, typically the throttle cable needs to be changed. Many people have installed a high-rise intake manifold, or a tall carburetor spacer, and found out that the throttle cable no longer reached the throttle linkage on the carburetor. The old-school approach to this problem was to simply install an extra-long throttle cable from a Slant-6 car.

Unfortunately, the Slant-6 throttle cable is no longer available over the counter, but a similar cable from a pickup truck can be ordered as Mopar PN 4088095. Several of the more common B-Body throttle cables are available in auto parts stores under the Pioneer, Inc. brand.

Mopar throttle cables used a round metal firewall fitting until 1972, and then the factory switched to a square plastic fitting at the firewall. Pioneer has cables in a variety of lengths with both types of firewall fittings.

Early B-Body vehicles used a unique throttle cable with a Clevis end that isn't compatible with the later-style cables. These early B-Body cables are not available from local auto parts stores, but Imperial Services does reproduce them. Imperial Services also produces a selection of other hard-to-find throttle cables, such as the ones used with Max Wedge and Hemi cross rams. Imperial Services also builds custom-length throttle cables for any application if one of its standard cables does not work.

Carburetor Choices

B-Body muscle car engines were originally equipped with either Carter or Holley carburetors, and those choices are still available 40 years later. Strictly speaking, the Carter brand of carburetor is no longer available, but Edelbrock offers a line of carburetors based on the original Carter AFB and AVS designs. Holley is still in business and is still producing some of the original OEM muscle car carburetors, as well as a fully updated line of performance carburetors.

Both Holley and Edelbrock offer larger carburetor sizes to work with large stroker engines. The Edelbrock AFB and AVS carburetors are now available in sizes as large as 800 cfm. And what used to be an 850 double

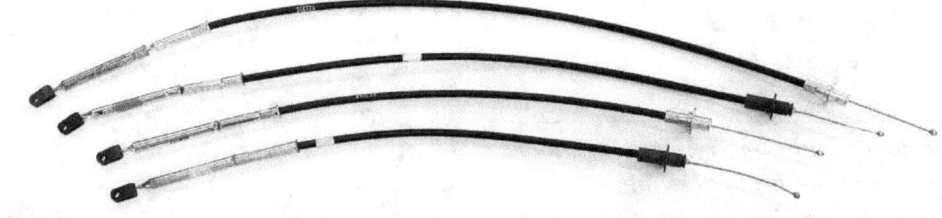

Throttle cables are available in a wide variety of lengths. Original cables are getting hard to find new, but various reproductions are available. Imperial Services can build most any throttle cable you might need.

CHAPTER 4

Holley carburetors were original equipment on many Mopar engines, but the OEM carbs have limited tuning capability when compared to modern carbs, such as this Holley 950 Ultra HP.

Edelbrock and Holley have brought back the classic Six-Pack combination. Carburetors, as well as intake manifolds, air cleaners, and linkage kits, are all available brand new.

pumper in the 1970s has now been smoothed and polished into a Holley 1000 HP. Holley has even brought back the original 2-barrel carburetors used in the factory 440+6 system. The original Six-Pack system is expensive, and can be a little tricky to tune, but it sure looks impressive.

Wide-Band Essentials

The fairly recent invention of on-board wide-band air/fuel ratio gauges has been a breakthrough for the shade-tree mechanic. For years, the only tuning aid available to low-budget mechanics was reading the spark plugs or looking at the color of the exhaust gases. Multi-gas systems to measure air/fuel ratio were priced too high for home use, and they didn't fit into a vehicle for operational testing. Commercial-grade wide-band systems came into use at professional tune-up shops over the past decade, but those systems were also out of reach of the average backyard mechanic.

Recently, however, several businesses, such as Innovate and AEM, released dash-mounted air/fuel gauges with a wide-band sensor located in the exhaust system. This on-board capability is priced well within the reach of the average hot rodder, and the capability is good enough for professional tuning results.

Oxygen Sensor

Installation of a wide-band system is fairly straightforward. The oxygen sensor (or sensors, if using a dual-channel unit) needs to be installed into the exhaust system. The sensor should be located in the collector of the exhaust header, or in the head pipe when using cast-iron manifolds. The sensor screws into a bung that must be welded into the exhaust system. The bung should be located so that the sensor can be changed without too much difficulty, as sensors do need to be replaced on occasion. Once the sensor is mounted in the exhaust system, the wiring harness is installed with a 12-volt source of power.

The oxygen sensor needs to be powered on whenever the engine is running, but it should not be left on when the engine is turned off. The sensor is heated and it burns out if left on without the engine running. If the sensor isn't turned on when the engine is running, the exhaust gases can foul the sensor. So, it is important to have a system that either turns on the sensor automatically or

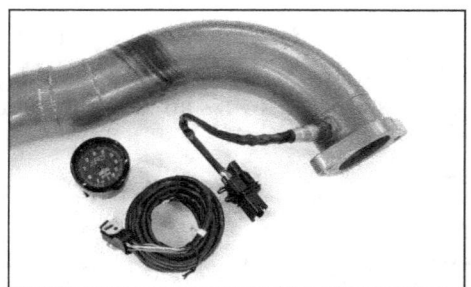

Adding a wide-band gauge kit should be one of the first performance upgrades made to any performance vehicle. A wide-band gauge provides precise data for performance tuning and economy.

This early B-Body has received a complete Magnum swap, including the factory fuel injection. (Photo Courtesy Richard Ehrenberg)

ENGINE SYSTEM UPGRADES

has a warning light that shows if the sensor is on or off.

Modern oxygen sensors react very quickly to a change in the exhaust gases, so the gauge can be used to tune steady-state conditions, as well as transient events.

A steady-state condition would be something such as idle, cruise, or wide open throttle (WOT). Steady-state conditions are fairly easy to monitor with an air/fuel gauge by just watching the gauge. Adjusting the idle mixture screws most often corrects a lean idle condition, and increasing the size of the main jets adjusts a lean cruise condition. For a Holley carburetor, changing the size of the restrictions behind the power valve adjusts the WOT mixture.

Transient events happen quickly, such as a sudden application of the throttle. During a transient event, the gauge might show lean, or rich, and then return to the baseline air/fuel ratio. Although these events might be a little more difficult to sort out, careful observation of the gauge, as well as some thought on the operation of the carburetor, should yield some answers.

For instance, if the accelerator pump isn't big enough, a sudden opening of the throttle results in a lean condition. A similar problem could result if the shooter nozzle is too small, limiting the amount of fuel. A temporary rich condition during hard acceleration, or hard braking, might be the result of fuel spilling out of the vent into the engine.

Cooling System Fundamentals

Although the cooling system on B-Body vehicles was usually adequate when new, 40 years of use takes a toll on even the best design. The early B-Body cars were handicapped with a small 22-inch radiator, so they are susceptible to overheating. The 1966 to 1972 B-Body cars could be equipped with an optional 26-inch radiator, which solved most cooling problems. The 1973-and-newer B-Body cars were equipped with large 28-inch radiators, so cooling problems are fairly rare with these high-capacity systems. But regardless of the year, as owners install 600-hp engines into vehicles designed for 300 hp, the cooling system is one of the first places for problems to occur.

Cooling system technology has changed dramatically since muscle cars first rolled out of Detroit. The typical B-Body radiator was constructed from brass and copper and was a down-flow design. The original cooling systems didn't even have a coolant recovery tank; the overflow tube just ran down the side of the radiator and dumped the overflow onto the road.

B-Body vehicles were all equipped with belt-driven fans, and early models did not have fan shrouds. After 40 years of engineering development, we now know that the shroud is essential, that electric fans provide significant benefits, and that cross-flow radiators work better than down-flows. We've also seen an almost total replacement of brass/copper radiators in the automotive industry by aluminum radiators over the past 30 years.

The primary function of the cooling system is to take heat from the engine and transfer it to the atmosphere. Flowing coolant through the engine block and cylinder heads to the radiator where the heat is transferred to the atmosphere via radiated and convection cooling accomplishes this function. The primary aspects of the cooling system performance are the flow rate of the coolant and the cooling capacity of the radiator. The more coolant that can be pushed through the system, the more cooling that takes place.

If the engine is making more power than what the factory originally specified, the radiator either needs to be larger to handle additional heat, or the airflow needs to be faster. There are just three items to adjust to increase the cooling

The cooling system in this NASCAR B-Body is heavily modified. The radiator was moved back, extensive ducting was installed to direct airflow into the radiator, and a Corvette expansion tank was added.

CHAPTER 4

system's capacity: the coolant flow, the radiator size, and the airflow across the radiator's fins.

Radiators

Size does matter when you're talking about radiators. The bigger the radiator, the better it is at transferring heat. Unfortunately, the Mopar engineers only provided a certain space for the radiator, so unless the front sheet metal is going to be modified, the radiator dimensions are fixed. Starting in 1966, a 26-inch radiator was optional in the B-Body. Higher-performance models usually received the 26-inch radiator; lower-performance models had either a 19- or 22-inch radiator. Generally speaking, vehicles with high-output engines, air conditioning, or a special rear-end option were upgraded to the wider 26-inch radiator core.

The sheet metal surrounding the radiator on a Mopar is called the radiator yoke support, or the core support. This sheet-metal stamping is welded into the front of the vehicle, so upgrading a car from a smaller 22-inch core support to the larger 26-inch opening does require replacing the two sheet-metal panels on each side of the radiator.

Converting a B-Body to the larger 26-inch size formerly required cutting a core support out of a donor car, but these days the aftermarket is producing replacement panels. AMD offers 26-inch core supports for 1966 to 1972 B-Body cars. Owners of early B-Body cars still need to custom-modify their existing core support to accommodate a 26-inch radiator.

For a B-Body car with more than 450 hp, you should seriously consider upgrading to the larger 26-inch radiator. The standard rule of thumb for radiator sizing is to use 1 square inch of surface area per engine hp. A 500-hp engine would, therefore, need a 500 square-inch radiator. Even with the 26-inch width, the factory height of 19 inches limits the total surface area to just 494 square inches. This size should be adequate for common street use with a modified engine, but the system might overheat when heavily loaded or on extremely hot days.

OEM radiators during the muscle car years were made exclusively from a copper/brass material. This is an excellent material for radiators, because it has high conductivity as well as decent strength-to-weight ratio, and it can be brazed or soldered together fairly well.

Over the years, additional research into the physics of cooling systems showed the design engineers that what they really needed for good heat transfer was a larger tube, and the copper/brass tube construction just becomes too heavy when the tube size is significantly increased. Therefore, over the years, there has been a shift to aluminum radiators made with two rows of large-diameter tubes, rather than the older copper/brass radiators, which had multiple rows of smaller tubes.

Currently, about 75 percent of automotive radiators are constructed from aluminum, and various aluminum radiators are available for B-Body vehicles. Vendors, such as Griffin, have the blueprints on-hand to produce aluminum versions of original B-Body radiators.

Thermostats and Restrictors

The primary function of the thermostat in an automotive engine is to help the engine come up to operating temperature as quickly as possible. During normal operation, the thermostat stays closed until the engine reaches operating temperature, and then it opens to allow coolant to flow into the radiator. Once the thermostat opens, its job is basically done.

People sometimes get confused about the purpose of the thermostat and blame it for various issues with the cooling system. If the engine is running too hot because the radiator is too small, changing the thermostat or eliminating the thermostat does not fix anything. The radiator controls how much heat is rejected

The aluminum radiator from Griffin Thermal Products on the left has a stock appearance and fits the original mounts. The radiator on the right is an original 22-incher from a 1965 Coronet with a 426W engine.

ENGINE SYSTEM UPGRADES

to the atmosphere; the thermostat just regulates how quickly the engine warms up. Another popular myth is that replacing the thermostat with a restrictor plate helps keep the engine cool. The use of a restrictor instead of a thermostat typically decreases the performance of the cooling system rather than improving it. Remember, more flow is better if additional cooling is required.

Water Pumps

The water pump is a very important part of the overall cooling system performance. For cooling effectiveness, the more coolant flowing through the system, the better. There is a popular myth that the coolant needs to move slowly through the radiator in order to properly "release the heat," but this isn't true at all. In fact, the higher the flow rate, the better the cooling system works. Increasing the volume of the coolant flowing through the system is one of the best ways to improve the cooling system's performance, especially when you are constrained with the size of the radiator. A high rate of flow for the coolant resolves other issues, such as steam pockets and localized overheating.

Centrifugal-Flow Water Pump: The Mopar V-8 engines used a centrifugal type of water pump. A centrifugal pump flows a higher volume of coolant as the speed increases, but the pump efficiency drops off quickly if the pump speed becomes too high. For a street-driven engine, the water pump should be overdriven slightly to keep the speed high enough to ensure adequate coolant volume is pumped through the cooling system.

The factory water pump drive ratio for the maximum cooling option was usually about 1:1 to the crankshaft. This ratio was increased for the later-model cars to a ratio of 1.2:1. The water pump was overdriven at a ratio of 1.4:1 for air-conditioning-equipped engines, but those engines had a smaller impeller in the water pump, so the overall coolant flow stayed about the same. For racing use, the crankshaft pulley size should be reduced to lower the maximum speed of the water pump.

The typical rule of thumb is to use 6,000 rpm as the maximum speed for a Mopar water pump. The Hemi engines were underdriven by either .84:1 or .95:1, depending on the year. The Hemi crank pulley does not retrofit to the wedge engines, due to the different dampener thickness, but underdrive pulleys are available from vendors such as March and Moroso.

The factory used a high-capacity water pump with eight impeller blades for most big-block engine packages. The engines equipped with air conditioning used a smaller-diameter impeller that only had six blades. This smaller impeller pumped less coolant, but the pump was driven at a faster speed to make up for it. Racers soon figured out that they could free up some horsepower by running the small air conditioning water pump at slower speeds. The combination of the small impeller blade with the slower speed reduced the power requirement of the water pump. It also reduced the coolant flow through the engine block, but this doesn't matter for most drag race vehicles. This trick was even used by the factory for the 426 Hemi engine in 1967. For that year, the factory engineers used the air conditioning water pump and a .84:1 water pump drive ratio to free up the maximum possible power from the cooling system.

A variety of water pump designs have been available for small and big-block engines. The factory water pumps used low-cost sheet-metal impellers; the aftermarket has generally adopted the scroll-type impellers shown on the left. The six-blade impeller in the lower right corner is noticeably smaller than the eight-blade impeller next to it.

Water pump pulleys are available in several different diameters, as are crankshaft pulleys. The factory engineers usually drove the water pump at crankshaft speed, but some Hemi cars used an underdriven water pump to free up some horsepower.

CHAPTER 4

At the other end of the scale, cars ordered with the towing option usually had an overdriven eight-blade water pump. In those situations, the factory engineers combined the biggest water pump impeller with an overdrive pulley ratio to make sure that the coolant flow through the engine was as high as possible.

Most of the aftermarket water pumps these days are a copy of the heavy-duty water pump, rather than the smaller air conditioning pump. Some vendors, such as Edelbrock, have improved the design even further by using a scroll-type impeller on their big-block pumps. Edelbrock also added a plate onto the back side of the small-block impellers for additional coolant flow. These design changes increase the volume of coolant that the pumps can move through the engine, and they help to improve the cooling capacity of the system.

Reverse-Flow Water Pumps: There is some interest in racing circles in the concept of reverse-flow cooling. In short, the concept of reverse-flow cooling is to send the cold coolant to the cylinder heads first and then to the engine block. The idea is that the cylinder heads run hotter than the block due to the combustion chamber and exhaust ports, and, therefore, should be cooled first. There are several vendors that offer reverse-flow cooling water pump systems for the big-block and Hemi motors, including Meziere, which sells a bolt-on reverse-flow pump.

Although reverse-flow cooling is a wonderful idea, in practice it has had a number of issues. The biggest stumbling block to implementing a successful reverse-flow cooling system is the problem of trapping air and steam in the cylinder heads.

Meziere sells a reverse-flow water pump for big-block engines. With a reverse-flow water pump, the coolant is first pushed through the cylinder heads, and then it exits from the front of the block.

Any air that gets trapped in the cylinder heads has to be flushed down through the engine block, and it is very difficult to force air bubbles inside the cylinder heads to flow into the block.

One trick that engine builders use with reverse-flow cooling systems is to install bleeder valves at the highest point in the water jacket in the cylinder heads. These bleeder valves can be used to purge the air from the system on a regular basis. This type of on-going maintenance is not an issue for a drag race motor, but would quickly become a hassle on a street-driven engine.

Electric Water Pumps: The use of electric water pumps has steadily increased over the years as electric motor technology improved. An electric water pump is an excellent choice for a drag race engine. It reduces weight, eliminates the complexity of the belt drive, and frees up a small amount of engine power. An electric water pump also provides an excellent way to cool down an engine between races because the pump can be left running to circulate coolant through the cooling system with the engine off.

Electric water pumps also provide some additional flexibility in cooling system design. The inlet position can be relocated on most electric pumps, and in many cases, the entire pump can be moved to a remote location rather than leaving it mounted to the engine. Vendors, such as Meziere, have electric pumps that can be mounted directly to the radiator for a simple system design. These remote pumps have provisions for hoses that can then be run directly to the engine inlet.

When using a remote water pump, the cooling system can be quickly configured for reverse-flow cooling or other designs, such as having the cold coolant enter the side of the engine block in one of the core plugs.

Although electric water pumps are an excellent choice for drag race engines, they typically are not used on circle track engines, and they are not necessarily a good idea for street cars. An electric water pump does not have the same durability of a belt-driven pump, and the electric water pump can't match the power capacity of a belt-driven system. Cars that are driven infrequently on the street, such as pro/street or cruiser-type vehicles, have used electric water pumps with varying degrees of success. As with any other modification to the vehicle, it is important to consider the application and to pick a solution that solves the most problems.

ENGINE SYSTEM UPGRADES

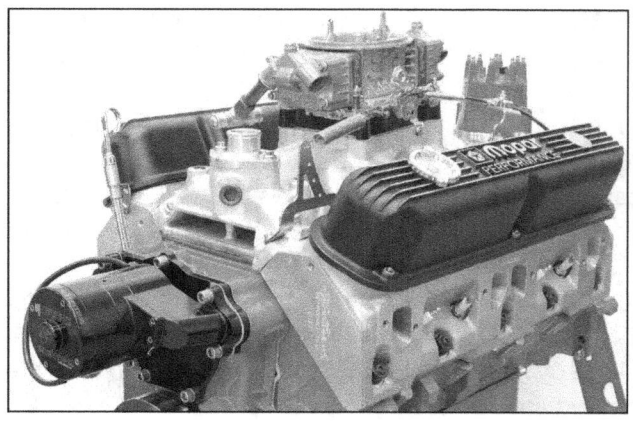

Bill Jenkins was one of the first to use an electric water pump. He did it by driving the water pump on the Old Reliable race car with a reverse-wired generator. These days, vendors, such as Meziere, offer bolt-on electric water pumps for both small-block and big-block engines.

Meziere also sells a remote water pump, which can be located on the motor plate or mounted directly to the radiator. A remote pump can help when trying to stuff a big engine into a small engine compartment.

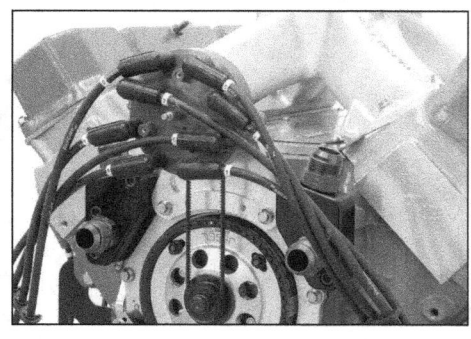

Water manifolds, such as this pair from Mancini Racing, are used to connect the output lines from a remote water pump to the engine block. The lines can be connected conventionally or for reverse cooling.

Fans, Mechanical or Electric

Mopar muscle cars all came from the factory with belt-driven engine fans, but those have become rare these days on any automotive engine. The electric engine fan technology has come a long way over the past 40 years and has made the belt-driven fan almost obsolete. Although the old fans were simple in design, they suffered from the basic flaw of being directly coupled to the engine. Direct coupling to the engine meant that the fan couldn't provide adequate airflow at idle without causing a lot of drag and noise at higher engine speeds.

Viscous-coupled fan drives were developed in the late 1960s, and they helped solve part of this issue. The viscous coupling (or fan clutch) was stiff enough to rotate the fan at low speeds but allowed the fan to slip at higher engine speeds. This approach provided better cooling at low speeds without forcing the fan to run at high engine speeds.

The fan clutch design is still a simple, reliable, and fairly inexpensive way to operate a cooling fan. With the addition of a large-diameter aluminum fan, you can build a perfectly adequate fan system for an updated B-Body vehicle.

Electric cooling fans are decoupled from the engine speed, which allows them to be turned on and off by a thermostat. Typically, the engine needs extra airflow at lower engine speeds, such as idling on a hot day; at freeway speeds, the airflow across the radiator is high enough that the fan can be turned off.

Electric fans consume a lot of power, so the electrical system in any Mopar muscle car usually needs to be upgraded. A higher-amp alternator is often required, and the wiring needs to be upgraded to handle the extra current. Pull-type fans work best,

Factory fans were available in a variety of sizes and styles. Late-model fans, such as this one, were usually at least 20 inches in diameter; they had aluminum blades to reduce the weight and a non-symmetrical pattern to reduce noise. A thermal clutch is an excellent idea for most street-driven cars.

A fan shroud should be used whenever possible. In most cases, a factory-style shroud can be adapted to radiators that didn't originally have a shroud. This C-Body shroud has been adapted to an early B-Body radiator.

and the fan should be mounted in a shroud in order to improve the efficiency. There are several vendors that offer complete fan kits for Mopar applications.

Electric engine fans also provide a way to free up some space in the engine compartment. Some engine swaps, such as big-block A-Body cars, do not have very much room for a water pump and engine fan, so an electric fan provides a little extra room around the engine.

A fan shroud is highly recommended for either a mechanical fan or an electric fan. The shroud helps to ensure that the airflow is directed across the radiator core rather than flowing around the radiator. Many of the original Mopar muscle cars did not have a factory-installed fan shroud, so this would be one of the very first steps to take in improving the cooling system performance.

Coolants

Water is the best coolant to use for heat transfer, but pure water has problems with freezing and corrosion. Pure water with a corrosion-resistance additive, such as Prestone Super Radiator Anti-Rust, works the best for a racing engine or a summer-only driver.

Another option is to use water mixed with a special additive, such as WaterWetter. WaterWetter is designed to reduce the surface tension of the water in order to increase the heat transfer from the engine to the water. WaterWetter also contains anti-corrosion additives, so other additives do not need to be added to the mixture. If the engine is going to be exposed to freezing temperatures, a high-quality antifreeze must be used, or else severe engine damage can result.

Oiling System Modifications

As the performance output of the engine increases, the demands on the lubrication system also increase. More engine power means more heat, and unless that heat is removed from the oil, the oil can overheat and fail. Another item to consider is that as the suspension system is updated, the cornering ability is improved, and oil control can become a major issue. If the oil pickup in the pan is uncovered during cornering, the oil pressure drops to zero, and engine damage quickly follows.

External Oil Lines

Any type of oil cooler installation requires the mounting and running of oil lines from the engine to the oil cooler. Once the external lines have been installed, it is easy to also add a remote oil filter and, possibly, an accumulator into the system. All of these devices require some method of plumbing the oil out of the engine and through the devices and then back to the engine. The first place to start is at the engine block, where the oil lines are most accessible to the outside.

The big-block is fairly easy to set up with external oil lines, due to the external oil pump, but the small-block engine requires some additional effort. The size of the external oil lines becomes critical, depending on the length and the oil flow. For lines that are kept fairly short, #10 AN lines should be adequate. For engines making more than 600 hp and/or for situations where the lines need to be several feet long, then it would be wise to use #12 AN lines and fittings.

Big-Block and Hemi

The external oil pump on the big-block and Hemi engines makes it fairly easy to install an oil cooler or a remote oil filter. An inexpensive solution is to install an oil line adapter onto the existing oil filter mount. This is a cheap and easy solution, but oil filter adapters like this suffer from potential leaks, and they add some restriction to the oiling system.

A much better approach is to purchase a special oil pump cover that is designed with ports for external oil lines. Milodon makes a big-block pump cover that is threaded for oil fittings. The Milodon cover bolts onto an existing oil pump and provides a direct path for the engine oil to flow to a remote cooler.

Small-Block

The small-block motor presents a bit more of a challenge than the big-block, because the oil pump is located inside the oil pan. There is an external oil filter mount on the rear passenger's side of the block, but this area on a production block is not designed to accommodate external oil lines. As with the big-block, the easy approach is to use an oil filter adapter with fittings for the external oil lines.

Big-block oil pumps can be easily converted for use with remote oil filters by just changing the pump cover. This cover is an older Milodon unit, but several other vendors offer similar products.

ENGINE SYSTEM UPGRADES

One fairly easy alternative for the small-block is to replicate the factory-style oil cooler plumbing. For factory-installed oil coolers, an oil feed line was taken off the oil pressure fitting at the back of the block. Once the oil had been fed through the oil cooler, it passed back into the oil sump through a hollow fuel pump bolt. This open-loop design is fairly easy to install, but it does need to be properly designed to maintain oil pressure. Because the oil path is open to the sump, the flow must be restricted or else the oil pressure is too low.

For racing applications, the oil filter pad on the engine block can be drilled and tapped for external lines. Typically, a portion of the pad has to be cut away in order to clear the fittings, which means that once a block has been modified this way, it cannot be converted back to a screw-on filter.

Oil Coolers and Remote Filters

An oil cooler is a fairly simple device resembling a small radiator. One significant difference between the two is that an oil cooler must be able to withstand more than 100 psi of pressure, while the cooling system operates at much lower pressures.

When choosing an oil cooler, select one that is large enough to dissipate the anticipated heat. The size of the cooler depends on the application of the engine, as well as its output. Typically, a 1,000-hp drag race engine doesn't need an oil cooler, because it only operates for a few seconds at a time. On the other hand, a 500-hp circle track motor, which operates at peak power for several hundred laps, requires a very large oil cooler.

On a street engine, or on any high-performance engine that has to be run in cold weather, the use of a thermostat in the oil cooler system should be considered. On a cold day, it can take quite a bit of time before the engine oil reaches the proper operating temperature. During the warm-up process, the oil pump is under high stress while pumping cold oil, so you want the oil to warm up as quickly as possible. Several types of thermostats are available on the market to bypass the oil cooler until the oil heats up to a set temperature. In addition to controlling the flow of the oil with a thermostat, it is possible to use a thermostat to control a fan mounted on the cooler. For example, the oil cooler could open at 180 degrees for oil flow, and then at 200 degrees a fan could turn on to provide extra cooling capacity. As always, your imagination and the depth of your pocketbook are your only limits.

Once the engine block has been modified for external oil lines, the oil filter needs to move to a remote location. Once again, a large number of solutions are available for remote oil filter mounts. The high-quality mounts are constructed from billet material rather than cast, and they have AN fittings rather than pipe. If the system is going to be plumbed with AN fittings and lines, it makes more sense to buy a mount that accepts the AN fitting directly rather than use adapters on each threaded port.

When choosing a remote filter mount, you need to consider the type and size of oil filter that is going to be used. There is a very wide selection of oil filters on the market with varying size and flow rates. Oil filters have different pad sizes as well as different center threads. The filter mounts typically are designed for Chevy filters,

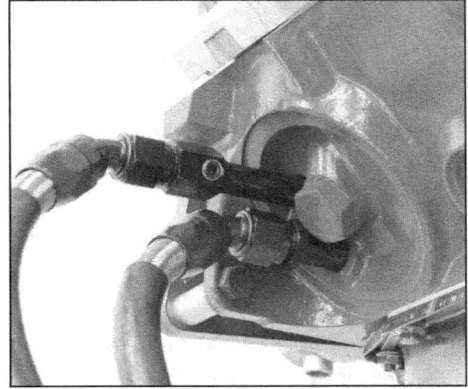

Installing external oil lines on a small-block engine involves drilling and tapping the existing oil passages for 3/8 NPT fittings. Bo Laws makes these oil inlet fittings with #12 AN ends for high-flow systems.

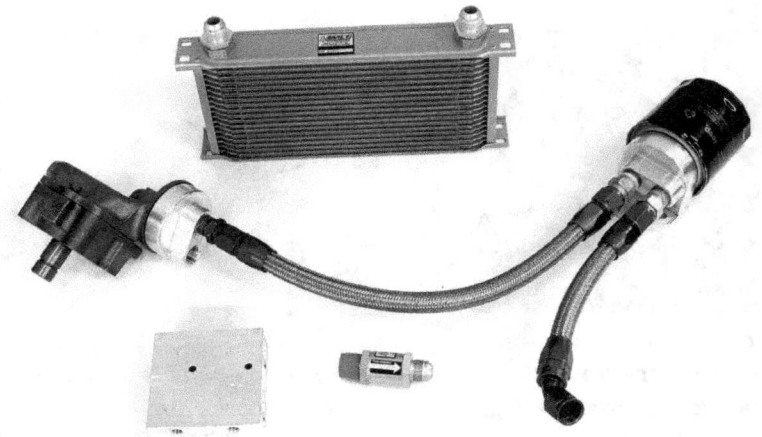

A complete oil cooler system from Earl's includes the cooler, as well as adapters for the oil pump and remote oil filter. Also shown is a thermostatic switch that blocks off the cooler until the oil temperature reaches 180 degrees F.

but there are special mounts available for special racing filters. The Chevy truck filter is an excellent one to use, if you have space for it. Pay attention to see if the oil filter is designed for bypassing or not.

Oil Accumulators

The installation of an oil accumulator is an excellent way to provide an extra margin of safety for a wet sump system. The oil accumulator is a sealed reservoir that is connected to the pressure side of the engine's oiling system. When the engine is started, the oil, under high pressure, flows into the accumulator and stays there under pressure. If the engine were to lose pressure during braking or cornering, the pressurized oil in the accumulator would flow back into the engine and provide a few moments of lubrication.

An accumulator is typically a machined cylinder with a floating piston inside. The oil is kept on one side of the piston by a seal, and the other side has air. As the oil pressure in the engine builds up, the oil flows into the cylinder until the air pressure equals the oil pressure. The simplest systems operate just like this; using a shut-off valve offers a more sophisticated approach. If the valve is closed just before the engine is shut down, several quarts of pressurized oil are trapped behind the valve. When the engine is started, the valve is then opened to provide full oil pressure at the main bearings before the engine is cranked over. Studies have shown that a significant amount of bearing wear occurs during start-up, so a pressurized accumulator can reduce wear.

The accumulator can be plumbed into the oil system anywhere on the pressure side. One good place to hook up the accumulator is at the back of the engine block where the oil pressure gauge mounts. The fittings in the block are normally too small to plumb the accumulator, so they need to be drilled and tapped to a larger size in order to accommodate a #8 or #10 AN line. With the accumulator plumbed into the back of the block, the pressurized oil can flow directly into the main galleries and to the bearings.

It is also possible to plumb the accumulator into the lines for the oil cooler, or the remote oil filter, but if that approach is taken, attention needs to be paid to the possibility of the oil flowing backward through the system, rather than into the engine.

Oil Pans

Using a deep sump pan is the classic solution for oil control problems in a wet sump system. By moving the sump of the pan lower, more oil capacity is added, and the oil is moved farther away from the spinning crankshaft. The deep sump pan is very effective for drag racing in which the acceleration is just in a straight line. A deep sump oil pan can be designed to control the oil being tossed back as the vehicle accelerates down the drag strip, and then also control the oil as the vehicle is under heavy braking at the end of the race.

Much like an egg beater, the crankshaft whips the oil into a froth, so moving the oil away from the rotating assembly improves power and reduces air in the oil. Also, a deeper oil pan means more oil capacity, which then provides additional oil to be available in the sump around the oil pickup.

The primary issue with deep sump oil pans is that they hang below the K-member and are prone to damage. This is especially true with cars that have been lowered for better handling. In this situation, the only way

A pressurized remote oil reservoir is an excellent performance upgrade for both drag racing and road racing. A remote reservoir can also be used as an engine pre-oiler to extend bearing life.

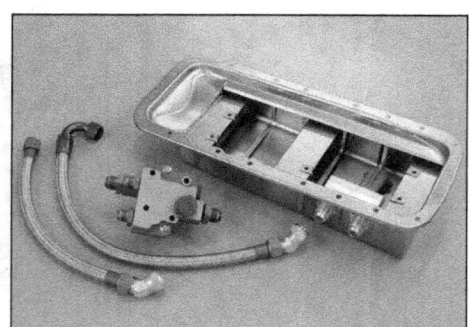

A full range of oil pans is available for both small-block and big-block engines. This big-block pan is designed for cars with rack-and-pinion steering and external oiling.

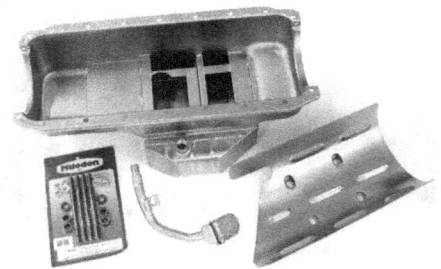

Milodon has road-race-style oil pans for both small-block and big-block engines. These road race pans are excellent for use on a high-performance street-driven car. The road race pans have an extensive system of trap doors to keep the pickup submerged in oil at all times.

ENGINE SYSTEM UPGRADES

to control the oil is to use a road-race type oil pan with extensive baffling.

Pan Baffles

Wet sump pans can do an excellent job of controlling the oil system with a system of baffles and trap doors. Baffles on the sides of the oil pan keep the oil in the sump from surging up the side of the pan during cornering or acceleration. The baffles are typically sloped to encourage oil to run back into the sump, but prevent the oil from traveling up and out of the sump.

Trap doors are a more sophisticated application of the baffle. By putting a series of trap doors in the oil sump, the pan designer can slow the flow of oil from one side of the pan to another. The trap doors are set up to allow oil to freely flow toward the pickup, but the doors slam shut when the oil moves away from the pickup.

A drag race pan might only have trap doors to the front and the rear of the pickup to control the oil flow under acceleration and deceleration. A road race pan, on the other hand, has trap doors on each of the four sides of the pickup so that the oil is controlled during cornering as well as straight-line acceleration.

Milodon sells road race oil pans that fit both the small-block and the big-block engines in B-Body applications. The Milodon pans are the best compromise between ground clearance and oil control for high-performance street use. For dedicated drag race duty, one of the deep sump pans would work fine and cost less than the road race pan.

Oil Pump Pickups

The clearance between the internal pickup and connecting rods is often an issue with larger stroker motors. On big-block and Hemi engines, the stroke is usually limited to about 4.250 inches maximum before the connecting rods begin to physically interfere with an internal pickup. On the small-block motor, the oil pump, as well as the pickup, starts to interfere with the connecting rods at strokes over 4.125 inches.

Windage Trays and Scrapers

Windage trays are available for both small-block and big-block Mopar engines from a variety of vendors. The original Direct Connection handbook claimed an increase of 15 hp by using a windage tray on a big-block engine, but this seems a little optimistic. However, certainly, power is to be gained by stripping oil off the rotating assembly and directing it back to the sump in the oil pan. Ideally, the windage tray should be installed so that it is close enough to the rotating assembly to effectively strip off the oil. Sometimes, it helps to pry open the louvers on the windage tray to provide more room for the oil to flow through.

When using a windage tray with a stroker motor, the tray position must be adjusted to clear the larger stroke. The small-block tray can be positioned on the main studs for

A windage tray should be used with most oil pans to prevent excessive whipping of the oil in the sump. Stock replacement windage trays are available, as are ones designed for stroker engines.

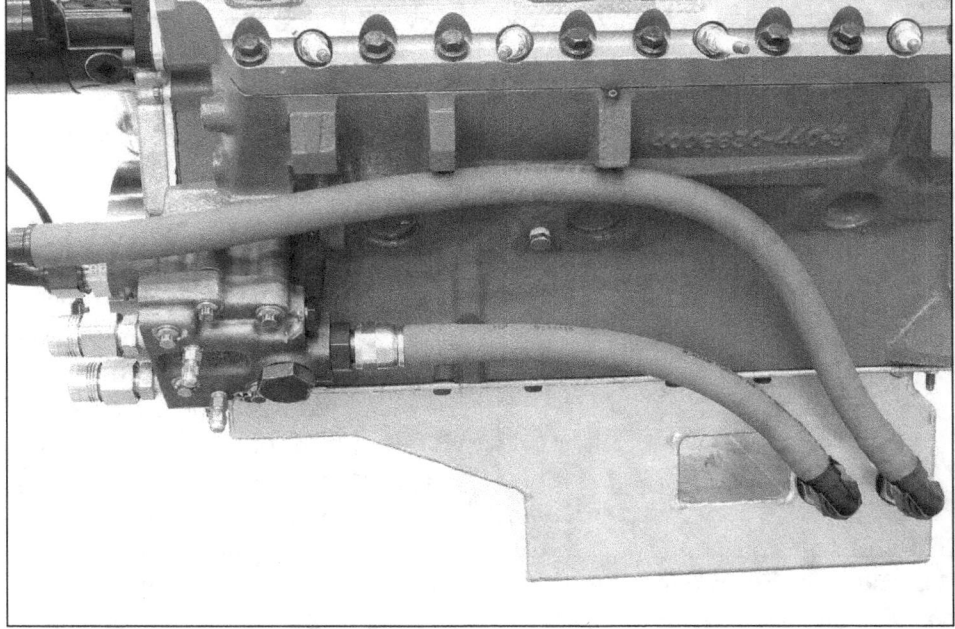

Drag race engines work best with rear sump oil pans, but the rear sump interferes with the steering linkage. One solution developed years ago is to weld a tube into the oil pan for the steering linkage to run through.

proper clearance, but the big-block tray might need to be dimpled for clearance. Milodon offers a stroker windage tray for big-block motors that accepts a 4.500-inch stroke.

Steering Linkage Clearance

The center link on B-Body vehicles runs underneath the engine in the exact spot where the oil sump should ideally be. To provide clearance for the steering linkage, the original Chrysler engineers moved the oil sump to the middle of the engine. This middle sump arrangement isn't ideal for drag racing, because the oil wants to end up in the back of the pan during hard acceleration.

A number of oil pan vendors such as Milodon have created rear sump oil pans with an internal tube for the steering linkage to pass through. This no-compromise-type oil pan design works very well for drag race motors, but it does slightly complicate engine work, because the steering linkage needs to be removed before the engine can be removed.

As discussed elsewhere in this book, there are alternative front suspension designs available for B-Body vehicles that move the steering linkage to the front of the K-member. With the steering linkage out of the way, a large rear sump oil pan can be used.

Dry Sump Systems

When the cornering ability of a vehicle approaches the 1-g mark, it becomes very difficult to control the oil in even the very best wet sump systems. During high-g cornering maneuvers, the oil pulls away from the pickup and plasters itself on the side of the oil pan. Although a swinging pickup system can compensate to some extent for this, there still comes a point where the engine designer needs to use a dry sump system.

Dry sump oiling systems were once considered rather exotic, and they still are quite rare on street-driven muscle cars, but many of the exotic car manufacturers, such as Ferrari, Porsche, and Lamborghini, use dry sumps on their production vehicles. Even the LS7 engine in the 2010 Corvette uses a dry sump system, so they are starting to be a little more common.

The basic concept behind a dry sump system is to evacuate the oil from the crankcase and store it externally. The engine's internal oil flow remains the same, but the oil that isn't in the internal passages in the block is stored in a tank, rather than allowed to slosh around in the oil pan. Having the oil stored in a separate tank provides a number of advantages, such as improved quality and better cooling. There are some disadvantages, such as complexity, cost, and weight, when compared to a wet sump system.

Improved Oiling

One very important benefit of a dry sump system is that the oil tank allows the oil to de-aerate and to cool down. Dry sump tanks are typically tall and cylindrical so that the oil is cooled as it flows down the sides of the tank. Removing the oil from the egg-beater environment of the oil pan also allows the oil to give up some of the air that has been beaten into it. The dry sump tanks are equipped with a system of baffles and breathers that are designed to separate the air from the oil. If the tank is working correctly, the cone-shaped area at the bottom of the tank is filled with oil that is cool and does not contain excess air. The pressure section of the pump is then able to pull this high-quality oil from the tank and pump it back into the engine.

Weight, Cost and Complexity

A dry sump system typically weighs a little more than a wet sump system. This is because of the extra weight of the external oil tank, as well as all of the lines necessary to route the oil from the engine to the tank and back again. However, there is a compensating effect, due to the fact that the external oil tank can be located toward the rear of the vehicle, which in turn can improve the weight distribution. Many circle track cars place the oil tank behind the driver or in the trunk area. Drag race cars often put the tank up front near the radiator in order to keep the lines as short as possible.

A complete dry sump system often costs a slight premium over a wet sump system, but the difference isn't very large when high-quality parts are used for both cases. Also, a vacuum pump system is often purchased with a wet sump system, but it might not be required with a dry sump system, as a good dry sump

A dry sump oiling system is the best choice if the budget and/or rules allow it. This big-block engine is fitted with a three-stage pump and a custom drive system.

ENGINE SYSTEM UPGRADES

A view from below shows how the two scavenge lines from the belt-driven oil pump are attached to the oil pan. These lines send the oil to the remote tank mounted on the motor plate. (Photo Courtesy Gary Beineke)

pump can be used to pull a vacuum in the crankcase.

No doubt, a dry sump system is more complex in terms of hose routings than a production-type wet sump system, but once again, the difference narrows when compared to a fully developed racing system. Most serious race engines use external oil lines on big-blocks to feed the oil pump, and many use an external filter and cooler already. There really isn't a huge difference in complexity between a wet sump system with external cooler and filter and a dry sump system. Some engine builders even use a belt-driven external oil pump with their wet sump systems; in that case, the only difference is the external oil tank and its associated plumbing.

Electrical System

The electrical system used for most Mopar muscle cars was a marginal design, even when new. The original design works okay if kept in top condition, but it degrades quickly in corrosive environments. Even when in the best working order, the original system was designed to operate with a 37-amp alternator, and it is not capable of carrying the higher loads required by modern accessories.

The Firewall Hazard

The weakest point of the OE wiring harness concerns the dash-mounted ammeter and the associated requirement that the full alternator output must run through the firewall in order to pass through the ammeter. The original design required that the entire electrical load for the vehicle passes in and out of the firewall on two flat-blade connectors, which were only rated for 15 amps continuous duty. As the vehicle aged, these connectors became corroded, and the resistance within the connector increased. It used to be quite common to find Mopar vehicles in wrecking yards with melted firewall connectors and burnt ammeters.

Eventually, the factory engineers realized that this was a weak design and upgraded the harness. The design changes included increasing the wire gauge for the charge circuit and using higher-rated connectors for the charge circuit.

There was a variety of charging circuit designs used for B-Body vehicles over the years. The early cars came with a very simple charging system with a 12-gauge wire running to the ammeter, and then another 12-gauge wire running back to the positive side of the battery. By 1978, these charge wires were upgraded to 10 gauge for the standard alternator and 6 gauge for the heavy-duty 100-amp alternator. Obviously, the factory engineers understood the need to upgrade the wiring harness when the alternator output was increased.

There are a variety of ways to improve the factory firewall connector, depending on what type of system you desire. The least amount of change required would be to stay with the factory ammeter in the original location, but improve the connectors at the firewall. In this case, the easiest fix is to drill a new hole in the firewall and feed the charge lines directly to the ammeter without connectors. Heavy 6-gauge wires that run directly from the output stud on the alternator to the ammeter, and back to the starter relay, greatly reduce the resistance in the system. The wires should be fed through a grommet to avoid chaffing the wires on the firewall, and the grommet should be sealed with RTV to prevent fumes from entering the cabin.

Ammeter or Voltmeter

At some point, the ammeter becomes the weak link, as there are only so many amps that can flow through the ammeter before it melts. In the mid 1970s, the 100-amp alternator system was deployed on a variety of Chrysler vehicles. A close examination of this system shows the separate firewall connectors used, as well as shunts on the ammeter to

CHAPTER 4

This Magnum engine is upgraded with a 60-amp Denso alternator. These Denso alternators are smaller and lighter than the original Mopar alternators, but they produce more amperage and work better at low speeds. That is the great thing about 40 years of engineering development.

bypass excessive current. These are all Band-Aids that can be used to extend a rather flawed initial design, but a conversion to a voltmeter is probably the best idea.

The ammeter can be thought of as a gauge showing how many amps are flowing in the system, just as a flow meter shows gallons per hour. A voltmeter, on the other hand, is best thought of as a pressure gauge; that is, it shows the pressure in the system, and then the flow depends on the resistance.

Although there is some debate about which monitoring system is the best, most vehicles have switched to a voltmeter arrangement because it is simple and effective. A voltmeter requires just a simple sense wire to "see" what the voltage level is in the electrical system. There is no need to pass the entire electrical load through a dash-mounted gauge.

The addition of a sensor light to show if the alternator is producing the correct voltage can be valuable when switching to a voltmeter. The warning light provides a quick way to alert the driver if the alternator is not maintaining system voltage.

Alternator

The alternator design used for most B-Body production was an inadequate design, as it did not produce very much current at low speeds. It was fairly common to watch the headlights in an original B-body dim at a stop light, only to brighten back up when the engine speed increased.

Newer-design alternators not only produce more amps, but they are also smaller and lighter. Modern alternators from Denso or Bosch produce 60 amps or more while weighing less and taking up less space than the original 37-amp alternators. Mounting kits are available from vendors, such as Mancini Racing and Hughes Engines, to install late-model Denso alternators onto any small-block, big-block, or Hemi motor.

The traditional Mopar alternator design used a voltage regulator mounted on the firewall to regulate the output of the alternator. Originally, these regulators were a mechanical device, but in the early 1970s, an electronic design was developed. The electronic regulators were a fairly good design, but they are an extra part that takes up space, so the OEMs made a switch to internally regulated alternators in the 1980s.

When a modern internally regulated alternator is retrofitted to an earlier Mopar muscle car, a minor change needs to be made to the wiring system. Basically, the switched 12-volt feed wire that used to go to the external regulator just needs to be extended to the regulator inside of the alternator.

Mancini Racing sells a kit to adapt a 120-amp Denso alternator to any big-block engine. A large alternator like this is required when using accessories, such as dual electric fans, large electric fuel pumps, or mega-watt stereo systems.

CHAPTER 5

BRAKE SYSTEM FUNDAMENTALS

The next several chapters deal with different aspects of Mopar brake systems, ranging from factory replacement parts to high-performance brake systems suitable for track cars. In order to properly understand the different brake systems and how they work, I first need to discuss some fundamentals of brake systems. I only have enough room in this chapter to just skim the surface of the subject, but there are a number of reference books on brakes. One of the more detailed reviews of brake system concepts can be found in *High-Performance Brake Systems: Design, Selection, and Installation* by James Walker.

An automotive brake system is nothing more than a simple hydraulic system, with the master cylinder providing a volume of pressurized fluid that drives the brake pistons located at each wheel. The key to successful operation is to have the correct pressure and volume available at each wheel to safely stop the vehicle. B-Body brake systems, starting in 1967, are dual systems consisting of separate hydraulic circuits for the front and rear brakes. Mopars built earlier than 1967 used a single-pot brake system, with a "jelly jar" type of master cylinder, rather than a dual-circuit system. Unless the car is just for show, these older single-pot systems should be converted to a modern dual-circuit system.

There are two very important principles that you need to understand when modifying the brake system of your car. First, the front brakes need to be balanced to the rear brakes. This front-to-rear balance is called bias, and it is a very important, although often overlooked, principle. The second fundamental principle is the hydraulic balance between the master cylinder and the wheel cylinders. The master cylinder and the wheel cylinders need to be considered together as a system; you should not change part of the system without understanding the effect on the other parts.

The key to a successful brake swap is to maintain the proper balance among all of the parts. That is, the master cylinder size must be balanced with the wheel cylinder size, and the front brakes must be properly balanced with the rear brakes. For some reason, many enthusiasts

Late-model aluminum master cylinders have been available with at least four different bore sizes. Aluminum master cylinders have a two-bolt mounting flange; cast-iron versions use a four-bolt arrangement.

routinely ignore this extremely important point. Internet forums are full of people asking about the price or fitment of disc brake kits, but you hardly ever see a question about piston size or bias ratio.

Master Cylinder Bore Size

Judging by the number of questions you see on web chat boards, selecting the correct master cylinder size for a given disc brake swap is a fairly confusing task. With a little bit of education, the process should be much easier to understand.

Given a standard pedal force, the master cylinder bore size controls the volume and pressure of fluid delivered to the wheel cylinders. A master cylinder with a large-diameter bore delivers more volume for each inch of travel, but at a lower pressure. A master cylinder with a smaller bore size delivers less volume, but at a higher pressure. The wheel cylinders need both the correct volume and pressure in order to operate the brakes correctly, so the master cylinder size is critical.

Master cylinder sizing can be calculated with an engineering formula, but for the average person, it is easier to just duplicate the factory solutions. A good starting point is the design that Chrysler engineering used for the late-model B-Bodies. These vehicles came from the factory with 11¾-inch front brake rotors, 10-inch rear drums, and a 1 1/32-inch master cylinder. The front calipers used a single 2.750-inch-diameter piston, and the rear drums had 15/16-inch-diameter wheel cylinders. This combination creates a well-balanced system that is easy to duplicate on any B-Body vehicle. The Mopar aluminum master cylinders are currently available in several sizes, ranging from 15/16 to 1 1/32 inches. Pedal feel can be tuned to the driver's preference by varying the master cylinder bore size; just don't get too far away from the baseline design.

Caliper Design, Fixed or Floating

Mopar vehicles have used both fixed and floating calipers over the years. The Bendix system, used on the 1966 to 1969 B-Body cars, was a fixed, four-piston caliper design. The fixed caliper design is used for high-performance applications as a way to save weight and space. Also, having the caliper location fixed eliminates any sliding friction between the caliper and the adapter. The only problem with a fixed caliper design is that manufacturing costs are higher, due to the extra machine work.

In 1970, due most likely to cost considerations, Chrysler engineers changed over to floating calipers rather than fixed calipers. At the same time, they also went to a caliper with one 2.750-inch-diameter piston rather than four smaller pistons. The floating calipers, sometimes called sliding calipers, work okay for street driving and mild-performance use, but they are not well-suited for high-performance applications. The primary issue with the use of sliding calipers in high-performance applications is that the small amount of sliding friction inherent in the design can lead to unpredictable brake performance. If the caliper on one side of the vehicle sticks a little bit, the driver experiences a sudden pull to one side during heavy braking. An initial pull to one side or the other doesn't really cause an issue at highway speeds, but it can be very unsettling at high speeds, especially when racing door to door with other vehicles on a tight race track.

Rotor Size

For high-performance use, the bigger the rotor, the better. The rotor is a heat sink for the brake system, and generally speaking, the bigger the heat sink, the better. During braking, the kinetic energy of the vehicle is converted into heat energy by the friction of the brake pads. This heat energy is then dissipated into the mass of the brake rotors. If the rotors do not have enough mass to absorb the energy, the rotors overheat. The rotors must be heavy enough to absorb the maximum energy that is dissipated, but they should not be any heavier than necessary. The brake rotors are unsprung weight, so any additional weight in this area creates extra work for the suspension to control.

For a street car, the wise approach is to use a rotor that is a little heavier than required, thereby providing an extra margin of safety. A racing

The largest OEM rotor ever used on B-Body cars was the 11¾ x 1.0-inch rotor (bottom). Chrysler engineers are now using much larger rotors for performance vehicles. At the top right is a 14 x 1.250-inch rotor from a new Charger; on the left is a massive 15 x 1.375-inch rotor from a Dodge Ram SRT. Larger rotors improve brake capacity and reduce pedal force, but they also add unsprung weight.

car, especially one with a dedicated maintenance budget, can reduce the rotor size until the margin of error approaches zero.

Piston Area

One very key item to pay attention to is the size of the pistons in the brake calipers. The aftermarket brake systems that are currently on the market for B-Body cars vary in terms of total piston area. This doesn't mean that the kits are poorly engineered; it just means that you need to understand the basic concept of brake system balance before purchasing one of the kits. Matching brake components to each other is no different than picking the correct camshaft profile to work with the engine's displacement and compression ratio.

Sliding Caliper

The B-Body sliding caliper, with its single 2.750-inch-diameter piston, has a total piston area of 5.940 square inches. Rounding off this figure to 6 square inches of piston area should be firmly imprinted on the mind of anyone who is going to be changing the brake system, because it provides the baseline for all brake system modifications.

For example, consider an aftermarket brake system caliper with two 1.500-inch-diameter pistons. A casual observer might think that two pistons would have more area and more braking ability than a single-piston caliper, but some quick calculations show that the total area of those two pistons is only 3.530 square inches. Because the piston area has been reduced by 40 percent, this aftermarket system only generates 60 percent of the braking force of the factory 2.750-inch system. Losing 40 percent of the braking force was probably not the intention of the brake swap, but that can easily happen if you aren't paying attention to what you are buying.

Fixed Caliper

One item that tends to confuse people is the calculation of piston area for a fixed caliper. Piston area is easy to calculate for a sliding caliper because the piston is on just one side of the rotor. Fixed calipers have pistons on both sides of the rotor, so people naturally think that the area of all of the pistons should be included in the calculation. Regardless of what seems natural, in both cases the piston area is calculated by just totaling up the surface area of the pistons on one side of the caliper. So, for a six-piston caliper with three pistons on each side, you only calculate the surface area of the three pistons on one side of the caliper.

The fact that the pistons on the other side of the caliper do not add any braking force is one of the reasons why sliding-type calipers are so popular. After all, why should the vehicle manufacturer pay for the extra caliper pistons when they do not add any braking force? There are plenty of reasons to use a fixed caliper, but additional braking force from the additional pistons is not one of them.

Matching Brake System Parts

In the earlier example, new calipers with 40-percent smaller pistons are going to be used. How should you compensate? In such a situation, you should re-balance all of the components based on the new piston area to create a matched system. So, if the new front calipers have a 40-percent reduction in area, the master cylinder size needs to be reduced by 40 percent, as do the rear wheel cylinders.

Remember, the matching has to be by area, not by diameter. A master cylinder with a bore size of 15/16 inch is about 40 percent smaller than one with a bore size of 1.125 inches. So, in this example, if the caliper piston size is going to be reduced from roughly 6 square inches to 3.500 square inches, the master cylinder bore size needs to be reduced from a diameter of 1.125 inches to .875 inch.

At this point, we've ignored the effects on the rear brakes, but they

Caliper piston size is very important. The larger the piston diameter, the more brake force is applied to the rotor. The large single-piston design used in factory B-Body brake systems usually provides more braking force than aftermarket multi-piston calipers.

Many of the modern high-performance calipers use staggered pistons to even out the pad wear. The caliper must be installed so that the rotor spins from the small piston to the large piston.

also need to be matched to the front brakes, so they also need to have the piston size or the wheel cylinder size reduced a proportional amount.

Bias

The bias of the front-to-rear brake systems is an extremely important aspect to consider when changing brake parts. Bias refers to the amount of brake force that is applied to the front wheels versus the amount that is applied to the rear wheels. The front wheels on a typical B-Body perform about two-thirds of the braking, due to the nose-heavy design of these cars. Not only are most Mopar muscle cars nose-heavy to start with, but during deceleration, weight transfers forward, putting even more load on the front brakes. Therefore, brake systems must be selected to provide a proper split of force between the front and rear brakes. If the rear bias (rear braking force) is too high, the rear brakes lock up and cause the vehicle to spin. If the front bias is too high, the rear brakes are not doing their share of the work, and the stopping distance is longer than necessary.

The piston size and rotor diameter of the front and rear brakes primarily determine the brake bias for a four-wheel disc brake system. For drum brakes, the bias is determined by the size of the drums and the diameter of the wheel cylinders. Larger-diameter pistons increase braking force, as does increasing the rotor or drum diameter. Smaller piston size, smaller wheel cylinders, or a smaller brake drum diameter all reduce the braking force.

The brake bias on any Mopar can be adjusted a fair amount with production parts, due to the variety of parts produced over the years. Switching to the larger 11¾-inch-diameter rotors from the 11-inch rotors increases front braking force. Replacing the small 2.600-inch-diameter front caliper pistons with the larger 2.750-inch-diameter caliper pistons also increases front brake bias. In the rear, 10-inch drums can be replaced with 11-inch drums for more rear bias. The size of the rear wheel cylinders can also be changed to adjust the rear brake bias.

The proper amount of front-to-rear bias for the brake system on any vehicle depends on various factors, including weight distribution, the height of the center of gravity, and the rate of deceleration. A rear-engined vehicle, such as a Porsche 911, can use more rear brake bias than a nose-heavy B-Body car. A taller vehicle transfers more weight to the front wheels during braking, and a car that has been lowered transfers less weight. And, of course, the harder the vehicle is stopping, the more weight is transferred to the front wheels.

A universal rule of thumb for brake bias is difficult to provide, given all of the variables, but the typical B-Body Mopar muscle car should perform well when the front-to-rear split is 2:1. That is, the fronts should be set up to provide twice as much braking as the rears. Another way to think about it is that the fronts apply two-thirds of the total brake force while the rears apply one-third of the force.

The 2:1 brake distribution result is based on a typical Mopar muscle car with 54 percent of the weight on the front wheels, a center of gravity that is 20 inches high, and a maximum deceleration of .80 *gs*. The front bias needs to be increased if the vehicle has more weight on the front wheels than 54 percent or if the center of gravity is higher than 20 inches. Conversely, the more weight on the rear or the lower the vehicle then the more rear brake bias can be used.

Bias can be calculated in a four-wheel disc brake system by just comparing the area of pistons in the front calipers to that of the pistons in the rear calipers. If the rotor diameters are different from the front to the rear, that factor also needs to be taken into account. Assuming the rotor diameters are the same at both ends of the car, the front piston area should be twice as large as the rear piston area in order to provide the desired 2:1 bias.

There is no easy way to calculate bias when working with a disc/drum system, so the best approach is to stay with factory combinations and tune as required.

Historical Note

The 1974 Imperial was one of the earliest Chrysler vehicles with four-wheel disc brakes. The engineers who designed the brakes for that vehicle certainly understood all of the available brake theory, but rather than going with a 2:1 ratio, they selected a brake bias of 10:7. The 1974 Imperial had front calipers with 3.100-inch-diameter pistons, and the pistons in the rear calipers were 2.600 inches in diameter. The front and rear rotors were roughly the same diameter, so the calculated brake bias is almost exactly 10:7 front to rear.

The resulting brake bias is too heavily weighted toward the rear to be considered a good candidate for heavy braking, although it worked just fine at lower rates of deceleration. Most likely, the engineers who designed the brakes assumed that the big Imperial wasn't a likely candidate for road racing and, therefore, optimized the brakes for lower-speed operation.

Proportioning Valve

The proportioning valve is a very important part of a modern brake system. It is a requirement with disc/drum systems, because disk brakes operate significantly different from drum brakes. Disc brakes are proportional; that is, if you push twice as hard on the pedal, you have twice as much braking force at the wheel.

A drum brake is different, because it has an extra "self-energizing" or "self-applying" force caused by the design of the brake shoes inside the drum. This self-energizing force inside the drum brake is a result of the brake shoes wedging against the drum. The wedging action of the brake shoes results in an amplified braking force. That is, if you push twice as hard on the brake pedal, you might get three times the braking force. This extra braking force is a nice feature of the drum brake design, because it lowers the necessary pedal pressure. However, this self-energizing force also makes drum brakes difficult to modulate during a panic stop. Consequently, a drum brake is much more prone to locking up than a disc brake, due to the self-energizing force.

In order to reduce the likelihood of rear-wheel lockup during a panic stop, a proportioning valve is installed in the rear brake line. The proportioning valve reduces the amount of brake pressure that is being applied to the rear drums in order to keep them from locking up prematurely. The proportioning valve only affects the pressure to the rear drum brakes; the full pressure is still applied to the front disc brakes at all times. If you test a factory proportioning valve by applying pressure to the input port and observing the pressure on the output port, you see that the output pressure is the same as the input's until a "split point" is reached. Once the split point is reached, the rear pressure increases at a slower rate than the input pressure.

Viper Example

The 1999 Viper field service manual provides a good example of a proportioning valve's operation. According to the manual, the Viper proportioning valve has a split point of 680 psi and a proportioning rate of 43 percent. Given these values, you can see that when the front line pressure is 680 psi, the rear line pressure is also 680 psi. But if the front line pressure is 1,000 psi, the rear line pressure is 680 + (320 x .43) or 818 psi. If the front line pressure is 1,500 psi, the rear line pressure is only 680 + (820 x .43), or 1,030 psi.

The 1999 Viper has a front piston area of 2,520 square mm and a rear piston area of 1,020 square mm for a brake bias of almost 2.5:1. The proportioning valve further decreases the rear braking force under heavy braking. As the line pressure increases (higher pedal force), the rear brake bias is reduced.

The Viper provides an excellent example of brake system design for a high-performance street car. The caliper pistons are sized correctly to create a front bias for moderate braking, and then the proportioning valve decreases the rear brake force during heavy braking. Duplicating a system like this is difficult for the average hot rodder, but with enough research and thought, you should be able to achieve similar results.

Adjustable Proportioning Valves

It is possible to replace the factory pre-set proportioning valve with an aftermarket adjustable proportioning valve, such as the one that Mopar Performance sells. An adjustable valve can be useful for tuning a brake system to minimize stopping distance, providing that the initial bias is correct.

High-performance cars that see serious track duty often have the proportioning valve within reach of the driver, so that adjustments can be made at the track. A car with a very sensitive brake system might need to have the proportioning valve adjusted during the race as the gas tank empties in order to keep the brake balance right on the razor's edge.

The typical street car would not need this type of constant adjustment, because the brakes are rarely used at full capacity on the street. So for a street car, the stock proportioning valve works just fine; if an adjustable one is used, it can be adjusted once and then left alone.

Many vendors of aftermarket proportioning valves do not publish the split point or the proportioning rate of their valves. Without knowing these values, it is impossible to properly engineer the brake system. Evidently, valve vendors assume that the average person is not capable of properly calculating the amount of proportioning that their brake system needs. Given this lack of information, you are left with the option of just trying various valves until you find one that works, or searching for a vendor that actually publishes the engineering values for its valve.

CHAPTER 6

BRAKE UPGRADES WITH FACTORY PARTS

Brake design almost seemed to be an afterthought for Chrysler engineering during the years that the B-Body was in production. Although disc brakes did become available in 1966, they were optional for most vehicles during the 1960s and 1970s. Even the premium-option brake packages available in those years were barely adequate for anything more than spirited street driving or drag racing. Fortunately, a number of factory parts used on later-model Chrysler vehicles can be combined into a cost-effective performance braking system for any B-Body vehicle.

Factory Brake System

Chrysler engineers started to install disc brakes onto production vehicles in the early to mid 1960s, depending on the make and model. Starting in 1966, B-Body owners could order a four-piston, fixed-caliper, Bendix disc brake package. Although these brakes were adequate for the time, the Bendix system is no longer a good choice for high-performance use. Replacement parts for the Bendix system are difficult to find, and tend to be expensive. Even if parts were commonly available, the combination of the heavy cast-iron caliper and the small rotor size makes the Bendix system a poor choice for anything other than mild street use.

The sliding caliper system introduced in 1970 was a slightly better design than the Bendix system, but it is still fairly expensive to maintain. The 1970 to 1972 brakes used a unique two-piece rotor with a smaller inner wheel bearing, and production volumes for this rotor were limited. Due to the low production volumes, these rotors are much more expensive to replace than the later-model uni-cast rotors. Besides being expensive, the 1970 to 1972 rotor is too small for high-performance use under a heavy B-Body car. These small-bearing rotors perform okay for street use, but there isn't really any reason to use this design when the later-model brakes are both cheaper and more robust.

Chrysler engineers changed the design of their disc brakes in 1973 with the adoption of a larger inner wheel bearing and the introduction of a uni-cast rotor. The 1973 design was used for the rest of B-Body production, and then it continued on for the FMJ cars until rear-wheel-drive production ended in 1988. Because the uni-cast rotors were produced in fairly high volumes for more than 15 years, repair parts are commonly available and are reasonably priced. The low cost of these uni-cast rotors makes these later-model brake systems a very attractive swap option for the earlier vehicles.

Richard Ehrenberg of *Mopar Action* magazine wrote the seminal work on retro-fitting the 1973 brake design to earlier Mopar vehicles. His article, "Disc-o-tech," is available on the Mopar Action website in the tech section. Even though the article was written several years ago, it remains a must-read for anyone who is contemplating a brake swap using factory hardware.

The new uni-cast rotors originally came in a 10.78-inch-diameter version. Starting in 1976, a larger 11¾-inch version was offered on the B-Body cars. Any 1973-or-newer B-Body with the 10.78-inch rotors can quickly be upgraded to the larger 11¾-inch rotors by installing the

BRAKE UPGRADES WITH FACTORY PARTS

larger rotors and the corresponding taller caliper brackets. The caliper brackets are held on with two 1/2-inch bolts, so the swap process is very quick.

At the moment, nobody is reproducing the 11¾-inch caliper brackets, so you must find them in a wrecking yard or purchase them used. The 11¾-inch brake systems can be found on B-Body and R-Body cars built after 1976. (Look for a Cordoba or similar vehicle when trying to find these parts in a wrecking yard.) The uni-cast rotors can be retrofitted to any earlier B-Body vehicle by installing the correct large-bearing spindles with matching caliper adapters.

The 11¾-inch brake setup is a very effective system, especially when combined with a late-model aluminum master cylinder. This is the very best system that can be created with factory parts, and it works very well on lighter vehicles. In fact, the factory 11¾-inch system handles the rigors of mild road-race duty in a lightweight B-Body car, provided that the proper brake pads are used and some air ducting is fabricated to cool the rotors.

One nice thing about using the factory system is that replacement rotors are quite inexpensive, so using up a pair of them on a weekend at the track is not a major hit to the pocketbook.

Knuckle Interchange

Before discussing brakes in more detail, I need to discuss the front spindle, or to be more precise, the front knuckle. Understanding the features and interchangeability of the front knuckles is the key to understanding B-Body brake swaps.

B-Body vehicles from 1962 to 1972 used a short front knuckle with a small 1.250-inch-diameter inner wheel bearing surface. In 1973, the inner wheel bearing diameter increased to 1.375 inches, and the overall height of the knuckle was increased by roughly .375 inch. Although the spindle diameter was only increased by 10 percent, it reduces the bending of the spindle by almost 50 percent. The earlier

The 1970 to 1972 B-Body disc brake knuckle on the left looks very similar to the 1973 A-Body knuckle on the right. The primary difference is the size of the inner wheel bearing. The spindle on the left uses a 1.250-inch-diameter inner wheel bearing, while the bearing size on the right-hand spindle is 1.375 inches.

Mopar spindles weren't known for breaking, but a 50-percent increase in stiffness seems well worth a very slight increase in weight.

The upper ball joint taper, as well as the bolt pattern for the lower ball joint, stayed the same for all years of B-Body production. Due to the ball joint dimensions staying the same over the years, any B-Body knuckle bolts into any B-Body car.

The A-Body big-bearing knuckle on the left has more material around the caliper mounting holes than the B-Body knuckle on the right. The lightweight version of the tall knuckle showed up in the late 1970s. Virtually all of the FMJ vehicles have this tall, lightweight, big-bearing disc brake knuckle.

If you cannot find original big-bearing disc brake knuckles in your local salvage yard, you can purchase reproduction knuckles, as shown on the left. Magnum Force makes the 2-inch dropped knuckle on the right. The Magnum Force knuckle is designed to the same specifications as the 1973 big-bearing design, so all of the uni-cast brake parts swap over to this knuckle.

The tall big-bearing knuckle has casting numbers 3402638 and 3402639. These knuckles came on late-model B-Body cars, as well as all of the FMJ vehicles. The short big-bearing knuckle from a 1973-or-newer A-Body or E-Body vehicle has casting numbers 3402627 and 3402626.

CHAPTER 6

Although any knuckle bolts into any car, the difference in knuckle height between early- and late-model vehicles has caused a certain amount of controversy over the years. Some people believe that the 1962 to 1972 cars should only be retrofitted with short knuckles because that is what they were designed to work with. Those in this camp point out that the taller knuckles might cause the upper ball joint to "over angle," or that the suspension geometry is harmed by the taller knuckle.

Others tout the benefits of the taller knuckles, including lighter weight and a better camber curve. People in this camp also point out that vendors sell "tall knuckle" conversions for various GM muscle cars with the intent of improving the suspension geometry. On a personal note, I've used the taller knuckles on several cars and have never seen a problem, but, of course, that is not definitive proof.

Although the debate is somewhat interesting, there are practical answers for people in both camps.

For those who wish to stay with the shorter knuckles on the 1962 to 1972 cars, they are in luck, because the 1973 to 1976 A-Body cars came with exactly what they need. These A-Body cars, as well as E-Body cars after 1973, came with short knuckles that had the larger inner wheel bearing surface. So by using the A-Body knuckles, an owner of a 1962 to 1972 B-Body car can install the later-model uni-cast rotors without changing the front suspension geometry. If you cannot locate the correct A-Body knuckles used, new knuckles are available from a variety of vendors. Magnum Force even sells a version of these knuckles with a 2-inch drop for those who want to drop the front ride height.

For those who want to try the taller knuckles, reproductions are not available, so used parts have to be found. Fortunately, Chrysler engineers used the same tall knuckles under the 1977 to 1988 FMJ cars as they did on the 1973-and-newer B-Body cars. These FMJ cars are still fairly easy to find in wrecking yards, and the front knuckles are usually fairly easy to remove. For those who want to use the taller knuckles but are worried about the possibility of over-angling the upper ball joints, Firm Feel makes upper A-arms that have the upper ball joint slightly tilted. These conversion upper A-arms move the ball joint position slightly so it stays within its range during full suspension travel.

Chrysler started to use phenolic pistons in 1975. They are lightweight, corrosion resistant, and insulate the brake fluid from the hot brake pad. These are 300 grams lighter than the standard chrome pistons. Using phenolic pistons in both calipers saves 1.3 pounds of unsprung weight on the front suspension.

The adapters are available for pin-type and slider calipers. The bolt pattern is the same, so the adapter type can be changed, if necessary. Both adapters are available in two heights to work with the 11- or 11¾-inch rotor. One fact that isn't well known is that there are also heavy-duty versions of the adapters, which are thicker and use longer mounting bolts.

Both of these caliper castings are designed to be used on the driver's side of the car. The housing on the left is a rear-hung design, while the one on the right is a front-hung design. The bleeder always has to be at the highest point on the housing, and the hose fitting should be pointed to the rear.

This is a rear-hung slider housing designed for driver's-side use. There aren't any stock hoses that fit these calipers properly on a B-Body, so custom hoses need to be used. Shown is a stainless steel hose with the correct banjo fitting. DoctorDiff sells these hoses, or they can be purchased from a brake hose dealer.

Calipers

Chrysler engineers used two mounting styles for the 1973-and-newer disc brake calipers. Either mounting system seems to work fine, but the type of bracket is important, because the caliper must match the bracket, and some parts are harder to find than others.

Type

The first style was a pin-guided caliper in which the caliper rides on two hard steel pins. This style lasted well into the 1970s, but it was eventually replaced with a simple mounting bracket where the caliper slides directly on two smooth surfaces in the cast-iron bracket. Because nobody is reproducing the taller 11¾-inch caliper mounting bracket, it is possible that you will be forced to just use whatever bracket you happen to find. If that is the case, you also need to find a caliper that fits the bracket.

Location

One question that often comes up during a brake swap using factory parts is whether to locate the caliper ahead of or behind the spindle. The ball joint mounting locations on the disc brake knuckle are symmetrical, so the knuckle can be installed on either side. Depending on which side of the car the knuckle goes on, the caliper is installed to the front or to the rear of the spindle.

The brake hose routing on the 1962 to 1972 cars tends to work best if the caliper is mounted to the front of the spindle. The front-hung position allows the brake hose to be longer and to be routed in a straight line from the frame to the caliper. A front-hung caliper interferes with the mounting bracket for the anti-sway bar linkage on the 1966 to 1969 cars, so people are sometimes forced into a rear-hung solution.

Although the brake caliper works perfectly fine in a rear-hung position, the hose routing is often done improperly. Chrysler engineers designed a caliper for rear-hung applications for the later F-Body cars, and this caliper is the one that should be used when building a rear-hung system. The F-Body rear-hung caliper design has the bleed screw at the top as needed, and it has the hose inlet at the bottom of the caliper for easy hose routing.

There is no factory replacement brake hose that retrofits properly to the earlier vehicles, so a custom hose is required. People sometimes try to jury-rig a brake hose from another vehicle just to save a few bucks, but there is no reason to do that when excellent options are available.

There is also no reason to have brake hoses with big loops in them jammed behind the knuckles, and there is absolutely no reason to have the calipers mounted upside down with the bleeders pointed down. The proper parts do exist to mount factory brake calipers either in a front-hung or a rear-hung location, so there is no excuse for a poorly executed brake swap.

Master Cylinders

Any drum brake vehicle that is being converted to front disc brakes needs a disc/drum master cylinder and a proportioning valve for safe operation. One easy option is to just acquire a master cylinder and proportioning valve from the same donor vehicle that is providing the front disc brakes. As long as the donor vehicle is approximately the same size and weight as the vehicle that the parts are being swapped onto, this should work fine.

The large chamber for the front discs identifies disc brake master cylinders. The rear chamber feeds the front brakes, while the front chamber feeds the rear brakes. This particular disc brake master cylinder has the brake lines exiting toward the engine. A cast-iron master cylinder weighs about 7 pounds, and an aluminum master cylinder weighs 2 pounds.

Cast Iron

B-Body master cylinders during the muscle car era were all made from cast iron and used a four-bolt mounting pad on the firewall. These master cylinders work fine, but they are heavy, and the cast-iron housing is prone to corrosion.

Aluminum

Toward the end of the rear-wheel-drive era, Chrysler engineers switched from the heavy cast-iron master cylinder design to one made from aluminum and plastic. The new aluminum master cylinders are considerably lighter than their cast-iron counterparts, and they are less likely to corrode. The brake fluid tends to stay cleaner in the plastic reservoir, which is an important consideration for muscle cars that spend a lot of time in storage. The aluminum

CHAPTER 6

A variety of aluminum master cylinders and adapters are available from vendors, such as Mancini Racing. Adapters with four holes are used when the vehicle has mounting studs on the firewall. If the vehicle has holes in the firewall, the adapter with studs is used. The offset adapter is used to move the master cylinder over to provide clearance for valve covers or the exhaust system.

Master cylinder pushrods were originally available in several different lengths, depending on the make and the model of the vehicle. You must use the correct-length pushrod so that the pedal is at the right height. Do not forget the rubber retaining ring that holds the pushrod into the master cylinder. Without the retaining ring, the pushrod can fall out of the master cylinder and disable the brakes.

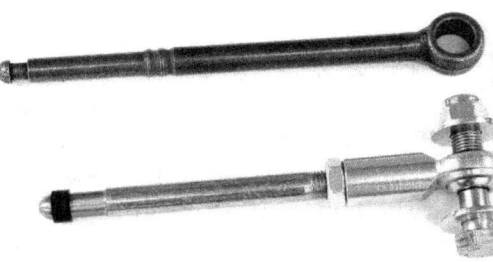

An adjustable pushrod is handy to have when building a custom brake system. This kit is from DoctorDiff.

master cylinders are also available in a variety of bore sizes, if system tuning is required.

New aluminum master cylinders can be purchased from any auto parts store or from a variety of aftermarket suppliers. They can also be found in a wrecking yard under the hoods of most FMJ cars. I wouldn't recommend using similar-looking master cylinders from a front-wheel-drive vehicle, because the fluid volume bias probably is not correct for a muscle car. The master cylinders from the FMJ cars work just fine when transplanted to earlier rear-wheel-drive vehicles, especially when combined with a late-model disc brake system.

The aluminum master cylinders do use a two-bolt mounting system, which is different than the older four-bolt mounts. Fortunately, there are a variety of adapter plates available that allow the aluminum master cylinders to be bolted directly to the four-bolt-style firewall.

An offset mounting bracket is available for the aluminum master cylinder. The offset bracket moves the master cylinder away from the engine 3/4 inch for increased clearance. Originally designed for Hemi cars, the offset master cylinder bracket can also be used any time that extra clearance is required around the exhaust system or valve cover. An extra-length pushrod is required, and the pushrod has to be moved to the other side of the brake pedal.

Vendors, such as DoctorDiff or Mancini Racing, carry these offset master cylinder adapters, as well as the special pushrod, which is required.

These same vendors also carry a heat shield, which attaches to the bottom of the master cylinder. The heat shield is an excellent way to protect the seals and the fluid in the master cylinder from engine heat.

Brake Pads

One limitation to using the factory brake system is that brake pad choices are fairly sparse when compared to what is available for aftermarket brake systems. Firm Feel carries a performance metallic brake pad for the pin-type caliper and the slider-style caliper. Carbotech doesn't currently list pads for the slider caliper, but it can build pads using any of its compounds on a customer's backing plates.

Firm Feel carries metallic pads for pin-type and slider calipers. (Photo Courtesy Firm Feel)

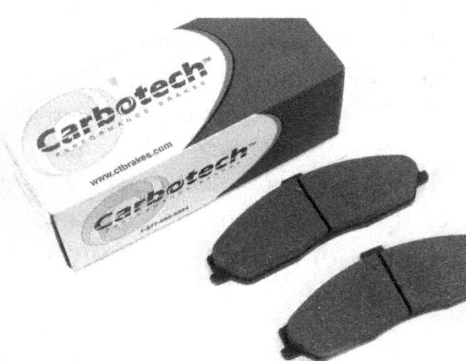

Carbotech has a wide selection of pad compounds, which can be applied to existing backing plates. This process can be expensive, but it is the only option for pads when using obsolete calipers.

---

60 MOPAR B-BODY PERFORMANCE UPGRADES 1962–1979

BRAKE UPGRADES WITH FACTORY PARTS

Rotors

OEM brake rotors and factory replacement rotors were high-quality castings produced to factory specifications. The original rotors were available in either standard-duty or heavy-duty (HD) configuration. The HD rotors had additional reinforcement ribs on the inside of the hub area. The factory replacement rotors were discontinued some time ago, but high-quality rotors used to be available from the better auto parts stores. Sadly, over time, it appears that the high-quality rotor suppliers have given way to some rather cheap imitations.

Although the "el cheapo" brake rotors might be fine on a grocery getter, anyone interested in high-performance use should carefully examine new rotors before purchasing them. It isn't uncommon to find new rotors that have a variety of casting flaws or machining errors. It has also become common to find rotors that crack or wear out quickly, possibly due to poor-quality material.

In my experience, the best rotors are the ones that say "Canada" on the inner surface. I have had fitment problems with rotors made in Mexico, and I wouldn't try to use off-shore rotors in a high-performance application. If the high-quality Canadian cast rotors are no longer available, it might be time to seriously consider switching to an aftermarket brake system.

There is an on-going debate about the virtue of slotted or drilled rotors. High-performance vehicles, such as those from Porsche, Ferrari, and Mercedes-Benz, often have drilled and slotted rotors. Seeing these rotors on high-end cars naturally leads people to desire these features on their own cars. Although some critics claim that holes and slots are useless, in reality the slots are designed to clean the brake pad, and the holes reduce weight and provide extra cooling for the pads. Neither of these features is a requirement for a daily driver, but if you're willing to pay extra for the looks, that is fine. Beware of cheap imitation parts, though. Rotors that have been improperly modified with slots or drilled holes can crack or break. If you really need high-end rotors for your vehicle, purchase them from a reputable manufacturer such as Brembo or Baer.

Stainless Steel Brake Hoses

As with drilled and slotted rotors, there has always been a bit of a debate over the value of stainless steel braided brake hoses. Some argue that the braided hoses provide a firmer pedal feel, and others dismiss them as nothing more than bling. The truth is probably somewhere in the middle, as there are actual benefits to, as well as concerns about, the use of stainless steel brake hoses.

One clear benefit is the ability to easily build proper-length hoses with the correct fittings for custom brake installations. Adapting rear-hung calipers onto most Mopar vehicles is a good example of where a custom hose is required for proper fitment. I'd much rather use custom-braided hoses in this application than use some of the rather bizarre hose routings that I've seen at car shows. A set of custom hoses rarely costs more than a nice dinner, yet they can literally save your life.

There are a few potential problems with braided-steel hoses, though, that you should be aware of. The braided-steel hoses can be very abrasive if they are allowed to

Originally, just the heavy-duty brake rotors had the reinforcement ribs cast into the hub, but now it seems that all of the replacement rotors come with these ribs.

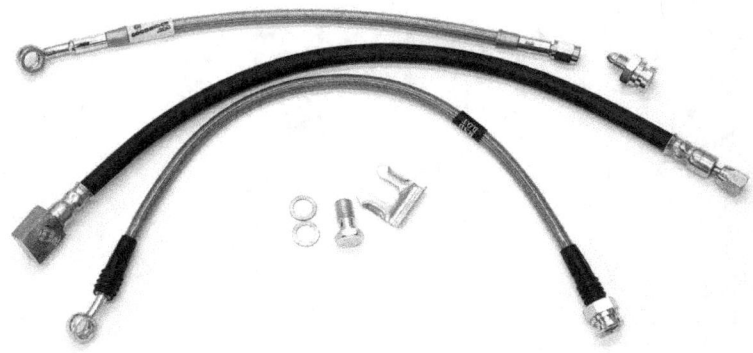

Brake hoses are available in multiple styles and lengths. Using front-hung calipers on 1962 to 1972 B-Body cars allows the use of stock brake hoses. Hanging the calipers to the rear requires custom hoses. When ordering custom hoses, carefully measure the length, and make sure to order the correct hose ends. Adapters are available to mate AN fittings to the factory steel lines.

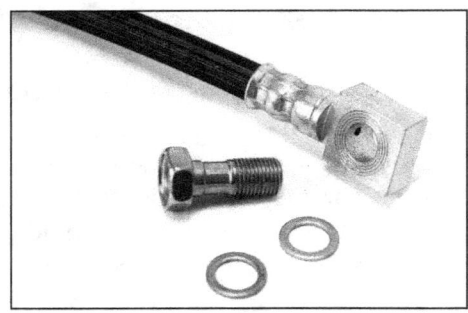

Banjo block fittings are available in different sizes and shapes. The banjo bolts are also available in different lengths to work with different calipers and hose ends. Don't forget to use new crush washers on each side of the banjo fitting.

rub on anything during normal suspension movement. Also, although braided-steel hoses are considered tough, they are actually quite easily damaged if they are improperly installed or if they come in contact with sharp objects, such as the edge of the frame. Some vendors now cover their braided brake hoses with a plastic cover to minimize abrasion damage. This plastic covering helps protect the hose as well as anything that the hose might come in contact with, but even with the covering, the hoses need to be carefully routed away from any sharp edges.

Power vs. Manual Brakes

Most new-car buyers prefer power brakes, but they are not required for performance applications. In fact, a manual brake system usually replaces a power brake system for high-performance use. The factory almost always installed power boost with disc brakes, but most people do not require power boost, as long as the brake system is properly balanced.

Experienced drivers tend to prefer the "feel" of manual brakes. With manual brakes, an experienced driver can modulate the braking force to keep the wheels from locking up. The power boosters, installed by the factory during the 1960s and 1970s, were highly boosted and left the brake pedal feeling "mushy" or "numb" and difficult to modulate. The power boosters are also heavy. They take up valuable space under the hood, and they require engine vacuum for operation.

The use of the larger rotors helps reduce the required pedal pressure because the larger rotor diameter gives the brake pad a longer lever arm to push on. A manual brake system with 11¾-inch rotors works just fine in any vehicle weighing less than 3,500 pounds, as long as the brakes are properly installed and adjusted. For vehicles heavier than 3,500 pounds, power assist is desirable, if larger rotors cannot be fitted.

Summary

There are factory disc brake systems for both small-bearing spindles as well as large-bearing spindles. However, the factory brake systems offered for the early small-bearing spindles have become obsolete over time, while the late-model factory brakes are a very viable option. For this reason alone, I always recommend that people swap on a set of late-model (1973-or-newer) disc brakes onto any B-Body that they intend to drive. The large-bearing design was made in substantially greater volumes than the earlier designs, making repair parts easy to find and much less expensive.

CHAPTER 7

AFTERMARKET BRAKE SYSTEMS

Although the factory 11¾-inch brakes are a very cost-effective solution, the cast-iron calipers are rather heavy, pad choices are limited, and the rotors are heavy. Furthermore, because no one is reproducing the tall caliper adapter brackets required for the 11¾-inch conversion, it can be difficult to find the parts necessary for the swap. Sensing an opportunity, the aftermarket has stepped in with a variety of solutions to fill this gap.

Street Kits

Several vendors, such as Master Power, SSBC, and Baer, have introduced entire kits that are designed for the muscle car owner who wants one-stop shopping for a conversion kit. These turn-key solutions typically use 11-inch-diameter rotors, so they have a slightly less braking capability than a factory 11¾-inch setup. But, these brake kits use the smaller rotor, which allows it to fit inside of a 14-inch wheel, and that's important to some customers. Also, these kit systems can be installed "out of the box" without having to locate used parts in a wrecking yard.

The Master Power kit uses a reproduction A-Body disc brake knuckle, an 11-inch rotor, and a cast-iron, single-piston sliding caliper. This kit is basically a reproduction of the 1973 A-Body disc brake system that is ready to bolt on.

SSBC has a variety of solutions, which use 11-inch rotors and cast-iron, four-piston brake calipers. The SSBC system is designed to bolt to factory drum brake knuckles and fit under some 14-inch wheels.

The Baer solution is also based on an 11-inch-diameter rotor, but Baer uses a two-piston, aluminum caliper sourced from PBR. These calipers are similar to the ones used on newer Mustangs, so repair parts are readily available. The Baer rotors are available drilled and slotted for extra cooling and curb appeal.

Baer offers a street kit that fits a wide range of Mopar muscle cars. The Baer SS4 kit uses an 11-inch-diameter rotor, in order to fit under 14- and 15-inch wheels, and a two-piston sliding caliper.

The Baer kit mounts on the 1962 to 1972 drum brake knuckle. The early knuckles are too short to be used on 1973-or-newer B-Bodies.

CHAPTER 7

Drag Racing Kits

There is a fairly long list of vendors that provide lightweight brake packages for Mopar knuckles. These lightweight brakes are designed for drag racing, where the car only has to stop once from high speed. Depending on the number of cars at the track, a drag race car can cool down in the pits for a fairly long period of time before the brakes need to be used again. Given this low-duty cycle, manufacturers have been able to significantly reduce the amount of mass in the brake rotors and calipers.

The drag race brakes typically have aluminum hubs; thin, lightweight rotors; and small aluminum calipers. These systems are easily capable of stopping a race car once, but they overheat if used repeatedly. Most of the drag race designs are labeled as "race only," and the components may not meet applicable DOT standards. These lightweight brake systems can be used on a hot rod driven on the street for cruise nights, but they are not designed for a family car headed to the mountains for summer vacation. Vendors that specialize in these types of brake systems include Wilwood, Aerospace, Strange, and Lamb.

A complete drag race system with aluminum hubs and thin rotors can save about 40 pounds or more when compared to an original 11-inch disc brake system. Drag race systems are available to fit most of the possible knuckles, so there should be a kit available for any B-Body vehicle.

On a drag race car, it would probably make sense to replace the heavy disc brake knuckles with the lighter drum knuckles and then install an aftermarket disc brake kit. This approach requires some extra work to swap the knuckles, but the drum knuckles should save another 5 pounds off the front end of the car.

Caliper Upgrades for Factory Rotors

Another possible approach that can be taken is to use lightweight aftermarket calipers on the factory rotors. This hybrid solution uses the low-cost and highly reliable factory cast-iron rotors, but saves weight by replacing the factory cast-iron calipers with aftermarket aluminum calipers. The weight savings with this type of approach can be up to 20 pounds off the front end.

Mancini Racing sells several bracket kits that are designed to mount lightweight Wilwood calipers directly to factory disc brake rotors. The existing cast-iron rotors provide sufficient brake mass to absorb the heat from repeated use, but the aluminum calipers reduce the unsprung weight on the front of the car. Mancini Racing has systems for both the big-bearing 11-inch rotors and the larger 11¾-inch rotors.

Another option is a bracket kit sold by Mancini Racing that adapts calipers from the Dodge Viper to the factory 11¾-inch rotors. The Viper caliper is a fixed-position, F-piston caliper designed for high-performance use. A large selection of pad

Wilwood sells several different brake kits that are designed for drag race vehicles. These kits feature a very lightweight construction with aluminum hubs, thin rotors, and lightweight calipers. Typically, the drag race kits use a four-piston caliper with an 11-inch-diameter rotor and fits under a 15-inch wheel.

Mancini Racing sells an adapter kit that mounts Wilwood Dynalite calipers onto the factory 11¾-inch-diameter rotors. This kit fits any of the 1973-or-newer disc brake knuckles.

The combination of the factory 11¾-inch rotor and the lightweight Wilwood caliper creates a low-profile assembly that fits under most 15-inch wheels. The mass and strength of the OEM rotor provides an extra margin of safety, while the lightweight caliper saves about 20 pounds of unsprung weight at the front of the vehicle.

AFTERMARKET BRAKE SYSTEMS

Wilwood sells a line of DynaPro radial-mount calipers, which have weather seals. This caliper is PN 120-7381, and it can be mounted on a Mopar 11¾-inch rotor with a kit from Mancini Racing.

The DynaPro caliper is fairly lightweight, weighing just 5 pounds with pads. It has four 1¾-inch-diameter pistons and can be front-hung or rear-hung on either side of the vehicle.

compounds is available for the Viper caliper, including several racing compounds. Used Viper calipers are often available from owners who are installing higher-performance brake systems. Although the Viper calipers provide slightly less piston area than the factory sliding calipers, the fixed caliper design eliminates the sliding friction inherent in the factory design. The fixed Viper caliper is also stiffer than the sliding caliper. The extra rigidity improves the feel of the brakes and reduces the pedal travel.

Big Brakes for High Speed and Road Racing

A quick trip to a new-car showroom reveals the current design practice for factory-performance vehicles includes four-wheel disc brakes with at least a 13-inch rotor. A few vendors have designed kits that adapt modern 13-inch rotors onto any B-Body.

Mancini Racing

Mancini carries a variety of brake systems for B-Body vehicles. Among them is a 13-inch kit based on the radial-mount Viper caliper from the 1994-and-newer Viper vehicles.

The Mancini kit uses 13 x 1.250-inch cast rotors, late-model Viper calipers, and CNC-machined hubs. Viper calipers are forged-aluminum, four-piston units sourced from Brembo. Piston size is 40 mm for the leading piston and 44 mm for the trailing piston, for a total piston area of 5.480 square inches. The Viper calipers are side-specific, due to the staggered piston sizes. They can be purchased from any Dodge dealer as PN 5136152AA and PN 5136153AA.

Early ear-mount Viper calipers can be adapted to big-bearing drum-brake knuckles with a kit from Mancini Racing. The key to this combination is the adapter bracket, which bolts to the knuckle and provides a mounting location for the Viper caliper.

This Mancini kit fits any of the big-bearing disc brake knuckles. The lightweight knuckles from the late-model B-Body or FMJ vehicles are recommended, due to the improved camber curve and lighter weight.

One unique aspect of the Mancini Racing kit is that it was designed to work with wheels from a Ford Mustang. The wheel mounting surface in the kit has been moved outboard by about 3/4 inch so that Mustang rims with 5.720 inches of backspacing can bolt in place. The hubs in the Mancini kit use the rotor and wheel mounting dimensions from a Mustang SN-95 vehicle. The typical SN-95 rim (Mustang 1994 to 2004) is 17 x 8 inches with 5.720 inches of backspacing and 30 mm of offset. Because the wheel mounting surface has been pushed outboard to accommodate the Mustang wheels, stock Mopar rims no longer fit properly. Some fabrication is required to fit matching Mustang wheels on to the rear end. (See Chapter 14 for additional information on how to fit the Mustang 17-inch rims to a B-Body.)

The Viper caliper is a high-quality OEM part built by Brembo. It has weather seals and a banjo-type brake line fitting. The higher-quality construction adds some weight to the caliper; each weighs 8½ pounds.

CHAPTER 7

Baer Brake Systems

Baer is one of the larger aftermarket vendors specializing in brake conversions. Baer originally focused only on Ford Mustangs, but it now provides brake systems for most of the popular muscle car applications. Baer currently offers high-performance systems with 13-, 14-, and even 15-inch rotors to fit any B-Body. These higher-performance systems are based on the family of radial-mount Baer calipers and are very capable systems. The Baer systems use lightweight two-piece rotors as well as special hubs manufactured from high-strength aluminum alloy. The Baer systems are designed primarily for the 1973-and-newer disc spindles, but there are also some kits available for the older, small-bearing disc brake spindles.

Baer currently offers three calipers in its high-performance lineup. The smallest caliper is the T4, which is a four-piston design. The T4 uses brake pads from a newer Camaro, so pads are easy to find. The T4 caliper has four 1.625-inch-diameter pistons for a total effective area of 4.150 square inches.

The next step up in the Baer lineup is the six-piston 6P caliper, which is also a modular-aluminum caliper. The 6P uses a six-piston design with a total piston area of 4.700 square inches, and it uses Corvette C5 brake pads. The 6P is designed for a 1.150-inch-thick rotor, but it can be special-ordered for a 1.250-inch-thick rotor.

Baer's top-of-the-line, large, six-piston mono-block caliper is called

The 1994-and-newer Viper calipers are a radial-mount design and are sourced from Brembo. These calipers use a large brake pad that is thick enough to handle multiple track sessions. There is a very wide range of pad choices available for the Viper caliper, which uses staggered piston sizes to reduce pad taper. The Viper caliper is much larger than the factory cast-iron caliper, but due to its aluminum construction, it only weighs 10½ pounds. The pads are top-loaded and are held in place with a spring clip.

Mancini Racing also offers a big-brake kit for B-Body cars that uses 13 x 1.250-inch rotors. This kit fits big-bearing disc brake knuckles and uses late-model Viper calipers.

The Mancini kit includes specially designed hubs that move the wheel centers out to provide room for the large calipers. The caliper bolts to the steering knuckle using a fairly simple L-shaped adapter. The Viper calipers must be rear-hung to work properly.

The wheel mounting surface on the Mancini kit is moved out to work with 17 x 8-inch wheels from a 1994 to 2004 Mustang. The Mustang wheels look great and provide plenty of clearance for the large Viper calipers.

Baer two-piece rotors are an option with the Mancini kit. The two-piece rotors are 6 pounds lighter than the standard cast-iron rotors, but they are significantly more expensive.

the 6S. The 6S is a premium caliper that is carved from a single block of aluminum for the ultimate in rigidity. It is designed for rotors that are 1.250 inches thick with diameters ranging from 13.500 to 16 inches.

The Baer kits are all designed to fit on the Baer-supplied, CNC-machined aluminum hub. The Baer hub is designed to mount the wheel in the stock location and uses the Mopar hub register, so most wheels designed for a Mopar should fit properly. The Baer hub comes with the wheel bearings already packed with grease and the seals installed, so the kit is very simple to install. Also included in the Baer kits are the correct brake hoses and fittings, as well as all of the required hardware.

Wilwood Engineering and Magnum Force Racing

Wilwood focuses primarily on brakes for the drag racing and circle track crowds, but it does also offer some big brake kits for Mopar vehicles. Wilwood sells a six-piston kit that uses a 14 x 1.100-inch rotor. Kit number 140-10816 is designed to fit the 1962 to 1972 small-bearing

Baer Brakes also offers a high-performance, street-oriented kit based on its T4 caliper. This kit uses a more economical 13-inch cast-iron rotor, along with the Baer aluminum hub.

The T4 caliper is a four-piston, radial-mount design. It has staggered bore sizes, so it must be mounted on the correct side of the vehicle for proper operation. The T4 uses brake pads from a 1998 to 2002 Camaro, so there are plenty of pad compounds available for this caliper. The T4 caliper is fairly lightweight at just 8 pounds fully loaded. The pads are bottom-loaded, so the caliper must be removed to change the pads.

The T4 kit mounts to big-bearing disc brake knuckles. The 13-inch rotor requires a 17-inch rim to clear.

The 6P caliper is designed to be rear-hung, although it is possible to change the location of the bleed screw and run the caliper front-hung, if required. This kit uses a 14-inch rotor, which requires an 18-inch wheel, but the 6P caliper also works with a 13-inch rotor. This kit mounts to a big-bearing disc brake knuckle, so it can be installed on any B-Body car.

Baer offers several kits. The 6P caliper kits are slightly smaller and less expensive than the 6S kits, and they are generally aimed at high-performance street cars or street-driven track cars.

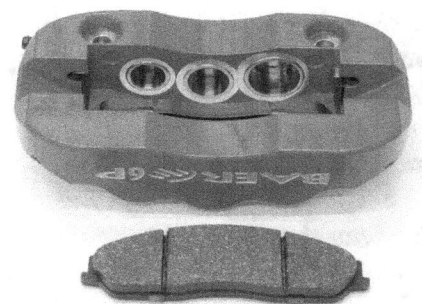

The 6P caliper is a radial-mount design with six staggered-bore pistons. The caliper must be mounted on the correct side of the vehicle to work correctly. The 6P caliper uses Corvette brake pads, so there is a wide variety of pad compounds available. It is a compact design that only weighs 8½ pounds fully loaded. There is just one bleeder screw, and the fluid passages are internal. The pads are bottom-loaded, so the caliper must be removed to change brake pads.

B-Body drum knuckle. The Wilwood kits all use a special aluminum hub for maximum weight savings.

The Wilwood calipers are designed as race-only units, and they do not have weather seals on the pistons.

Magnum Force Racing has taken the basic Wilwood offerings and "upsized" them with thicker rotors. With the increased rotor thickness, the Magnum Force kits are better equipped to handle high-powered cars and higher speeds. Magnum Force has also verified the fitment of these big-brake kits onto its 2-inch-dropped front spindle.

DoctorDiff

DoctorDiff offers several big-brake kits, including a 13-inch kit that uses production rotors and calipers from an SN-95 Mustang. The Mustang rotor is 1.100 inches thick, and the caliper is an aluminum two-piston, pin-mounted unit. This kit includes a custom hub that is CNC machined from aluminum and a special caliper adapter bracket. The hub face on this kit is designed to be in the stock location, so wheel offset needs to be similar to factory rims.

DoctorDiff also has a 14-inch kit using rotors from a late-model Dodge Charger matched with Viper

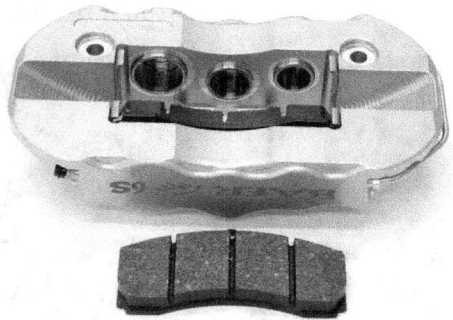

The 6S caliper is a work of art. It is a six-piston design carved from a solid block of aluminum. This mono-block construction makes it one of the most rigid calipers available. The brake pad has a lot of surface area and is thick enough to handle multiple track sessions. This caliper weighs 11½ pounds fully loaded, which is quite reasonable, given its massive size and strength. The 6S caliper is designed to work with a 1.250-inch-wide rotor that is at least 13½ inches in diameter.

Baer sells a variety of big-brake kits that fit Mopar muscle cars. Here is a kit consisting of the premium 6S caliper with a 15 x 1.250-inch rotor. Also shown is the aluminum Mopar hub, as well as the required caliper adapter bracket. This kit fits big-bearing disc brake knuckles.

A 19-inch wheel is required to clear the 15-inch rotor. The wheel also needs a generous amount of clearance for the large 6S caliper. Baer has wheel templates available on its website that can be used to verify the clearance required for its brake kits.

Magnum Force sells a variety of big-brake kits that are designed to work with its dropped knuckle. The Magnum Force kits are built from various Wilwood Engineering components but usually have thicker rotors than these used in Wilwood kits. The thicker rotors are better suited for use during track days or high-performance street driving. (Photo Courtesy Magnum Force Racing)

The Magnum Force brake kits are designed to bolt onto the Magnum Force dropped knuckle, as shown here. Kits are also available for different production knuckles. (Photo Courtesy Magnum Force Racing)

calipers. The rotor in the 14-inch kit is 1.250 inches thick and is a heavy cast-iron design capable of handling stops from very high speeds. The Viper caliper is the 1994-or-newer radial-mount design, which is available from any Dodge dealer. The 14-inch kit from DoctorDiff also uses a custom-made aluminum hub that mounts the wheels in the stock location. An 18-inch-diameter rim is required to clear the 14-inch rotor.

XV Motorsports

XV offers a 13-inch kit using a twin-piston PBR caliper and a 13 x 1.10-inch rotor. The XV kit fits the big-bearing disc brake knuckles, and the calipers are rear-hung. The kit is designed around a production-based cast-iron hub, which makes this kit fairly economical. The cast-iron hub is a very durable design, and it shares all of the bearing and seal sizes with a factory disc brake rotor. The use of the factory hub also means that the wheel register size remains the original Mopar size, although the wheel mounting surface does move out about .250 inch per side to accommodate the thickness of the rotor face.

The Charger's 14-inch rotors provide enough mass to safely handle a high-powered muscle car. The DoctorDiff kit fits the big-bearing disc knuckles, which can be retrofitted to any B-Body car. The 14-inch rotor requires at least an 18-inch-diameter wheel, and the Viper caliper requires a wheel with additional caliper clearance built in. The Viper calipers need to be rear-hung to work properly.

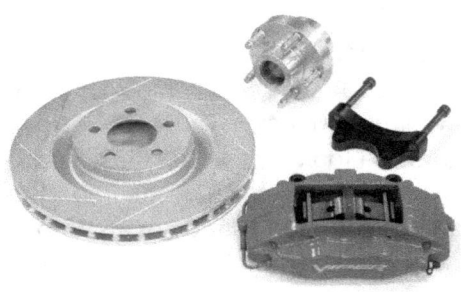
DoctorDiff has developed several big-brake kits designed for high-performance use. They use a clever blend of OEM hardware to provide excellent performance at very reasonable prices. This kit uses 14-inch rotors from a new Charger and calipers from a Viper.

DoctorDiff also offers a lower-priced kit, which is based on Mustang Cobra components. This kit uses a 13 x 1.100-inch rotor and a Cobra two-piston caliper. Aluminum hubs are included, as are the caliper adapters and the necessary mounting hardware.

The DoctorDiff 13-inch kit fits the big-bearing disc knuckle, so it is a very universal kit. The Cobra caliper is a front-hung, twin-piston, floating design. The aftermarket extensively uses these calipers, so a wide selection of pads is available. To use this kit, 17-inch wheels are required.

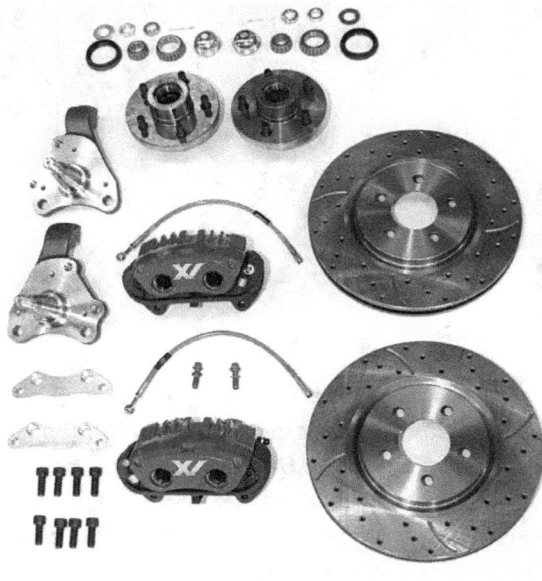
XV Motorsports sells a 13-inch brake kit for stock suspensions. This Level 1 kit includes a pair of disc brake knuckles to make it an easy bolt-on kit. The XV kit uses 13 x 1.100-inch rotors and twin-piston sliding calipers. The hubs are steel, and they work with factory parts, including bearings, seals, and dust cap. (Photo Courtesy XV Motorsports)

CHAPTER 7

Stainless Steel Brake Corporation

SSBC offers a 13-inch kit for the small-bearing drum brake knuckles used on the 1962 to 1972 B-Body cars. The SSBC kit uses a unique sliding caliper design with three 38-mm pistons. The total piston area with this three-piston caliper is 5.270 square inches, which is about 11 percent less than that of the factory 2.750-inch caliper. Given the larger-diameter rotor, this works out to be a roughly equivalent braking force, which means that the SSBC system should bolt in place with only minor adjustments to the bias.

Building a Custom Brake Kit

Designing and building your own big-brake kit might seem an odd thing to do when kits are available from different vendors, but building your own parts is a hot rodding tradition. Building your own parts provides a sense of accomplishment and pride and is also a great way to become more educated on the subject. This section illustrates the process used to engineer and fabricate a custom brake system based on commonly available 13-inch rotors and 17-inch wheels. These components are fairly universal on modern performance vehicles, so parts are easy to find and are fairly inexpensive. The combination of 17-inch rims and 13-inch brakes provides plenty of stopping power for a high-performance B-Body car.

A typical disc brake system consists of four primary components: the knuckle, the hub, the rotor, and the caliper. These four parts need to be selected in a logical manner in order to provide a working design. The wheel and tire dimensions also need to be carefully selected for both form and function.

Although brake system design might seem difficult to grasp, it really isn't if you copy what the factory engineers did on similar vehicles. The individual parts do not know what car they are bolted to; they just know how much pressure and volume the master cylinder is providing and how much force is being applied to the rotors. If the pressure and volume are correct, and the rotor dimensions are correct, the system works properly.

Knuckle

Any knuckle can be used because you are custom-building the parts, but it makes the most sense to start with a big-bearing disc brake knuckle. The late-model ones bolt into any B-Body vehicle, so their application is universal and they are fairly easy to find.

I recommend starting with a set of 638 and 639 castings from a 1973-or-newer B-Body. The 638/9 knuckles are slightly taller than the early knuckles, but they weigh less. The slight reduction in unsprung weight might not matter for most applications, but it never hurts. If you are going to look for the 638/639 knuckles in a wrecking yard, look for either a 1976-or-newer B-Body or an R-Body car. If the car has 11¾-inch rotors, it would also be a good idea to buy the caliper adapters at the same time, even though you don't need them for this project. The taller caliper

Different knuckles can be used as the basis for a big-brake system, but the late-model B-Body knuckle is probably the best choice. Not only is it slightly taller, but it is also a little lighter than the other choices. These knuckles usually weigh 7 pounds, although early castings, such as this one, have a little extra material around the caliper mounts.

SSBC sells a brake kit that is based on its three-piston sliding caliper and a 13-inch rotor. (Photo Courtesy Stainless Steel Brake Corporation)

A big-brake kit, such as this one, can be built from scratch. Porsche calipers and Baer rotors were used to build this custom brake system. A local machine shop fabricated the hubs and brackets.

AFTERMARKET BRAKE SYSTEMS

adapters are getting hard to find, so it is always a good idea to save a set from the crusher whenever possible. You also have a good probability of finding the 638/639 knuckles under an FMJ vehicle, as the wrecking yards often have plenty of those on hand.

When searching for knuckles in a wrecking yard, be sure to verify that the wheel bearing surfaces are in good shape. Sometimes, the spindle bearing surfaces are damaged, so double-check before you pay for them.

Hub

There are several options when it comes to hubs. You can design and fabricate a new hub, you can purchase an aftermarket unit, or you can recycle a hub from a different application. Designing a custom hub and having it fabricated by a competent shop is an excellent choice for people who have the proper skills. But, many people do not have the necessary CAD software or expertise required to design such a critical part, so one of the other alternatives is probably a wiser choice.

Buying a hub from a vendor such as Wilwood or Baer is an excellent option if you do not have access to any fabrication equipment. Of course, the issue with using a purchased hub is that you then are working with a fixed design. The other parts, such as the rotor and caliper brackets, have to be fabricated to fit the existing hub design.

The third alternative is to recycle a hub from an existing Mopar vehicle. Recycling is an easy way to get the project started. I suggest using this method for your first brake conversion project, and then once you gain some experience building big-brake systems, you will be more comfortable with creating your own hub on the next project.

Disc brakes before the 1973 uni-cast design actually had a separate hub and rotor assembly. For a project involving a 1972-or-earlier vehicle,

It takes a big lathe to turn 6-inch steel bar stock into a hub! Most large cities have a machine shop that is capable of doing this kind of work, but it needs a drawing or a CAD file to work from.

One advantage of making your own hubs is that extra offset can be built into the hub in order to work with late-model wheels. The custom hub on the left has an additional .750 inch of offset to work with Mustang wheels.

you can easily press off the brake rotor and start with the remaining hub. That solution does not work for this project, however, because you want to use the late-model knuckles with the larger wheel bearings. The late-model brakes use a uni-cast design, so you can't press off the rotor, but you can make a hub by machining away most of the rotor surface from a used rotor. By machining down the rotor until only a 6-inch-diameter hub is left, you have a great starting point for a big-brake kit.

The cast-iron hub that you are left with after machining off the rotor is designed to hold up a 4,000-plus-pound vehicle. This is the same hub that came on big, heavy B- and R-Body vehicles, so it has plenty of load capacity to meet your requirements. Because it is a factory hub, all of the mating parts, such as bearings, seals, and dust cap, properly fit. This is a big advantage over

Because the 1973 rotor is a uni-cast design, the rotor has to be machined away before the center hub can be used for a custom brake kit project. Cutting the rotor off the hub isn't a fun project, so expect to pay a machine shop to do this work for you. Once the rotor has been cut away, the cast-iron hub that remains, works just fine as the starting point for a custom brake project. The hub fits Mopar wheels, and the factory seals and bearings fit just fine. These cut-down hubs weigh about 9 pounds once they are fully loaded.

Baer makes this strong and lightweight aluminum hub. It is made for the 1973 spindle, and it only weighs 4½ pounds complete with bearings and seals. This hub is designed to fit Mopar wheels.

some of the aftermarket hubs that require special parts. It is always convenient to be able to purchase repair parts at a local shop rather than having to special-order replacements.

Because I'm planning to use 17-inch wheels from a Mustang with these brakes, the nose on the hub needs to be turned down slightly. The 1994 to 2004 Mustang wheels have an inner diameter of 2.780 inches, so the nose of the hub needs to be slightly smaller than that. If you turn the nose of the hub to an outer diameter of 2.775 inches, the wheel has .005 inch of clearance. This amount of clearance provides room for the wheel to slip on, but it is still precise enough to keep the wheel centered.

There also needs to be a slightly larger step machined onto the hub to center the rotor. As with the wheel, .005 inch of clearance works pretty well between the hub and the rotor. In this case, I'm going to machine a step onto the hub with an outside diameter of 2.795 inches in order to provide the proper clearance for a rotor with an inner diameter of 2.800 inches.

Rotor

Finding 13-inch rotors is fairly easy these days; just visit any new-car dealership, and you'll find a bunch of vehicles with 13-inch rotors on them. However, the choices for this project are reduced, because you need a 5 x 4.50-inch bolt pattern. It is also desirable to have the rotor be 1.250 inches thick because there are a lot of calipers available for that thickness.

The Ford Mustang comes close with a 13 x 1.100-inch rotor on 5 x 4.50-inch bolt pattern, but the Mustang rotor has a very shallow hat, which leads to complications when mounting a caliper.

There are a few Toyota vehicles that have a 5 x 4.50-inch bolt pattern, but most of them do not use a 13 x 1.250-inch rotor.

Mercedes uses a lot of large rotors that fit these criteria, but the only complication is that the Mercedes bolt pattern is 5 x 115 mm. 115 mm is the equivalent of 4.528 inches, which is very close to 4.500 inches. Because the rotor is centered by the register on the hub rather than the lug bolts, the bolt pattern does not need to be a perfect match. The wheel does need to have the correct hole pattern, but the rotor just needs to be able to slip on.

Given that extra freedom, you can make a rotor from a Mercedes vehicle work for this project with just minor machine work. If you're capable of re-drilling the rotors, potential rotors for use increases, as a rotor with a 5 x 4.750-inch bolt pattern often has enough material to be re-drilled with a 5 x 4.50-inch bolt pattern.

For this exercise I've selected a rotor from an S500 Mercedes. This is a big, heavy 13-inch rotor that is 1.250 inches thick. The Mercedes rotor has a large surface for the brake pad to ride on, and it has a deep hat section, which provides plenty of caliper clearance. This cross-drilled rotor is readily available from any Mercedes dealer and comes with a 5 x 115-mm bolt pattern.

The Mercedes rotor is a high-quality part, but the price is quite reasonable. The PN for the rotor I selected is A220-421-25-12, and the cost was $125 each at a local dealer. The center register hole in the Mercedes rotor did need to be machined slightly to open it up to 2.800 inches.

Caliper

Picking a caliper is an interactive process with picking the rotor. Calipers are designed to work with a specific rotor diameter, thickness, and annular ring. The brake pads in the caliper come in a variety of shapes and sizes. To work properly, the brake pad must fit on the machined area of

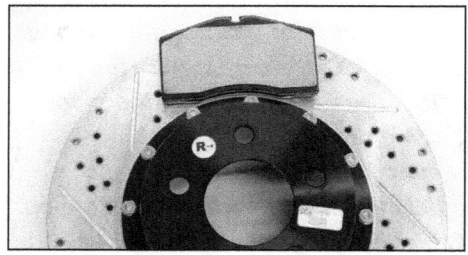

The rotor must have a wide braking surface to work with the large pad from the Porsche caliper. Not all rotors are wide enough in this area, so I made sure to specify this dimension when ordering the lightweight rotors from Baer.

Porsche "Big Red" calipers from a 993 Turbo are an excellent choice for a custom brake kit. These calipers are widely available, and the price is usually quite reasonable for such a high-quality kit. The Porsche caliper is physically quite large, but the aluminum construction keeps the weight down to 11 pounds. A Big Red caliper is a few pounds lighter than a Mopar cast-iron caliper. The Porsche caliper is a four-piston design with staggered piston sizes. The pads are very large and are thick enough to last multiple track days.

AFTERMARKET BRAKE SYSTEMS

the rotor. If the pad overhangs onto an un-machined part of the rotor, the pad wears incorrectly, and the rotor or the caliper might become damaged with use. Fortunately, most brake pads fit most rotors, but pay attention to this detail when you are considering a swap.

For this project, I selected a set of the rather famous Porsche "Big Red." The Big Reds are very popular calipers and are used for a lot of swap kits. The Big Reds are available from any Porsche dealer as PN 993 351 426 10 and PN 993 351 425 10. The calipers are side-specific and are designed to be front-hung. Pad choices for these calipers are excellent because they are so heavily used in club racing and high-performance street use.

Brembo makes these Porsche calipers, and they are very highly developed calipers. Even with that impressive pedigree, the Big Reds are available at a very reasonable price. Some people might not like the thought of Porsche parts on their Mopar, but others might enjoy the reaction that they get from people checking out the Big Red calipers.

Big Reds have a very large brake pad, which in turn requires a brake rotor with a wide annular ring. The Porsche brake pads are also quite thick because they are designed for endurance use. The caliper is a quick-change design, which means the pads can be popped out with just a simple twist of the wire spring clip. The wire clip design allows the pads to be changed in less than 30 seconds once the wheel is removed. Brembo design influences are obvious to experienced brake people when they look at a caliper like this. The fluid inlet uses an OEM-quality 10 mm banjo fitting instead of the pipe thread fitting used on cheaper aftermarket calipers. Big Red calipers have staggered piston sizes of 44 and 36 mm to reduce pad taper; the cheaper calipers use the same piston sizes front and rear. Big Reds are OEM quality, so they have full weather seals, anti-rattle clips, and wear indicators. Many aftermarket calipers do not have all of these features.

The Big Red is a radial-mount caliper, as are most high-performance calipers these days. With the radial-mount design, the hold-down bolts clamp the body of the caliper to the mounting bracket. The radial-mount design also allows the use of studs for mounting rather than bolts. Using studs can be beneficial if the caliper has to be removed on a regular basis, as there is less wear and tear on the threads in the mounting bracket. Cheaper calipers tend to use an ear mounting system. With the ear-mount calipers, the caliper body is cantilevered off two ears, which bolt to the knuckle. The ear-mount style is not as rigid as a radial mounting setup, and the mounting brackets are not as easy to fabricate.

Mounting Bracket

One really nice feature of the radial-mount caliper is that a very simple bracket design can be used. With the Big Red caliper, all you need is a simple L-shaped bracket that mounts the caliper to the back side of the knuckle. The Mopar disc brake knuckle has two 1/2-20 threaded holes located 3.125 inches apart on the back side of the knuckle. These holes provide a very solid mounting point for a caliper bracket.

Mounting dimensions for calipers and knuckles are not typically published, so you just have to sit down with the parts and reverse-engineer the measurements. A prototype bracket can easily be made from a piece of aluminum bar stock to get the caliper in the general location, and then the design can be adjusted for the final location.

The radial-mount system allows for easy adjustment in the vertical direction by using washers under the caliper to raise it to the correct height. The caliper bracket can also be spaced away from the knuckle to get it to the correct alignment. Once everything is in the right spot, it is easy to measure the final dimensions and put those onto a drawing for a machine shop to duplicate.

The mounting bracket can be made from either steel or aluminum. Steel is a better choice for highly stressed parts, but steel is also heavy and is prone to corrosion. Aluminum is lighter, easier to fabricate, and not as prone to corrosion. Aluminum is less rigid than steel, so the stress load needs to be carefully considered when designing with aluminum.

In this situation, the stress on the bracket is fairly low, so aluminum works just fine. You should not have an issue with stripped threads because the Big Red calipers have top-loaded brake pads. With the top-loaded design, the brake caliper does not need to be removed from the bracket to change pads. Some other caliper designs require the brake pads to be installed from the bottom, which means that the caliper needs to be removed from the bracket at each pad change.

Of course, aluminum could be used even in a high-maintenance environment, by either Heli-Coiling the threads or using studs to hold the caliper. Most of the radial-mount calipers use a 12-mm hold-down bolt. For this particular swap, I used a set of sockethead 12-mm bolts.

CHAPTER 7

Metric Dimensions

Brembo is an Italian firm, so the caliper dimensions are metric: piston diameter, distance between the mounting bolts, and size of the mounting bolts. The Big Red uses 12-mm mounting bolts, which is the same-size hardware that is used on Viper calipers and other Brembo radial-mount deigns. The banjo fitting is a 10-mm thread, so don't mess it up by trying to jam in something off your Mopar.

System Design Considerations

As stated earlier, the Porsche calipers use 44- and 36-mm pistons for a total piston area of 2,538 square mm, or 3.930 square inches. If you use the late-model sliding caliper as your reference point, the Porsche caliper's braking force is reduced by about 35 percent. Reducing the front brake force isn't your goal, so you have to find a way to re-balance the system. Using 13-inch-diameter rotors rather than 11s increases the braking force back up by about 20 percent. Porsche calipers are quite rigid when compared to the factory sliding calipers, so you gain back some braking force there.

You have the ability to purchase different pad compounds for the Porsche brakes. Selecting a pad compound with a higher coefficient of friction increases the front brake force.

You can also reduce the rear brake force, if necessary, by either downsizing the rear brakes or by using a smaller wheel cylinder in the back.

Finally, you have the ability to tune the brake bias with an adjustable proportioning valve.

Project: Installing a Custom Brake Kit

Designing and assembling your own custom brake system requires attention to detail so that the system provides adequate stopping power and the brake bias from front to rear is correct. If designing and assembling is beyond your comfort or skill, buy and install an off-the-shelf system. Brake systems are a safety device, and you should get the most suitable equipment for your particular application.

1 Once the stock rotor has been machined away, we are left with a cast-iron hub that is a perfect fit for our late-model knuckles.

2 The Baer rotor slides right onto the cut-down cast-iron hub, as long as the center hole was machined to the proper dimension.

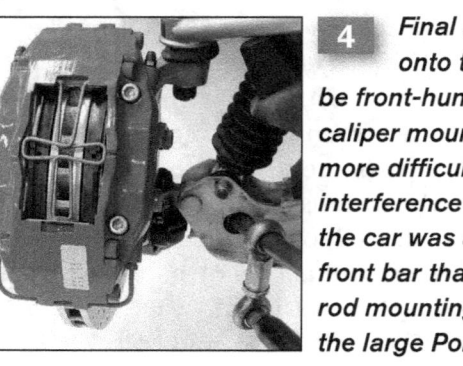

4 Final assembly begins by bolting the caliper onto the adapter. The Porsche caliper must be front-hung, so the knuckle is mounted with the caliper mounts forward. A front-hung caliper is more difficult to install, due to the possible interference issue with the sway bar. In this case, the car was already equipped with a custom-built front bar that mounts to the strut rods. The strut rod mounting provides some extra clearance for the large Porsche calipers, so we were okay.

3 Luckily, the mounting bracket, which is required to bolt the Porsche caliper to our Mopar knuckle, is actually quite simple to fabricate. The radial-mount design of the Porsche caliper means that we just need a simple L-shaped bracket. This bracket was fabricated from stainless steel, but mild steel or aluminum also works just fine.

AFTERMARKET BRAKE SYSTEMS

5 One advantage of the front-hung caliper is that the brake hose can follow the factory routing. These brake hoses were custom-built for us by the guys at Oil Filter Service Company. These are DOT-rated assemblies with a #3 AN fitting at the frame and the correct banjo fitting at the caliper end.

6 Porsche calipers are designed for quick pad replacements. The brake pads slide in from the top, just like bread into a toaster.

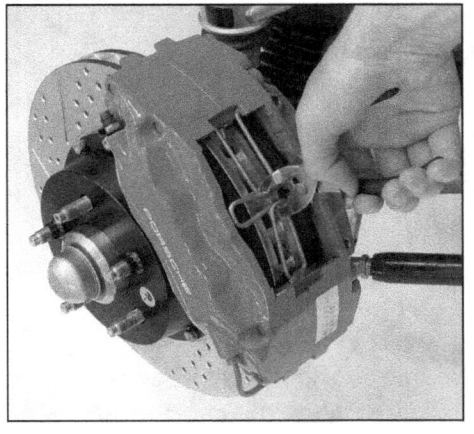

7 The pad retainer is a large, bent wire spring arrangement that can be easily squeezed into place with a pair of pliers.

8 The last thing to do after installing the new custom brake kit is to bleed the brake system. Porsche calipers have two bleeders per caliper, so it takes a few extra steps to complete both sides of each caliper.

Baer Builder Series

Another approach that can be taken when building a custom brake system is to work with a vendor to source some of the necessary components. Baer Brake Systems has a line of products called the Builder Series, which provides a tuner with the ability to get high-quality brake components built to specification. For the following track car project, Baer was willing to provide a wider version of its popular 6P caliper to fit a 1.250-inch-thick rotor. Baer also produced a set of 13 x 1.250-inch rotors with the proper offset and bolt pattern for this project. A local machine shop custom-fabricated the caliper mounting brackets and wheel hubs.

The vehicle used in this series of pictures is actually an A-Body, but the steering knuckles came from a late-model B-Body car, so this entire brake kit bolts onto any B-Body.

This Mopar track car is fitted with a home-built Viper conversion brake setup. This conversion uses re-drilled Viper rotors, Viper calipers, and custom hubs. The home-built brake kit works well, but the cast-iron rotors are quite heavy.

Custom Baer rotors and calipers can replace the heavy Viper rotors and calipers, saving a significant amount of weight. Baer's Builder Series provides parts necessary for custom swaps like this.

With the Builder Series parts from Baer in place, the 17-inch Mustang rims fit perfectly, and this Mopar is ready for the track. Replacing the Viper brake kit with Baer components saved 12 pounds of unsprung weight.

CHAPTER 8

REAR DISC BRAKES

The installation of rear disc brakes is becoming more common on Mopar muscle cars as more aftermarket options have become available. Rear disc brakes were never an option on any of the B-Body cars, but the factory did install a rear disc system on the 1974 Imperial. The Imperial brakes worked okay for the time, but the system wasn't a big success in the marketplace, so the engineers reverted to drum brakes for the next couple of decades. The Mopar rear drums are fairly simple, and they work fine for most applications, but they are heavy, and they don't have a lot of curb appeal. Over time, a number of options to retrofit rear disc brakes onto the Mopar rear ends have become available.

Design Considerations

Replacing the rear drum brakes with disc brakes is a fairly significant change to the brake system and should be approached with some caution. A four-wheel disc brake system operates significantly different than a disc/drum system because disc brakes operate in a linear fashion, and drum brakes are non-linear. When converting from drum to disc brakes in the rear, the rear discs no longer self-energize like drum brakes.

The good news is that a four-wheel disc brake system acts in a linear manner and has a more predictable feel. This is due to the fact that, in a four-wheel disc brake system, the driver directly controls the brake force at all four wheels with pedal pressure. Due to the lack of self-energizing brakes in the rear, the pedal force is increased, which is the downside to the conversion. Most people consider this to be a fair trade, as they prefer the more predictable brake pedal response.

Axle Shaft Bearings

The Mopar 8¾-inch and Dana 60 rear ends use a tapered roller bearing for the axle bearing. The tapered roller bearing design is an excellent design to handle side loads, such as those seen during cornering, but it is

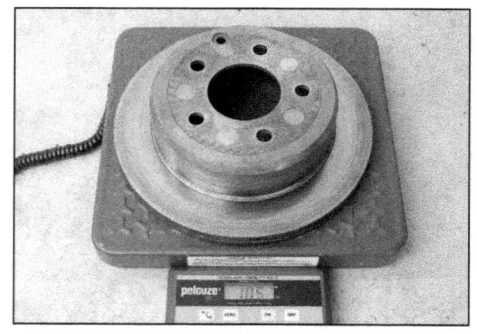

Less rotating weight can be a benefit with rear disc brakes. It depends on the replacement rotors and the drum brakes. This 11-inch brake rotor weighs 10½ pounds, which is lighter than most brake drums.

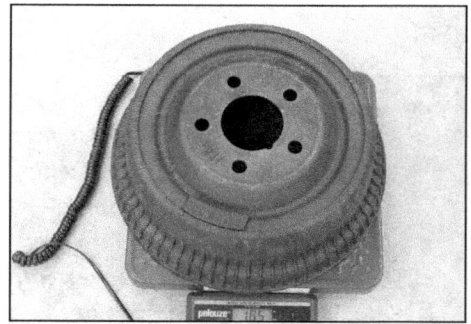

This 11-inch brake drum weighs a little more than 18 pounds. The brake drum is both unsprung weight and rotating weight. So, any reduction here is beneficial for both acceleration and suspension control.

REAR DISC BRAKES

Rear axles in both the 8¾-inch and Dana 60 rear ends use tapered axle shaft bearings. These bearings use an adjuster on the passenger's side to set end play. Some of the less-expensive rear disc brake kits require ball-bearing-type bearings, because they aren't designed to work properly with the tapered axle bearings.

a slightly complicated design, which requires some adjustment mechanism for setting end play. The net result of this extra adjustment is that either the rear disc brake kit needs to be able to accommodate the requirements of the tapered roller bearing, or the bearing needs to be changed to a ball bearing design.

Several vendors offer simple rear disc brake kits for Mopar axles that force a conversion to a ball bearing design. Other vendors accommodate the factory-style tapered roller bearing design. The type of rear axle bearing should match the intended use of the vehicle. Ball bearings are fine for straight-line duty, such as drag racing, but road racers usually prefer the tapered roller bearing design.

Bias

As you recall from Chapter 5, bias refers to the split of brake force between the front and rear systems. For a four-wheel disc brake system, front and rear calipers of different sizes control bias. My rule of thumb is that a typical Mopar muscle car wants to have roughly twice as much braking force on the fronts as on the rears. This means that if the rotor size is the same from front to rear, the piston area on the front calipers should be twice as large as the rear piston area. So if you have a system with 6 square inches of piston area at the front, the rear piston area should be 3 square inches.

Many aftermarket brake kits use a larger-diameter rotor for the front brakes than for the rear brakes. For example, the front rotor might be 13 inches in diameter while the rear brakes use a 10- or 11-inch rotor. This is not a problem as long as the piston diameters are adjusted to maintain the suggested 2:1 brake force ratio. When working with different rotor diameters, the brake force calculation has to take into account the extra leverage provided by the larger-diameter front rotor.

There should not be an issue with brake bias when purchasing a complete four-wheel disc brake system from a reputable vendor such as Baer. In the case where you are buying a complete four-wheel brake system, the vendor has the ability to properly match the front and rear piston sizes with the master cylinder to provide a safe design. A problem occurs when people purchase front and rear disc brake kits without having any understanding of how the particular brake kit affects the system bias on their car. Some of the rear disc brake kits on the market today use calipers with very large pistons, and other kits use rear calipers with fairly small pistons. Randomly matching a kit's unrelated disc brake setup on the front of the vehicle can lead to a dangerously unbalanced system.

Tuning a Rear Disc Brake System

The term "tuning" might seem odd to describe brake work, but it is an apt description for the task. Any time a complex set of parts, such as a four-wheel disc brake system, is installed, there needs to be some process of adjustment in order to get it to work properly. Just as the engine needs to be tuned for the intended application, the brake system needs to be tuned for its intended application.

For a race car, the brake system is typically tuned to minimize stopping distance on dry pavement. For street driving, the brake system should be tuned in a more conservative manner. That is, the brake system for a street car should be adjusted so that the car is safe when it is fully loaded and operating on wet pavement.

A conservative setup for a street car is to slightly increase the front bias

An adjustable proportioning valve is the easiest way to tune a four-wheel disc brake system. As long as the mechanical bias created by the piston sizes is correct, the proportioning valve reduces rear brake force to prevent rear wheel lockup. This Direct Connection proportioning valve is plumbed into the rear brake line and is located conveniently next to the master cylinder.

past the point where the minimum stopping distance is measured. The additional front bias does increase the minimum stopping distance, but it also makes the car less likely to spin during a panic stop. If the car can be kept straight during heavy braking, there is a better chance of steering around the problem than if the car spins and the driver loses control.

Tuning a new brake system can be accomplished by taking the vehicle to a large parking lot, or to a race track, and applying the brakes at different speeds. A second observer outside the vehicle can help to verify if the front brakes or the rear brakes are locking up first. If the caliper selection was performed correctly, the front brakes should always be locking up slightly before the rear brakes. If the rear brakes are locking up first, the rear bias needs to be reduced.

To change the rear bias, you replace the system components (to change the diameter of the wheel cylinders or caliper pistons), or the bias can be adjusted with an adjustable proportioning valve. One simple way to know what to do is to carefully observe how the vehicle reacts during testing. If the rear wheels lock up under moderate brake force, the mechanical bias needs to be adjusted. Either the rear brake force needs to be decreased or the front brake force needs to be increased to solve the premature lockup problem. The proportioning valve has no effect at lower line pressure, so adjusting it does not fix the problem.

On the other hand, if the rear brakes are only locking up during a very hard stop, decreasing either the split point or the pressure slope of the proportioning valve reduces the rear brake bias.

Master Cylinder Selection

Most aftermarket master cylinders are designed for disc/drum systems, so the proper selection for a disc/disc system can be slightly more difficult. Disc brake reservoirs tend to be larger than drum brake reservoirs, because the disc brake caliper pistons use more fluid than drum brake wheel cylinders. If you use a disc/drum master cylinder with a four-wheel disc system, be sure that you check the fluid level in the master cylinder on a regular basis. If the mechanical bias is correct, the pistons in the rear calipers are fairly small, and the smaller fluid reservoir from a disc/drum master cylinder is adequate.

I have had some success using the factory aluminum/plastic two-bolt master cylinder with four-wheel disc brake conversions. This master cylinder was not designed for use with four-wheel disc brakes, but it works okay as long as the rear piston size is fairly small.

Another option would be to retrofit a master cylinder from a

One of the late-model, lightweight, aluminum master cylinders should work okay for a four-wheel disc brake system, as long as the rear calipers aren't too big.

vehicle, such as a Viper, that was designed for four-wheel disc brakes. One potential problem with this approach is that most production vehicles with four-wheel disc brakes also have power assist. Installing a power assist system can be difficult, but running without it may require a lot of pedal force. A third option is to contact a vendor such as Baer or Wilwood. These vendors can supply master cylinders that are designed to work with the four-wheel disc brake systems that they sell.

Drag Race Kits

Many of the rear disc brake kits on the market are designed as lightweight replacements for heavy drum brakes. Some of these drag race brake kits are very lightweight and do not have parking brakes because they are for racing use only. Drag race kits are typically designed to provide adequate stopping power for just one application from full speed. The rotors are small and heat up when used, but because there is enough time for them to cool down between races, these lightweight brakes work just fine at the track. However, if you install one of these lightweight disc brake systems on a vehicle that sees repeated heavy braking, the lightweight rotors may overheat and warp.

Drag race kits are also designed for straight-line use only, so often times the original tapered roller axle bearings are replaced with less-complicated ball bearing units. There is nothing wrong with these lightweight rear disc kits when they are used in the appropriate application. Just don't buy a drag race kit if you're planning on street driving or road racing.

REAR DISC BRAKES

Wilwood has several rear disc brake systems. This Superlite system has a 12.88-inch-diameter rotor with an internal drum-style parking brake. Piston area is 2.46 square inches, which works fine with some of the track-style front caliper kits. (Photo Courtesy Wilwood Engineering)

Wilwood also has drag race–only rear disc brake kits, such as this Dynalite system. This system requires the use of ball-bearing-type axle bearings and does not have a parking brake. (Photo Courtesy Wilwood Engineering)

Road Race Kits

Road racing disc brake kits for the Mopar rear axle housings are not as common as drag race kits, but there are a few to choose from. Baer and DoctorDiff make excellent kits, which retain the factory tapered roller bearing. Weight reduction is important for road racing, as is brake balance, pad life, heat management, and several other variables.

If you are planning on road-racing your Mopar muscle car, you should spend some time at the track to see what other folks are using on their cars. The rear brakes are not heavily stressed on the average muscle car, so staying with drum brakes is a possibility until you've completed your research. I have worked on road race cars with top speeds of more than 130 mph that were equipped with rear drum brakes, so rear disc brakes are not an absolute necessity. Of course, the rear disc brakes run a little cooler, are more linear, more fade-resistant, and possibly a little lighter, so it is a worthy upgrade to have on the list.

Street Driving

Rear disc brakes are not really necessary for street use, but many owners want the look of a four-wheel disc brake system. If the primary focus is on looks rather than function, go ahead and purchase a kit that looks good. As long as the kit includes a parking brake, it should function okay on an average street car. My recommendation would be to only use a rear disc kit that uses the factory tapered roller axle bearing, but there is some difference of opinion on that subject.

Another primary consideration for a street kit would be the availability of replacement parts. Several kits, such as the one made by DoctorDiff, are based on OEM parts, so repair parts are available from local auto parts stores. Some kits on the market use specially designed parts that are only available from the kit vendor. If you buy a kit with unique parts, you might want to buy a set of spare parts also, so you aren't sitting by the side of the road waiting for FedEx to bring you spare parts.

XV Motorsports' Level 1 rear disc kit uses 11¾-inch rotors. This kit has a parking brake and is designed to work with XV's 13-inch front brake kit. (Photo Courtesy XV Motorsports)

CHAPTER 8

A close view of this DoctorDiff rear disc kit shows a steel mounting bracket and a vented rotor. The DoctorDiff kits are available in three sizes of rotors. (Photo Courtesy DoctorDiff)

The XV Motorsports rear kit makes an attractive statement with the drilled rotors and red calipers. (Photo Courtesy XV Motorsports)

Project: Installing a Rear Disc on a Track Car

A complete 10.7-inch rear disc kit was purchased for our project vehicle from DoctorDiff. This car has an 8¾-inch rear end and uses the stock tapered roller axle bearings. Because this is a track car, we wanted to stay with the tapered axle bearings. We also needed a parking brake, as the vehicle is driven occasionally on the street. The DoctorDiff kit comes complete with calipers, pads, hoses, rotors, and brackets. The brackets are machined from solid billet and they serve as both the backing plate and the caliper adapter.

1 *Once all of the drum brake hardware is removed, the first step is to install the caliper brackets. The brackets are designed to hang the calipers to the rear of the axle. The caliper brackets fit in place of the drum backing plates, so the normal assembly process using the OEM gaskets and bearing adjustment is used.*

2 *With the brackets installed and tightened in place, the axle shaft end play can be adjusted. The procedure is the same as that specified in the service manual, and therefore, an adjuster assembly on the passenger's side of the vehicle is used to set the end play. The caliper bracket makes a handy place to mount a dial indicator. The service manual specifies .005 to .015 inch of end play, so we dialed in this setup with .009 inch of play.*

REAR DISC BRAKES

3 With the end play set and everything tightened in place, the caliper can be installed to check fitment. At this point, the hose routing should be laid out. The brake line on the rear end needs to be cut and flared to accept the #3 AN adapter, which is included in the kit. The best solution is to weld a small tab onto the rear end housing to hold the hose adapter, but a large hose clamp can also be used. The caliper slides a small amount during operation, which is why a flexible line is needed.

4 Final assembly can begin once the caliper bracket fit has been verified and the hose routing is laid out. The rotor should fit properly on the locating shoulder in the axle. The shoulder on the axle, rather than the wheel studs, needs to center the rotor. There needs to be plenty of clearance in the rotor for the wheel studs to ensure that the rotor is sitting squarely on the axle face.

5 The caliper is mounted back on the adapter after the rotor has been installed. Carefully check for proper clearances and operation. The caliper can be bled, and the operation of the parking brake can be verified. Once everything has been properly installed, the brakes are ready to be bedded in. Follow the pad vendor's recommendations on pad bedding.

6 For this project vehicle, we used a Mopar aluminum master cylinder, complete with an adapter plate and a heat shield. The entire assembly was purchased from DoctorDiff. The aluminum master cylinders are available in several bore sizes. They are fairly inexpensive, so changing master cylinders to get the best brake "feel" is often the best approach. Larger bore sizes move more volume, but they require additional pedal pressure. Smaller bore sizes require more pedal travel, but the pedal force is lower. Some drivers prefer the additional pedal travel for modulation, and others like the brake pedal to be "high and hard." There isn't a wrong choice as long as the master cylinder can provide enough fluid to operate the caliper pistons.

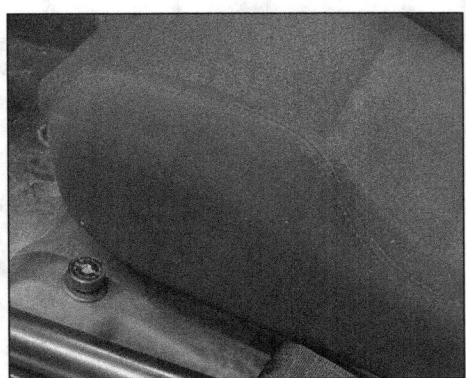

7 An adjustable proportioning valve was installed in the brake line running to the rear end. The valve was installed under the floor near the driver's seat, with the knob coming up through the floor. This placement allows the driver to reach the adjuster knob while seated in the car. The driver is able to reach down and twist the knob to adjust the brake bias during a track session.

CHAPTER 9

FRONT SUSPENSION UPGRADES

Chrysler muscle cars were equipped with an excellent double-wishbone front suspension system from the factory. When combined with the asymmetrical rear leaf springs and front torsion bars, the factory design makes a very capable suspension system. Nevertheless, there are some simple modifications that can be made to the original design that offers a noticeable improvement.

The Mopar front suspension is a double-wishbone design, even though it doesn't quite look like it at first. The upper control arm is a classic wishbone design, and the strut rod and the lower control arm combine to make the bottom wishbone.

Torsion Bars

One fairly simple modification that can make a dramatic improvement in vehicle performance is to install larger-diameter torsion bars. Torsion bars are the springs that support the front of the vehicle, and they are much easier to change than the coil-over springs used in most GM and Ford vehicles. The torsion bars are quickly removed in the unloaded position with a few blows from a hammer on the appropriate torsion bar removal tool. The whole process only takes a few minutes for someone who is experienced at the task of changing torsion bars and has the necessary equipment.

The factory selection of torsion bars was matched with the engine package installed in the vehicle. In production B-Body cars, four torsion bar diameters were used, ranging from .860 to .920 inch. These four sizes are commonly referred to as the Slant-6, small-block, big-block, and Hemi bars. This terminology is not perfectly precise, because it was possible to get an upgraded

FRONT SUSPENSION UPGRADES

Several vendors are now producing torsion bars for Mopar vehicles. This rack at Firm Feel holds torsion bars that are ready to be shipped to customers.

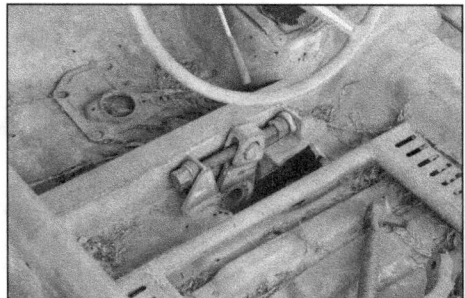

The torsion bar mount is adjustable on the left side of this old B-Body race car. The driver is able to use a wrench during the race to change the suspension pre-load.

suspension package with one of the smaller engines. Nevertheless, when people mention that they have "Hemi bars" for their B-Body, most everyone understands that they are talking about the .920-inch-diameter torsion bars.

At one time, the Mopar Performance catalog listed a wide selection of torsion bars, ranging from super-lightweight drag racing bars all the way to extremely stiff circle track bars. Mopar Performance has cut back on its product selection these days, but several aftermarket vendors have stepped in with replacement parts.

The spring rate of a torsion bar is a function of the diameter of the bar raised to the fourth power. So, if you double the diameter of a torsion bar, the spring rate increases 16 times. A common production size for the 1962 to 1972 B-Body torsion bar is .880 inch in diameter. If these .880-inch bars are replaced with 1.000-inch-diameter bars, the front spring rate increases by 67 percent. A 67-percent increase in the spring rate is a very large change and is very noticeable. In fact, passengers may dislike the change, because the ride can become overly stiff and a little harsh. The moral of the story with torsion bars is to remember that a small change in diameter goes a long way, and bigger isn't always better.

One rule of thumb when picking torsion bars is to select a spring rate that is 10 percent of the front-end weight. For example, if the front-end of a 3,500-pound B-Body car weighs 1,800 pounds, you would select a set of torsion bars with a wheel rate of 180 pounds per inch for a high-performance ride.

Remember, as the wheel rate goes up, the ride becomes harsher with more high-frequency movement. Low spring rates make the ride smoother, but the suspension needs to travel farther to provide the same force. A car with low spring rates feels like a boat, and one with high spring rates feels like a go-cart. Neither extreme is very comfortable, so it is best to select a moderate spring rate for normal street driving.

Shock Absorbers

The Mopar front suspension uses a fairly conventional tube-type shock absorber, but the bayonet top mount does limit the number of aftermarket parts that will fit. Inexpensive replacement shock absorbers typically are a twin-tube design, which really isn't suitable for high-performance use. Upgrading to a higher-performance gas-charged shock absorber is best suited for a car that has stiffer springs and lighter suspension components.

A variety of vendors sell gas-charged shock absorbers for Mopar muscle car applications. Although these shocks are much better than lower-priced alternatives, they are non-adjustable, and the valving specifications are not published, so it can be a trial-and-error process to find a shock

Mopar 41-inch B-Body Torsion Bar Chart

Diameter (inches)	Color Code	Factory PN	Recommended Use	Wheel Rate (lbs/inch)
0.840	N/A	P5249156	Drag race only	92
0.860	Orange	1857774-5	Drag race moderate weight	102
0.880	Green	1857776-7	Fast drag race car	111
0.900	Aluminum	1857778-9	Street cruiser or fast drag car	122
0.920	Brown	1857780-1	Big-block street car	133
0.960	N/A	P5249158	Canyon car	158
1.000	N/A	P5249159	Serious G-machine	186
1.120	N/A	P5249160	Solo racing or road racing	292
1.160	N/A	P5249161	Flat-track race car	336
1.220	N/A	P5249162	Banked-track race car	411

CHAPTER 9

A variety of shock absorbers are available for B-Body cars. On the left is an adjustable shock from Strange. The middle shock is from Edelbrock, and the blue shock on the right is an inexpensive parts store replacement.

This track car has been lowered so much that a normal shock no longer fits. Bilstein shocks from an Impala SS were modified to work in this application.

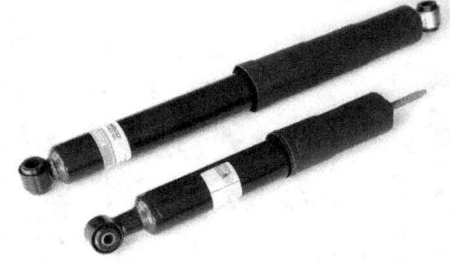

RCD can supply custom Bilstein shocks to fit most Mopar applications. These Bilstein mono-tube shocks have a large piston size and split valving. The RCD shocks are available in different lengths to fit different ride heights.

that works properly with a specific vehicle. There is also an aspect of driver preference to shock valving, so even if your buddy swears that Brand X shocks are great on his car, they may or may not feel great on your car.

There are a few vendors that sell adjustable shocks for Mopar muscle cars. Many of them are designed for drag racing applications, but with some careful searching, you can find road race shock absorbers that work. Single-adjustable shock absorbers allow the valving to be changed for one direction, and double-adjustable shocks are able to adjust both rebound and compression valving independent of each other.

XV Motorsports has done extensive research on Mopar muscle car suspensions, and it used that research to design a full line of shock absorbers for B-Body cars. The XV shocks are available in twin-tube and mono-tube designs. Both versions are available in single-adjustable, double-adjustable, and non-adjustable styles. Specialty shocks, such as the XV-designed ones, are several times more expensive than department store shock absorbers.

Race Car Dynamics (RCD) is one company that specializes in shock absorbers for muscle cars. It offers a very broad range of shock absorbers for most popular muscle cars, including 1962 to 1972 Mopar vehicles. Several vendors, such as Firm Feel and Hotchkis, carry the RCD Bilstein shocks for Mopar vehicles. These Bilstein shocks are a cost-effective, large-diameter, gas mono-tube, non-adjustable design. Although the Bilstein shocks are non-adjustable, RCD is capable of coming up with custom valving for unique applications.

Edelbrock has recently introduced its own line of Mopar shocks. The Edelbrock shocks are also a large-diameter, mono-tube, gas-charged design, but with an inertia-activated system (IAS) for additional control on rough roads.

Ride Height

The shock absorber selection for Mopars is fairly decent for vehicles with the stock ride height, but the majority of vehicles modified for performance applications have a lower-than-stock ride height. Depending on how the vehicle was lowered (see Chapter 14), the shocks probably need to be slightly shorter than stock. You definitely need to prevent the shock absorber from bottoming out before the frame hits the bump stops. The shock absorber and its mounting brackets are not designed to carry the full weight of the vehicle. If the shock bottoms out during use, it fails and may cause damage to the vehicle.

It isn't very easy to change the shock absorber mounts, especially on the front of a Mopar, so take the proper measurements and search for shocks that fit your particular car. For a vehicle that has been heavily modified, it is probably best to work with a specialty vendor, such as Race Car Dynamics, to find a shock absorber that fits. RCD has the ability to cross-reference multiple applications to find a shock that fits your particular vehicle.

Upper Control Arms

Over the past several years, a number of vendors have jumped into the marketplace with fabricated upper control arms for various Mopar vehicles. The stamped sheet-metal control arm that came on

FRONT SUSPENSION UPGRADES

production vehicles was a compromise design. Although certainly a low-cost item to produce, the factory design was not adjustable, and the sheet-metal threads can be damaged when replacing the ball joints. The various aftermarket offerings solve these problems by providing additional caster and camber, as well as using thicker wall tubing where the upper ball joint screws into the arm.

A variety of control arms are available in the marketplace, so it is best to shop around and see what the options are. Some arms are adjustable, and others have fixed ends. Several vendors offer upper control arms designed to change the suspension geometry slightly for higher-performance applications. Be sure to discuss with the vendor your intended use for the vehicle, as well as what your ride height is. Some upper control arms are designed to work with the tall knuckle conversion, as well as provide extra room for large-brake conversions and wheels with extra backspacing.

Lower Control Arms

The lower control arm is a very important piece of the Mopar front suspension, because it carries the weight of the front end of the vehicle. Many high-performance vehicles use the original lower control arms, but several vendors do offer special lower control arms that have been lightened or otherwise modified. The lower control arms need to be modified significantly when replacing the

The Firm Feel arms have the upper ball joint positioned at a slight angle in order to accommodate the late-model knuckle. This allows the lighter and taller 638 knuckle to be used on the 1962 to 1972 B-Body cars.

Firm Feel makes these non-adjustable A-arms. They have a gusset in the web area for extra strength. Aftermarket arms have been known to fail in this critical area, so the gusset adds a little extra strength.

QA1 sells these double-adjustable upper A-arms with Heim ends. (Photo Courtesy QA1 Performance Products)

These B-Body lower control arms illustrate the two most common mounting locations for the sway bar link. The control arm at the top, with the sway bar tab located at the end, fits 1966 to 1969 cars. The control arm at the bottom, with the sway bar tab located near the center, is from a 1970 to 1972 B-Body.

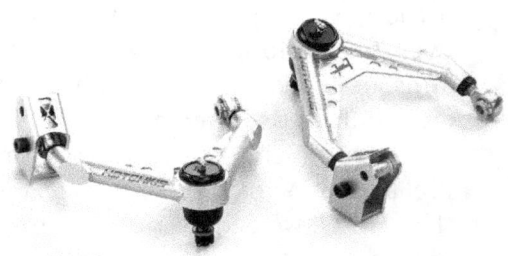

Hotchkis relocates the pickup points on its B-Body upper A-arms. The relocated pickup points are designed to improve the camber and caster curves. (Photo Courtesy Hotchkis Performance)

Boxing the lower control arm is a good idea when using a stiffer-than-stock sway bar. Boxing the control arm helps it to withstand the torsional stress created by the force from the sway bar. (Photo Courtesy Gary Beineke)

CHAPTER 9

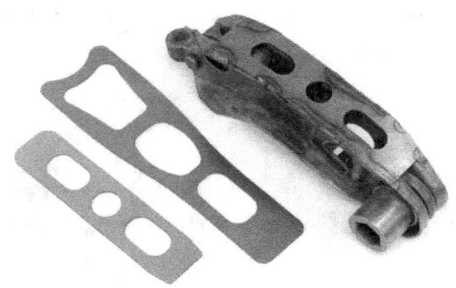

The plates used to box the lower control arms are simple flat sheets available from Mancini Racing. They are clamped onto the bottom of the lower control arm and then welded in place. Plates are available for all B-Body cars.

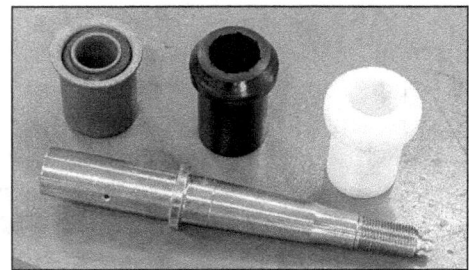

Several bushing materials are available for the lower control arm pivot pin. This pin has been drilled for a Zerk fitting so that the poly bushing can be greased.

torsion bar suspension with a coil-over suspension, so lower control arms designed for that application are significantly different.

Several vendors, such as Firm Feel and Mancini Racing, offer plates that can be welded onto the bottom of the factory lower control arms to fully box the arms. The factory design is a U-channel shape. The U-channel design is strong enough to support the vehicle weight, but it wasn't designed to handle the torsional load created by a stiff sway bar. Welding a plate onto the bottom of the lower control arm boxes in the structure and makes it strong enough to transmit the force from the sway bar to the chassis without twisting open.

Strut Rods

The front strut rod is a fairly simple part that connects the front of the K-member to the lower control arm. The strut rod primarily operates in tension, transmitting the braking force from the tires to the K-member. Several types of strut rods are available in the aftermarket, including lightweight versions for drag racing and adjustable units for performance applications. The OEM design is made from solid rod and is fairly heavy. Lighter, stiffer, tubular units can replace the original bars. Another option is to purchase strut rods that are adjustable, in order to compensate for other issues with the suspension.

For example, some replacement strut rod bushings are thicker than the factory ones, which pushes the lower control arm back slightly and results in reduced caster. An adjustable strut rod can resolve this issue by allowing the lower control arm to be reset into the correct position.

The front strut rod plays a key part in the suspension by keeping the lower control arm properly located. Vendors offer several types of front strut rods, including these Firm Feel adjustable rods. Shortening the strut rod pulls the end of the lower control arm toward the front bumper and increases caster.

The strut rod needs to be the correct length, and it needs to swing properly through the entire range of motion in order to properly control the position of the lower control arm. If the lower control arm is allowed to float back and forth, the front alignment settings vary as the suspension moves, and the handling feels sloppy. It is also possible to use the strut rod as a place for the sway bar to attach, but only if the strut rod has been specially designed for that load.

Sway Bars

Sway bars were available for all generations of the B-Body, but it was a fairly rare option in the early years. The design of the sway bar, as well as the mounting brackets, changed several times over the years.

Early B-Body cars used a design that mounted the end links directly to the strut bars. These early sway bars are fairly rare to find, and replacement parts are even more difficult to find.

A second B-Body design was used from 1966 to 1969. This second-generation design mounted the end links toward the outside edge of the lower control arms.

The third B-Body design used from 1970 to 1972 moved the end

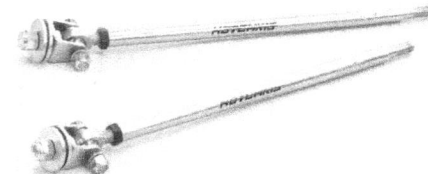

Hotchkis offers these adjustable strut rods for 1962 to 1972 B-Body cars. The front of the rod is secured with a 5/8-inch high-articulation rod end. (Photo Courtesy Hotchkis Performance)

FRONT SUSPENSION UPGRADES

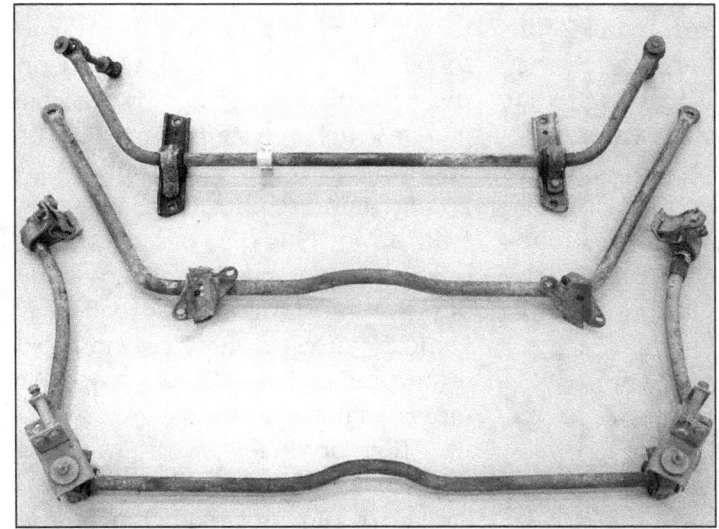

Three versions of B-Body sway bars illustrate the different mounting methods used by the factory. The early B-Body bar at the bottom was mounted to the K-member on long studs, and the ends of the bar are attached to the strut rods. The middle bar is from a 1966 to 1969 B-Body and is designed to mount on the front of the K-member. The short arms on the top bar identify it as a 1970-or-newer sway bar, which runs through the K-member.

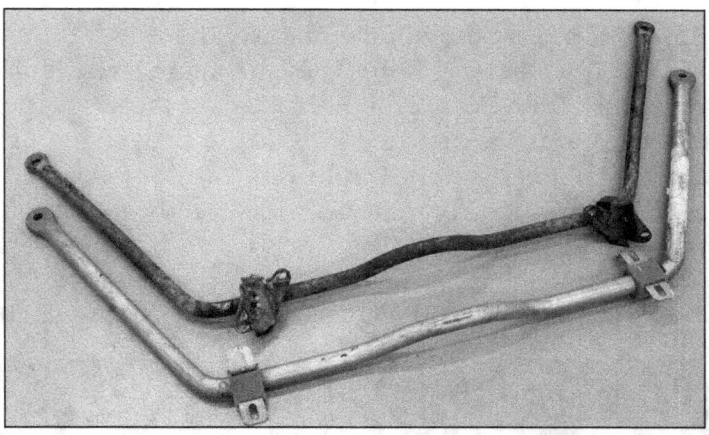

A 1.250-inch-diameter aftermarket bar (bottom) dwarfs a factory sway bar from a 1969 B-Body car. A large bar like this usually works fairly well when matched with good shocks and modern radial tires.

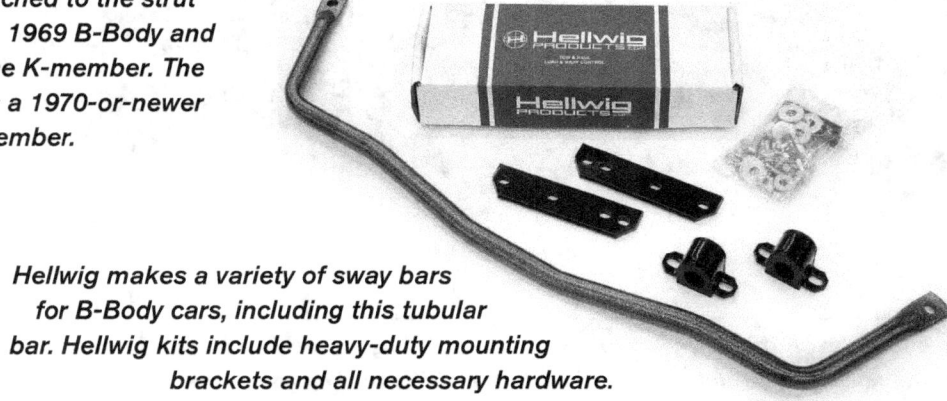

Hellwig makes a variety of sway bars for B-Body cars, including this tubular bar. Hellwig kits include heavy-duty mounting brackets and all necessary hardware.

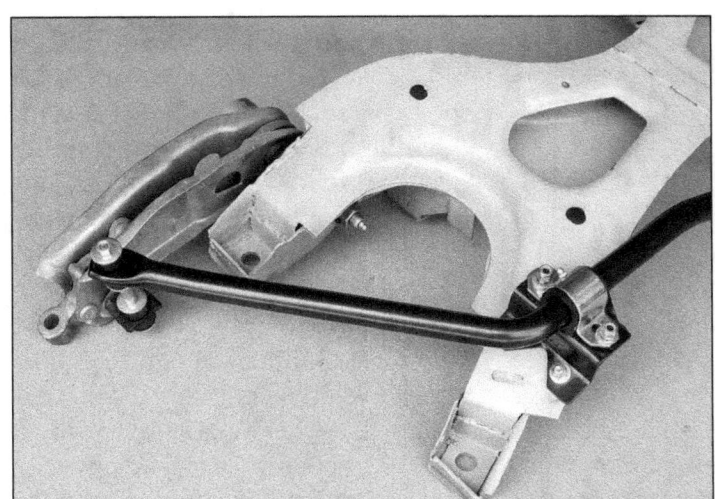

Firm Feel sells a variety of anti-sway bars for Mopar vehicles, including this 1966 to 1969 B-Body setup.

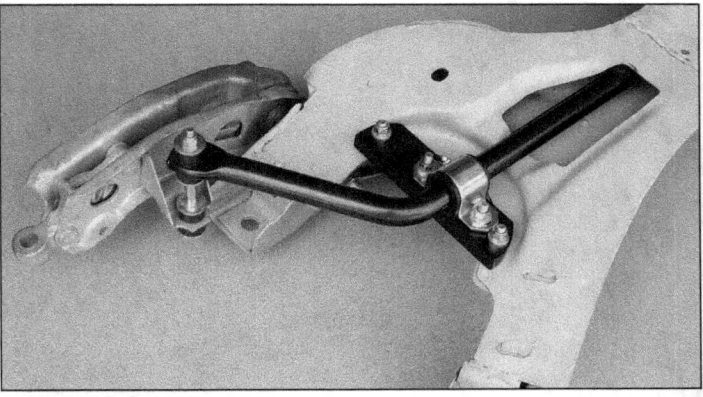

This 1970 K-member is upgraded with a Firm Feel sway bar and mounts. The 1970 to 1972 sway bar runs through the K-member, with the end links attached to the middle of the lower control arms. This is a very simple and effective design.

links inboard to the middle of the lower control arms. This third design provided more clearance for the brake calipers and is the preferred method for general street use. The E-Body cars shared suspension components with the 1970 to 1972 B-Body vehicles, so sway bars interchange between them.

The closer the end links are to the end of the control arms, the more leverage that the sway bar has on the suspension. This means that a smaller and lighter bar can do the same work as a thicker bar operating on the middle of the control arms.

If you have the ability to fabricate the necessary mounts for a custom sway bar, the best solution is to use rear-hung brake calipers and to push the end links outboard on the control arms. It is also possible to construct a system that ties the end links to the strut arms, but this arrangement requires some custom fabrication. This type of custom fabrication is not needed on anything but the most dedicated road race vehicle, though, as the standard mounting systems should work for most situations.

The original factory-installed sway bars were fairly small in diameter and did not add much roll stiffness to the suspension. For high-performance applications, multiple aftermarket vendors offer B-Body sway bars. Firm Feel is one of the original suppliers of sway bar systems for Mopar vehicles, and it carries a full line of bars and mounting kits. Firm Feel currently offers large-diameter sway bars for all generations of B-Body cars, and it can build custom bars, if needed.

For the weight-conscious car builder, Hellwig makes tubular sway bars for various Mopar applications, including most B-Body cars. The tubular design shaves about 6 pounds off the nose of the car while still providing a high degree of roll resistance. Making a sway bar from a tube is actually a very good idea, as the inner material in a torsion spring doesn't provide a significant amount of stiffness. A hollow tube only needs to be slightly larger in overall diameter to equal the stiffness of a solid bar, but the hollow tube is significantly lighter. The tubular design does cost more to produce than a solid-bar design, but the weight savings is a valuable benefit. The Hellwig sway bars are available in diameters up to 1.500 inches, and it has patterns for 1962 to 1972 B-Body vehicles.

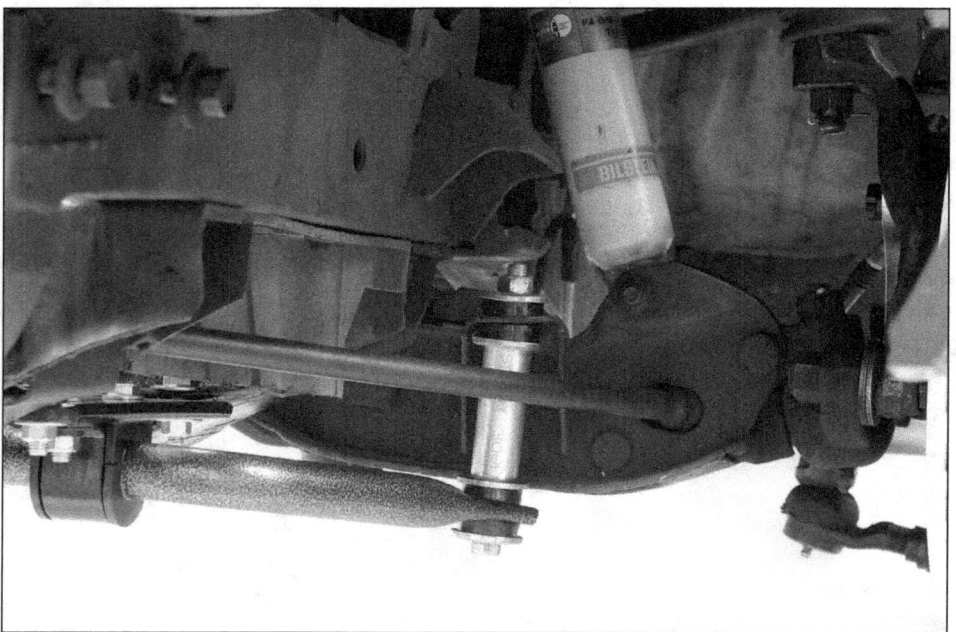

The end links on this sway bar are upgraded with large-diameter aluminum bar stock. The large-diameter end links are stiffer and increase the bar's effectiveness.

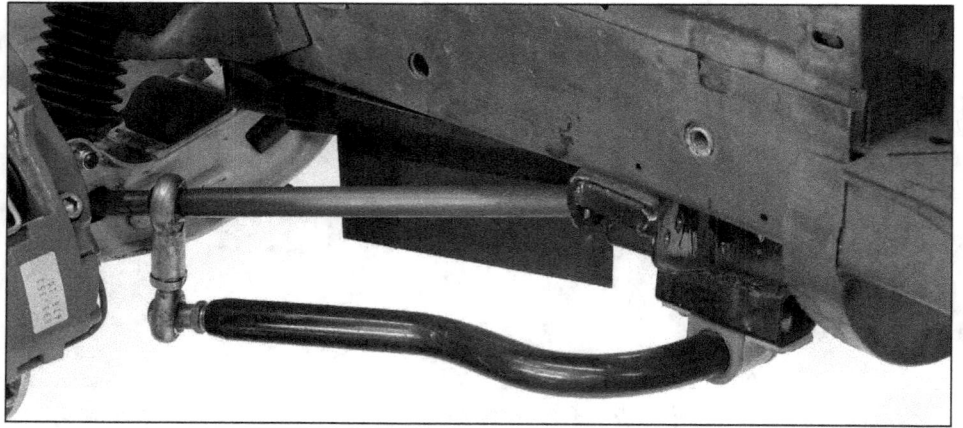

This custom-built sway bar has a curved section to clear extra-wide front tires. Also notice the solid Heim joint end-link design and how it is attached directly to the strut rod. This is a very effective end-link design, but it is noisy and probably too harsh for most street-driven cars.

FRONT SUSPENSION UPGRADES

Frame Isolators for Late B-Body Cars

The 1973-and-newer B-Body cars had rubber isolators between the front frame section and the rest of the unibody. The factory isolators can be replaced with machined aluminum spacers to reduce body flex. Firm Feel carries these isolator plates for the late B-Body cars.

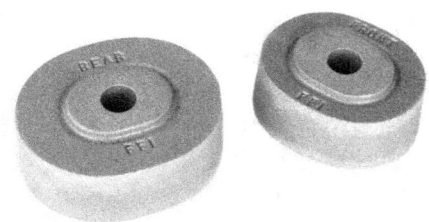

Firm Feel offers solid subframe bushings for third-generation B-Body cars. Using these solid bushings to replace the factory bushings reduces some of the "rubbery" feel from late-model cars.

Coil-Over Front Suspensions

The original torsion bar design is quite good for general handling and road racing, but it does have some limitations for drag racing. Drag racing requires high-powered engines, which in turn require large exhaust headers and oversize oil pans. These items all end up competing

One cheap way to increase negative camber for autocross or road racing is to install washers between the lower ball joint and the knuckle. Firm Feel has these 2-degree spacers, if you don't want to make your own.

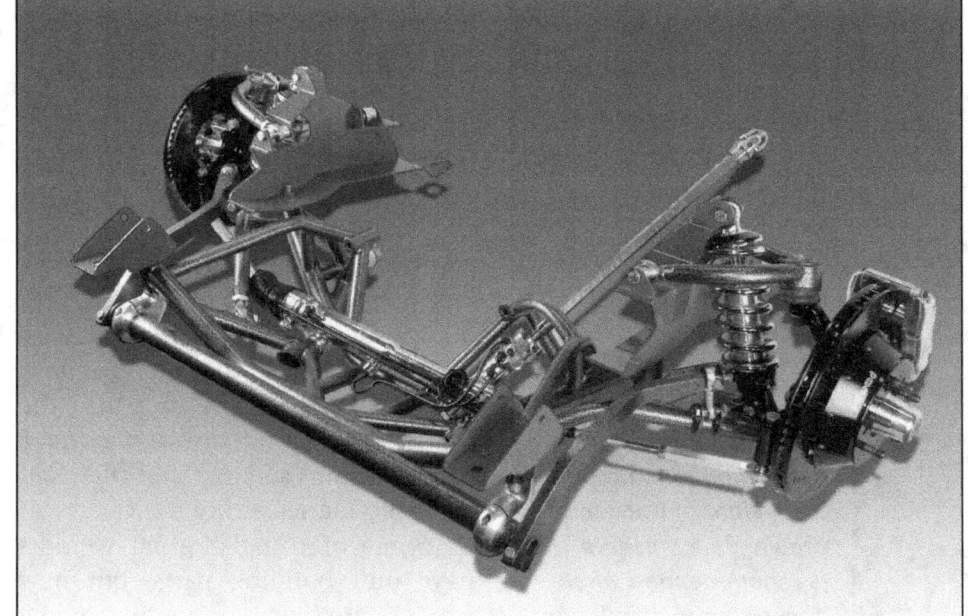

Magnum Force Racing offers coil-over-suspension kits for the 1973 and 1974 B-Body cars. The Magnum Force suspension eliminates the torsion bars and converts the steering system to a forward-located rack-and-pinion design. (Photo Courtesy Magnum Force Racing)

for space with the torsion bars and the steering linkage. The original Mopar steering system is a rear-steer arrangement with a center sump oil pan. The rear-steer design works well for moderate performance use, but a rear sump oil pan works better on faster cars. Years ago, vendors such as Milodon began to build rear sump oil pans with tubes installed in them for the steering linkage. This arrangement is a compromise to both the oil pan and the ability to work on the vehicle, but it does get the job done.

Eventually, several vendors figured out how to fabricate replacement front suspension systems, which resolved most of the issues enthusiasts have with the factory system. There are a number of vendors for these replacement suspension systems, but generally they all use coil-over springs to replace the torsion bars, and they change to a front-steer arrangement using modern rack-and-pinion steering.

The use of coil-over springs eliminates the torsion bars from under the car by moving the springs out to under the inner fenders. Eliminating the torsion bars not only frees up some extra space for the exhaust system, but it also eliminates the need for the torsion bar crossmember. As explained in Chapter 16, the torsion bar crossmember is a stumbling block to swapping in a larger transmission, such as a Tremec T-56 6-speed. Another benefit to the coil-over suspension is that the spring rate can be easily changed, as can the pre-load.

The coil-over spring is a very popular design, so there is a large vendor base making springs and shocks. The large supply base means that prices are lower and that parts are readily available.

Magnum Force Racing also has suspension systems for the 1962 to 1972 B-Body cars. It offers drag race kits, as well as road racing and Pro-Street–type designs. (Photo Courtesy Magnum Force Racing)

Replacing the original torsion bars with coil-over springs opens up the area under the car for large-tube headers. Moving the steering linkage to the front of the K-member provides space for a large-capacity oil pan. (Photo Courtesy Magnum Force Racing)

Rack-and-Pinion Steering

Although the original Mopar steering box is quite well regarded as a recalculating ball design, it still can't quite compare to the precision of a rack-and-pinion steering setup. Almost all modern cars are designed with a rack-and-pinion steering system, because it performs well and is cost effective.

A rack-and-pinion steering system could be developed for a rear-steer application, but almost all of the aftermarket vendors have gone with a front-steer design in order to move the steering linkage away from the oil pan. In a front-steer design, the rack is moved ahead of the spindle center line, which in most vehicles puts it slightly ahead and below the nose of the crankshaft. The result of eliminating the torsion bars and moving to a front-steer design is a wide-open space for the oil pan and exhaust headers.

In a coil-over suspension design, the K-member is replaced with a new subframe built from either round or rectangular tubing. The replacement frame needs to have all of the various mounting points for the steering rack, as well as engine mounts and pickup points for the front suspension. These are not terribly difficult tasks to accomplish for a skilled fabricator, but some of the first products on the market did generate a lot of complaints about general fit and finish.

The weight reduction with an aftermarket coil-over suspension can be quite significant. Reducing front-end weight on a drag race car can really help the 60-foot times. The reduced weight up front helps the nose to lift and transfer weight to the rear tires. If a drag racer has to carry some extra weight to meet the rules, generally it's better to place the weight on the rear of the car and not on the nose.

One slight drawback to the coil-over suspensions is that some of them are based on a Mustang II front spindle. Although the Mustang II spindle isn't necessarily a bad thing, it does mean that the existing Mopar brake system cannot be installed onto the new suspension. The Mustang II spindle is actually much more popular than the Mopar spindle, so there are lots of options for brakes and related items, but many Mopar owners already have a large investment in Mopar components.

Obviously, the front suspension is a rather critical design with a lot of items competing for space and complex geometry issues that need to be resolved. Some of the early customers of coil-over conversion kits ran into problems with turning radius, bump steer, and alignment issues. Early customers reported geometry so poor that they couldn't turn the car while backing up, or having a turning radius so large that they had difficulty maneuvering the car.

Some of those original vendors have quit building parts, but new vendors are always emerging in the marketplace. It pays to be careful and to search for product reviews before making such a significant change to your car.

The shock towers in the B-Body unibody were not designed to hold up the weight of the car, so bracing, such as this, is recommended when converting to a coil-over type of suspension. These down bars tie the shock tower to the front frame rail and the firewall area. (Photo Courtesy Magnum Force Racing)

CHAPTER 10

REAR SUSPENSION UPGRADES

The rear suspension used on B-Body cars was actually a very advanced design for its time. While almost every passenger car during that era used a live axle hung on parallel leaf springs, Mopar vehicles were different, as the Chrysler engineers had a few extra tricks up their sleeves. The Chrysler leaf springs were biased front to back with the rear axle located at about the one-third point on the spring rather than in the middle of the leaf. Also, the Chrysler engineers put additional leaves on the passenger's side to bias the leaf springs from side to side. Some high-powered vehicles came with additional right-side bias to further improve axle control under heavy acceleration.

The rest of the rear suspension was fairly typical with shock absorbers mounted at an angle and a small pinion snubber to control spring wrap. Rear sway bars became available on B-Body cars starting in 1972, although the LAPD was ordering its B-Body police cars with rear sway bars as far back as 1967.

Leaf Springs

Changing rear leaf springs is slightly more work than changing the torsion bars, but it is a task that most people can complete with typical hand tools. A variety of rear leaf springs are available for most Mopar muscle cars, depending on the intended application. The advanced design of the Mopar leaf spring eliminates most of the problems that other car brands had with their leaf springs, but that doesn't make the Mopar design fool-proof. If the engine power output is increased significantly more than stock and more than what the original springs were designed to handle, the springs won't be able to control the rear axle. Another consideration is the age of the original leaf springs and whether they have been subjected to any abuse over the last 40 years. In many cases, the original leaf springs are just no longer up to the task of controlling the suspension.

The B-Body cars typically used a 58-inch leaf spring with a 22-inch front segment and 36-inch rear segment. However, there are some exceptions to this rule, which complicate matters. The early B-Body cars used a 55-inch spring with a 20-inch front segment in 1962 and

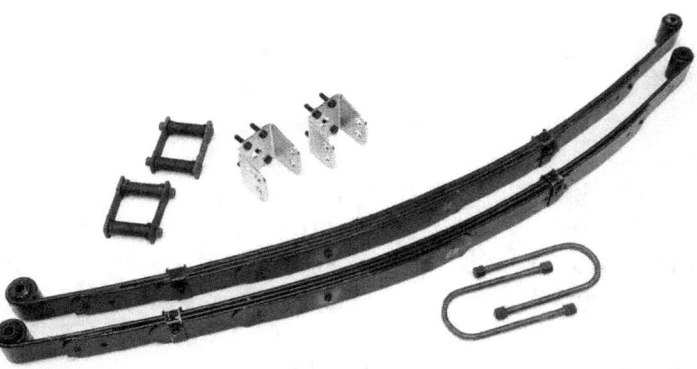

These oval track springs from Mopar Performance provide a good illustration of leaf springs designed for handling. They have a fairly flat design, and each side has the same number of leaves. These springs can be made to fit early B-Body cars by using special front hangers.

CHAPTER 10

Hotchkis offers leaf springs in its handling package for second-generation B-Body cars. The Hotchkis springs are a flat design, and they use hangers with a relocated eye bolt. (Photo Courtesy Hotchkis Performance)

1963. That changed to a 56-inch spring with a 21-inch front segment for the 1964 and 1965 cars. The different spring lengths can make parts selection confusing, especially when some vendors do not provide clear descriptions for their parts.

There is a fairly wide selection of springs available for the 22/36/58-inch-segment spring. These vehicles can also be converted over to the commonly available 20/36/56-inch Super Stock spring by installing a 2-inch-longer front hanger. The 1962 and 1963 vehicles with the 20/35/55-inch-segment springs are also fairly easy to work with because these dimensions are the same for A-Body springs. When ordering A-Body springs for an early B-Body car, be sure to specify the larger 5/8-inch-diameter eye bolt size.

A more difficult application to source leaf springs for is the 1964 and 1965 vehicles with the odd 21/35/56-inch-segment spring. There are two options for these cars, both of which work just fine, but neither is well known. The first option is to use a front spring hanger that is 1 inch shorter than stock with an E-Body leaf spring. The E-Body springs had 22/35/57-inch segments, so both front and rear segments fit perfectly if the spring hanger is 1 inch shorter. The other option for the 1964 and 1965 vehicles is to use a spring hanger that is 1 inch longer than stock with a 20/35/55-inch-segment A-Body spring.

Vendors, such as Mancini Racing and Firm Feel, carry the special front hangers for the 1964 and 1965 cars, which allows them to be converted to either A-Body or E-Body springs. The E-Body springs with the 22-inch front segment are best for general street performance, and the shorter A-Body springs are typically used for drag racing. One complicating factor is that Dodge cars used a different spring hanger than Plymouth cars. So, when ordering new spring hangers for your B-Body, you need to specify the make, model, and year.

One common mistake made with the 1964 and 1965 B-Body cars is to install B-Body Super Stock springs with the 36-inch rear segment. It seems natural to order a B-Body Super Stock spring for these B-Body cars, but the rear segment length is too long. If you install leaf springs with too long of a rear segment, the rear shackle might end up at too steep of an angle to work properly. The Mopar Performance catalog has never provided correct Super Stock spring application information for early B-Body vehicles, so be cautious. Measure twice, order once.

Street Performance

For "spirited" street driving, the XHD leaf spring from Mopar Performance is an ideal selection. Mopar Performance has the XHD spring available for 1966 to 1972 B-Body cars. Because this is a stock-replacement type of spring, it fits into the original spring hanger. The XHD spring has about the same spring rate as a factory Hemi car package. XHD springs are typically biased a small amount with one extra leaf on the passenger's side of the vehicle. This bias helps to counter the torque reaction of the rear end under acceleration.

If the Mopar Performance springs are not available in your area, other vendors, such as Mancini Racing, Firm Feel, and Hotchkis, can provide leaf springs for your vehicle. As pointed out earlier, the A-Body XHD springs can be used on the 1962 and 1963 B-Body vehicles without any modifications. The E-Body XHD springs can be used on the 1964 and 1965 B-Body vehicles if the front spring hanger is 1 inch shorter than stock. For 1964 and 1965 Dodges, order PN AR098. For 1964 and 1965 Plymouths, order AR105.

Oval Track Springs

Mopar Performance offers an oval track spring package. Each spring in it is not necessarily a super-stiff spring, but at 120 inch-pounds, it is a little stiffer than a standard factory spring. One significant difference between the oval track springs and the XHD springs is that the oval track springs are not biased. While the XHD springs have an extra leaf on the right side, the oval track springs are identical on each side. Having the same spring rate on each side of the car is more of a necessity for a road race vehicle than it is for a drag race car, which is why these springs are somewhat unique.

One significant issue with the Mopar oval track spring is that the front segment length is different than that of any production spring, and therefore, the production spring hanger does not work. The Mopar engineers picked a front segment length of 20½ inches for the oval track spring. Consequently, a special spring hanger is required to keep the re ar axle in the correct location. The rear segment length of the Mopar Performance oval track spring is 35 inches, which is too short to work with 1966-or-newer B-Body cars, but these springs can be fitted to any of the early B-Body cars. Firm Feel can custom-build oval track front hangers for the early B-Body cars.

The Mopar Winston Cup cars used a leaf spring package well into the 1970s. At one point, Direct Connection (DC) offered a very large number of leaf springs that were available for the circle track program. These springs are all long gone now, but it is still somewhat interesting to look over the old bulletins to see all of the various choices. A good leaf spring vendor should be able to match the spring rate to one of those old DC spring packages, if so desired. The older Direct Connection bulletin has charts showing which rear springs to combine with the front torsion bars and sway bars in order to achieve the required roll couple. The principle remains the same, even if the part numbers are no longer available from your local Dodge dealer.

Currently, Hotchkis offers a rear leaf spring package that is designed for road and track use. The Hotchkis springs use a different leaf package than production springs, and come with a spring rate of 130 inch-pounds. The Hotchkis spring kit includes new spring hangers, which alter the spring eye position slightly from the factory setting. The relocated spring eye in the Hotchkis package is designed to reduce roll steer and to lower the vehicle by about 1 inch.

Super Stock Springs

The Mopar Super Stock rear leaf springs are legendary at the drag strip. Created during the 1960s by factory racing teams, they are still in use today. Although there are more effective rear suspensions available today, the classic Super Stock spring setup is still a very simple and inexpensive way to get a drag race car down the track.

The Super Stock springs are available in several spring rates and applications. All of the Super Stock springs have a 20-inch front segment, but the rear segments are either 35 or 36 inches long, depending on the application. The Super Stock springs are highly biased toward the right side of the car with extra leaves. In fact, these are so highly biased that the passenger's side of the vehicle rides noticeably higher than the driver's side when first installed. Some people race with the car jacked up like this, and others adjust the front torsion bars to even out the car's stance. The Super Stock springs are designed to provide a high degree of body rise during launch, so it is important to install a shock absorber that has extra travel.

Due to their shorter 20-inch-long front segment, the Super Stock springs require a special hanger when used in most B-Body applications. The 1966 to 1972 B-Body chassis used a 22-inch front spring segment, so the spring hangers need to be 2 inches longer to make up the difference when using Super Stock springs. As mentioned above, early B-Body cars need to use the A-Body Super Stock springs.

Mancini Racing, as well as other Mopar part distributors, has a full selection of Super Stock hangers that should cover all of the popular body styles. For specialized applications, you most likely need to build a set of custom hangers in order to use Super Stock springs.

The Super Stock leaf springs were designed solely for drag racing, but

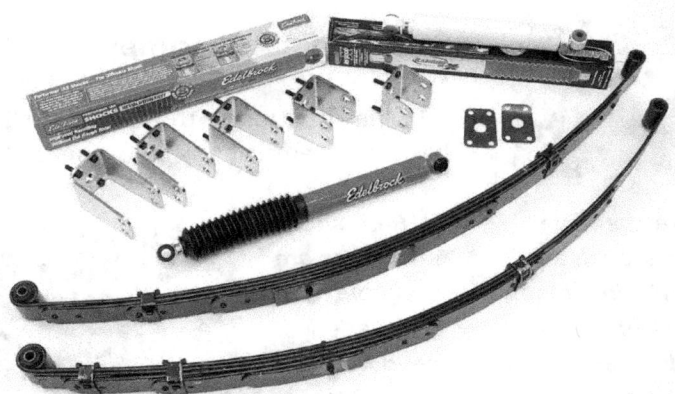

Installing the Super Stock springs from Mopar Performance is a classic modification for drag racing. The Super Stock springs use a 20-inch front segment, so most B-Body cars require longer front hangers. Super Stock springs are usually paired with longer shock absorbers, such as these from Edelbrock and Rancho.

CHAPTER 10

some people have successfully used them in oval track and road racing competition. Typically, you would use two identical springs for road racing, so two left-hand springs, or two right-hand springs, would be installed as a pair. Even a pair of left-hand Super Stock springs results in a fairly high ride height, so the springs may need to be de-arched. Of course, the Super Stock spring package can also be taken apart and re-assembled with fewer leaves in order to get just the right spring rate and ride height.

Although the Super Stock springs have been very successful over the years, the large number of leaves makes them very heavy. A set of Super Stock springs weighs about 70 pounds, which is a lot of weight for the shocks to control, as well as to be carrying down the track. To save weight, Calvert Racing has introduced a split-monoleaf leaf spring design, which is substantially lighter than the traditional Super Stock spring.

The Calvert design uses a single leaf, which is considerably thicker than the main leaf in a Super Stock spring, but because there is just one leaf, the whole assembly weighs about 10 pounds less per side than the Super Stock springs. The split-leaf design allows the suspension to be set up with a stiff front leaf segment and a softer rear segment. Mixing and matching spring rates allows the suspension to be tuned to the chassis.

Calvert also has a link-type rear suspension, which is very popular in certain drag racing classes. The Calvert system uses a reaction strut and a pivoting mount to prevent leaf spring wind-up. This concept works somewhat similarly to traction bars or pinion snubbers, but it is a more direct connection than either of those and is capable of being pre-loaded.

Spring Hangers

The factory spring hangers are often in poor shape after 40 years on the job. Not only are they in poor shape from abuse, but original hangers do not have any provision for adjusting the ride height.

Fortunately, a number of vendors, such as Mancini Racing and Firm Feel, carry a full line of replacement spring hangers made from heavy-gauge material and are zinc-plated to resist corrosion. Replacement hangers are usually available with an extra eye bolt hole, which lowers the car an inch or more.

Shock Absorbers

The situation with rear shocks is basically identical to that of the front shocks, which I covered in Chapter 9. The same vendors that make shocks for the front also make shocks for the rear, and the same basic technology choices are available.

The primary difference for the rear suspension is for drag race cars that use the Super Stock springs. That type of suspension relies on body separation to launch the car off the line. The body separation can be tremendous on powerful vehicles, especially those with high gear ratios, such as 4.56 or 4.88:1. In these cars, the rear end rises so much that the shock absorbers must be extra long, or else the shocks act as travel limiters and unload the tires. Mopar Performance sells extra-long shock absorbers for this application, but racers have also used C-Body or pickup truck shock absorbers for years as a substitute. The current practice is for drag racers to use adjustable shock absorbers from one of the aftermarket vendors such as Calvert. For drag racing, the primary concern is how well the shock controls the separation of the body during the launch, with the compression side considered less important. But of course, this depends to some extent on how fast the car is, as well as exactly what type of suspension is used on the vehicle.

During hard acceleration, higher-powered Mopars can still have problems with the leaf springs wrapping up and causing axle tramp. The Super Stock spring package was designed to

New spring hangers are available from a variety of vendors, such as Firm Feel and Mancini Racing. Most of these hangers come with dual eye bolt locations, so the ride height can be varied. Using the upper eye bolt location lowers the rear of the car by 1½ inches.

Rear shock absorbers are available from a variety of vendors, such as Bilstein, Edelbrock, and KYB. Longer shocks are usually used for drag racing, and shorter shocks are fitted for road racing and autocross applications.

REAR SUSPENSION UPGRADES

This older B-Body race car is fitted with dual shock absorbers at each rear wheel. Also notice the heavy bracing that supports the shock absorber mounts. This shows how much the chassis builder was concerned with providing a rigid mounting system for the shocks.

eliminate axle tramp for drag racing, but street cars and track cars might need another solution. One trick that controls axle tramp fairly well is to add a second set of shock absorbers horizontally from the rear axle to the frame. Adding shock absorbers in this manner greatly reduces axle hop under acceleration, as well as during heavy braking. Direction Connection sold a kit like this for off-road pickup trucks, but it has been discontinued for some time. Fortunately, Firm Feel now has a kit available for adding extra "kicker" shocks to the rear axle.

Moving the location of the end link adjusts the stiffness of this custom rear sway bar. The bar on this track car is mounted to the frame in an effort to reduce unsprung weight.

Another possible approach is to stagger the rear shocks to control spring wind-up and axle hop. With a staggered shock absorber mount, the passenger's-side shock is placed ahead of the axle, and the driver's-side shock is behind the axle.

One more idea would be to use two shocks on each side of the car, like the NASCAR chassis builders used to do.

Sway Bar

Rear sway bars were not available to the general public until the 1972 model year, so most cars do not have factory brackets in place. This can be easily fixed, though, as several vendors, such as Firm Feel, Hotchkis, and Hellwig, carry complete rear sway bar kits.

Rear sway bars are designed to be mounted either on the axle or on the frame. Mounting the bar on the axle is a little easier to accomplish, but it does add a small amount of unsprung weight. Mounting the bar to the frame is a better solution in terms of overall effectiveness, but a frame-mounted bar can interfere with the gas tank and/or exhaust system. Before ordering a rear sway bar system, it would be wise to take a close look at the pictures in the vendor catalogs to see if the bar fits. It would be even better

to look at a car similar to yours that has a sway bar installed. Be especially careful if you have upgraded to larger rear tires and/or a 3-inch exhaust system, as either of these modifications can cause interference with the sway bar. Many rear sway bar kits are designed to fit the 8¾-inch rear end and may not clear the larger housing on the Dana 60, so double-check with the vendor before ordering.

The installation of a rear sway bar requires more analysis than that of a front sway bar. Although bigger is usually better for the front bar, the rear bar size needs to be carefully selected. Too large of a rear bar results in excessive weight transfer to the rear suspension, which results in oversteer. An oversize front bar results in understeer, which isn't desirable, but at least with an understeering car you see what you run into. A car with excessive oversteer can be quite dangerous to drive for anyone other than a dirt track racer.

With a little extra work, the rear sway bar can be made adjustable. A rather simple design with multiple-link attachment points on the bar allows the spring rate to be adjusted. Of course, changing the diameter of the sway bar adjusts the bar rate, but it is handy to be able to quickly dial in more or less "rear bar" with just a few twists on a wrench.

This 1971 Charger is fitted with an axle-mounted sway bar. The end links are anchored on the inside of the frame rails. (Photo Courtesy Gary Beineke)

CHAPTER 10

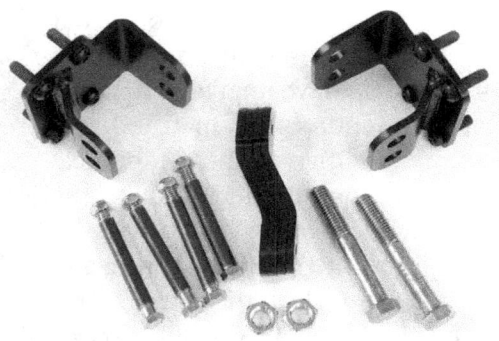

Offset hangers are a fairly easy way to move the leaf spring inboard for some additional tire clearance. These offset hangers are available from DoctorDiff.

Advanced Modifications

A variety of serious modifications can be made to the rear suspension to improve vehicle performance. They range from sheet-metal changes for additional clearance to a complete redesign of the suspension. One common issue that needs to be addressed with a Mopar muscle car is the ability to install a wider rear tire. A wider rear tire is desired for both drag racing and road racing, as well as general appearance for street vehicles because it provides a larger footprint for greater traction and a more aggressive appearance. There are a variety of ways to add room for larger rear tires, ranging from offset hangers to moving the leaf springs to modifying the sheet metal.

Offset Hangers

On a B-Body rear suspension, the leaf spring is almost always the first place that a wider tire hits. Fortunately, offset hangers are a fairly simple solution that provides some additional clearance. Mopar Performance, as well as other vendors such as DoctorDiff, offers a kit that moves the leaf springs inboard by 1/2 to 3/4 inch. The front and rear spring hangers are bent with a slight offset in order to move the leaf springs in, away from the tires. If the offset is slight enough, the pads on the rear end do not need to move, but typically, in order to gain additional tire space, the spring pads on the rear end housing need to be cut off and relocated. DoctorDiff offers a B-Body relocation kit that moves the springs in 1¼ inches on each side. With this kit, the spring pads on the rear end do need to be cut off and relocated.

Relocated Leaf Springs

Offset hangers are a fairly easy way to achieve about an inch of extra tire clearance, but if more space than that is needed, it is time for more substantial modifications. Moving the leaf springs directly under the frame rails is one fairly popular modification that gains room for the tires. Moving the leaf springs like this adds about 4 inches of space for the tires. This is a fairly advanced modification, because it does require fabrication work on the frame rails, including cutting and welding. Mopar Performance sells a relocation kit for this modification, which can be useful for the less-experienced fabricator. The mounting pads on the rear axle need to be relocated when moving the leaf springs in this much.

Typically, when the springs are relocated, the car continues to use a combination of Mopar Super Stock

For maximum tire clearance, the rear leaf springs can be moved into the rear frame rails. Moving the springs in requires careful fabrication work, because the frame rails are cut open for the front hangers. The front hangers need to be properly located before they are welded in place, or the car does not drive straight. Also visible is the CalTrac suspension and the fabricated wheel well tub.

This early B-Body street car has had the leaf springs moved into the frame rails in order to provide clearance for 13-inch-wide tires. A modified Mopar Performance kit was used for this installation. The second eye bolt hole in the frame allows the ride height to be raised, if desired.

springs and drag racing shocks. Having the springs closer together works fine for drag racing, but moving the springs under the frame rails is not a recommended approach for a serious road race vehicle. As the springs move closer together, they have less leverage on the car body during cornering. This means that either higher-rate springs need to be used, or a higher-rate sway bar has to be installed.

For road racing in which extra tire space is required, a chassis builder would probably change over to a NASCAR-style, trailing-arm-type suspension or a more advanced three-bar system with coil-over springs. Having said that, it is true that the Kit Car and other Chrysler-bodied circle track cars used leaf springs with very good results, even well into the 1970s, after other brands had moved to the trailing arm suspension. (The Chrysler Kit Car was a racing-type Aspen or Volare, and the owner or racer assembled the vehicle.)

Mini Tubs

When the leaf springs are moved under the frame rails, the inner fender wells need to be modified so wider tires can be installed. Although the entire fender well can be cut out and replaced with a fabricated wheel tub, this is a very intrusive modification that can significantly reduce the resale value of the vehicle. A less intrusive modification to make is to split the factory wheel well at the seam and to move the inner half inboard to provide the necessary clearance.

Typically, the inner wheel well area is moved inboard by about 2 inches to line up with the face of the frame rail. A patch panel is then seam-welded in place to restore the integrity of the wheel well. If a competent welder performs this job, the entire wheel well area retains a stock factory look. After some simple body work, the entire trunk area appears factory original to the majority of observers.

Back-Half

Back-halving a car is a serious modification in which the factory rear frame rails are removed and replaced with a fabricated set of frame rails. Typically, a car is back-halved for drag race applications so that the rear suspension is set up with clearance for large racing slicks. The original leaf spring suspension is usually replaced with ladder bars or a four-link system. Both the ladder bar and the four-link systems use coil-over springs rather than leaf springs. The coil-over systems are easier to adjust than a leaf spring suspension, and more spring choices are available. The coil-over systems are also lighter than leaf springs, and they provide additional clearance for large tires.

Street Lynx

Reilly Motorsports (RMS) has released a rear suspension kit for Mopar B-Body cars that is a radical departure from the factory design. The RMS Street Lynx kit replaces the existing leaf spring design with a coil-over spring setup. The rear axle is controlled with a four-bar system, but this is not a typical drag racing type of suspension. The Street Lynx design is loosely based on the rear suspension found in various General Motors and Ford vehicles in which the upper control arms are installed at an angle to form a triangle shape. The triangle arrangement provides side-to-side location of the rear end housing and locates the rear end front to back. This type of suspension is highly developed in various racing classes and has excellent capabilities. The coil-spring design allows fairly easy adjustments to spring rates, and the link bar design allows for roll center adjustments.

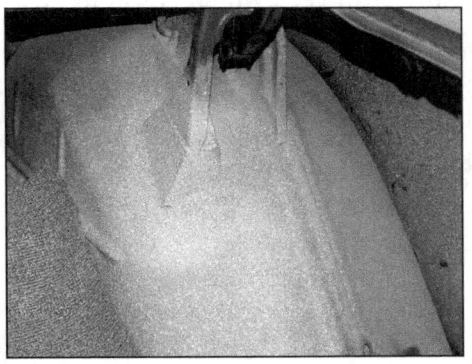

With the rear springs moved under the frame rails, the tires interfere with the wheel wells, unless they are widened. The wheel wells in this 1965 B-Body were split apart, and a strip of material was welded in the middle of each well to make the wheel wells wider. To keep the stock look, the welds were ground down, and the wheel wells were repainted with the original trunk paint. Dedicated race cars often use large wheel tubs fabricated from sheet metal to provide even more tire clearance.

Reilly Motorsports offers a triangulated four-bar system with coil-over springs for Mopar B-Body cars. There are a lot of advantages to a system like this, including lighter weight and easier tuning. This system from RMS is mostly a bolt-in operation, with some minor welding required. (Photo Courtesy Reilly Motorsports)

CHAPTER 11

PERFORMANCE STEERING SYSTEMS

Compared to modern steering systems, Mopar's steering system of the 1960s and 1970s leaves a lot to be desired. The factory power steering systems were over-boosted to the point that road feel was almost totally eliminated. The manual systems were not much better; they took so many spins of the steering wheel to change direction that the driver sometimes felt like a barge captain. Thankfully, both Mopar Performance and the aftermarket have developed products to improve these situations.

Power Steering

Although the power steering systems in passenger cars were over-boosted to the point of limpness, police cars received a different steering box with better road feel. Dick Ross, a long-time Mopar enthusiast and racer, took notice of this fact. He eventually figured out what the factory engineers had done to create the police car steering box, and he tooled up the parts necessary to recalibrate regular power steering boxes. Ross eventually established the company Firm Feel, which is still in business today, providing power steering boxes for Mopar muscle cars.

Firm Feel offers several levels of firmness for the power steering boxes, with the majority of customers opting for the Stage II level. Evidently, people have become comfortable with the higher-effort steering that is common in modern performance vehicles, and they like their older

The factory power steering box was highly boosted, which results in a "mushy" feeling. Vendors, such as Firm Feel, offer fully rebuilt power steering boxes that are calibrated to modern standards. The Firm Feel boxes are available in several stages of firmness. (Photo Courtesy Firm Feel)

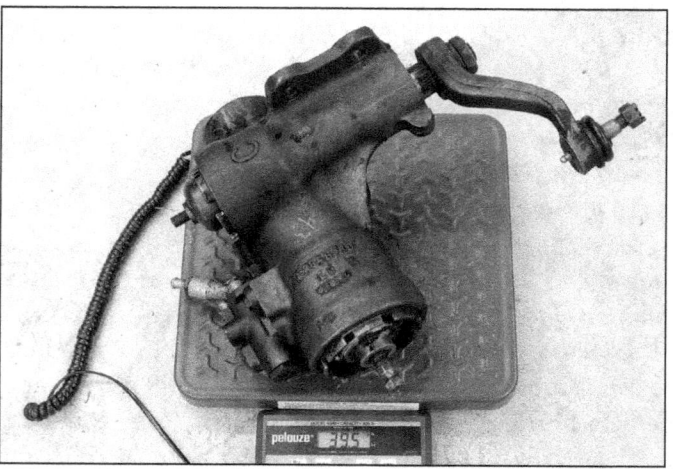

The power steering box is quite heavy, weighing about 40 pounds. Not only is the box heavy, but there is additional weight required for the pump and the hoses.

98   MOPAR B-BODY PERFORMANCE UPGRADES 1962–1979

PERFORMANCE STEERING SYSTEMS

Placing the original box (left) next to the Flaming River box (right) shows some of the slight differences in shape.

Three worm-and-ball nut chucks have been available for the stock manual steering box. Mopar Performance has a 20:1 chuck (middle) in the catalog, and Firm Feel offers a 16:1 chuck (bottom). The original 24:1 chuck (top) is only available used.

muscle cars to have the same type of feel. The Stage II box is designed to make the car feel similar to what a new Mustang or Camaro feels like when driving down the road. The older Mopar boxes do not have the ability to change ratio like a modern box, so low-speed parking lot maneuvers are heavier, but at normal highway speeds, the boxes feel similar.

B-Body power steering boxes used a 1⅛-inch-diameter sector shaft through 1971. In 1972, the sector shaft was upgraded to a larger 1¼-inch diameter. The two steering boxes are interchangeable, but the correct Pitman arm must be used to fit the sector shaft. The small-sector Pitman arms are much more expensive than the late-model ones, so if you are going to be upgrading the steering system, it makes sense to go to the large-sector system at the same time.

Manual Steering

The factory manual steering box is actually an excellent design. The aluminum case is lightweight, and it is a very nice part, considering how many years ago the original tooling was fabricated. However, the original steering ratio of 24:1 requires 5½ complete turns of the steering wheel to go lock to lock, which is very slow for performance driving. Any attempt of counter-steering to avoid a slide during high-speed corning requires rather dramatic spinning of the wheel, and it can lead to a loss of control.

The factory engineers recognized this in the 1960s when they introduced the 16:1 quick-ratio steering box for A-Body cars. It isn't known how many of these quick-ratio steering boxes were actually installed by the factory, but it doesn't appear to have been too many, considering how rare they are to find used. I came across one years ago that had been mounted in a B-Body car, and it is the only factory quick-ratio steering box that I've ever seen.

The 16:1 manual steering box is just about perfect for performance driving once vehicle speed is over 15 mph, but at speeds under 15 mph, it can be very heavy, especially in a nose-heavy vehicle.

If you combine a 16:1 manual steering box with a heavy big-block and wide front tires, you'll probably be able to cancel your gym membership because it takes a lot of effort to turn the steering wheel. It isn't uncommon to try the 16:1 box, and then decide that it is just a little too much steering effort. A reproduction 16:1 worm gear was available for a few years, but evidently, the supply on that item has now dried up. As with most items in the aftermarket, if the demand is there, someone will resurrect the tooling and make some more parts.

Evidently, the Mopar Performance engineers felt the same way about the 16:1 steering ratio, so they designed a 20:1 steering box as a compromise. At the time this book went to press, Mopar Performance still showed the 20:1 gear as available under PN P4007612, but there are not very many of these steering chucks left in the warehouse. Hopefully a vendor will continue producing these parts well into the future.

Flaming River offers a cast-iron manual steering box with a 16:1 ratio. It uses a cast-iron case, which increases the weight to 18 pounds.

CHAPTER 11

Aftermarket Steering Box

Flaming River produces an aftermarket version of the manual steering box for Mopar vehicles. The Flaming River box has a 16:1 ratio, so it is a quick-ratio box. However, this box is cast iron rather than aluminum, so it is noticeably heavier than an original steering box. The external appearance is slightly different than that of the factory box, which may or may not matter, depending on the application.

Quick-Ratio Pitman Arm

Chrysler engineers wanted to speed up the steering on the factory AAR 'Cuda and T/A Challenger to improve steering response. Presumably, the cost was too high to design a new steering box, so they designed a longer Pitman arm. This arm acts as a longer lever on the steering linkage, moving the wheels more for the same amount of steering input. The extra-long Pitman arm speeds up the steering ratio from 16:1 to about 12:1. Instead of 3½ turns lock to lock, the steering increases to only 2¾ turns from lock to lock. Of course, the extra length of this arm pushes the center link back, potentially causing interference issues with the exhaust system.

The original factory quick-ratio Pitman arm is no longer available, but the aftermarket has stepped in with reproductions. In fact, the aftermarket quick-ratio arms are better than the originals, because they are available with correct splines for both the small-sector-shaft boxes and the late-model large-sector-shaft boxes. This means that you can now install a quick-ratio Pitman arm on manual steering boxes as well as on all years of power steering boxes.

Curiously, the factory design only used a longer Pitman arm while leaving the idler arm the original length. This combination of a longer Pitman arm and a stock-length idler arm puts the center link at a slight angle. The slanted center link arrangement causes the wheels to point at different angles during hard cornering. To solve this issue, Firm Feel designed a matching longer-length idler arm. The longer Firm Feel idler arm fits any B-Body car with the through-bolt-style idler mount. Using the longer idler arm with the longer Pitman arm keeps the center link parallel to the K-member and maintains the proper geometry during hard cornering. Using the longer idler arm moves the center link back on the passenger's side, so the exhaust system needs to be checked for any interference.

Factory Steering System Upgrades

A variety of upgrades have been developed over the years for the factory steering system. These upgrades generally focus on improving geometry or on making the system more rigid. Rigidity is an important factor

A quick-ratio Pitman arm was used on the T/A (Trans-Am) cars to speed up the steering. Reproductions are available from several vendors. Firm Feel has developed a matching idler arm, which is the same length as the T/A Pitman arm.

The factory manual steering box is a very nice design. It is lightweight, compact, and provides excellent road feel for the era.

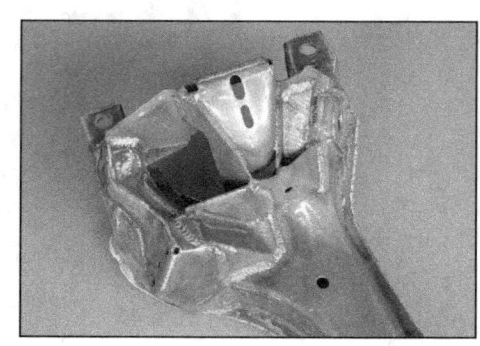

The force required to steer large tires can flex the factory K-member, so chassis builders usually gusset the steering box mount on a track car.

in how the steering feels and operates. If there is a lot of deflection within the steering system, the driver has a difficult time holding the car on a precise line through a corner and most likely complains about "steering a barge." Although the original steering system is an adequate match for narrow bias-ply tires, it does need a little help steering a pair of wide radial tires.

The steering box mounts to a stamped-steel bracket, which is welded to the K-member. This structure certainly appears to be rigid, but when examined during operation, you can see the steering box move as the wheels are turned lock to lock. Fortunately, welding in a few pieces of steel between the steering box mount and the K-member is a fairly easy way to gusset it. The guys at Firm Feel have reinforced so many K-members over the years that they have gone ahead and designed a kit of gussets for the task.

Also on the K-member is the mount for the idler arm. Prior to 1968, the idler arm had a stud, which mounted to a plate on the K-member. The stud-mount design does not resist side loads very well, so it was replaced in 1968 with a through-bolt design. The through-bolt design is very strong, and as an additional benefit, the idler arm is less complex and less expensive to manufacture. It is not very easy to rework an early K-member into a through-bolt design, so most people

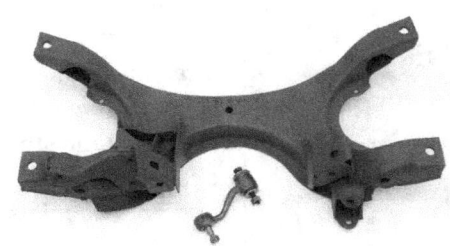

The idler arm bracket was changed in 1968 to a stronger double-shear-style mount. The double-shear mount uses a through bolt to retain the idler arm, as opposed to earlier designs that had the idler arm mounted on a stud.

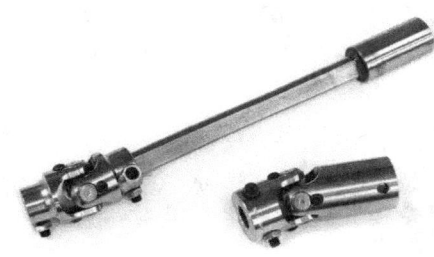

The original steering shaft coupling (bottom) can be replaced with a U-joint (top), if desired. The U-joint design has a slightly slimmer profile, which provides more room for large-tube exhaust headers.

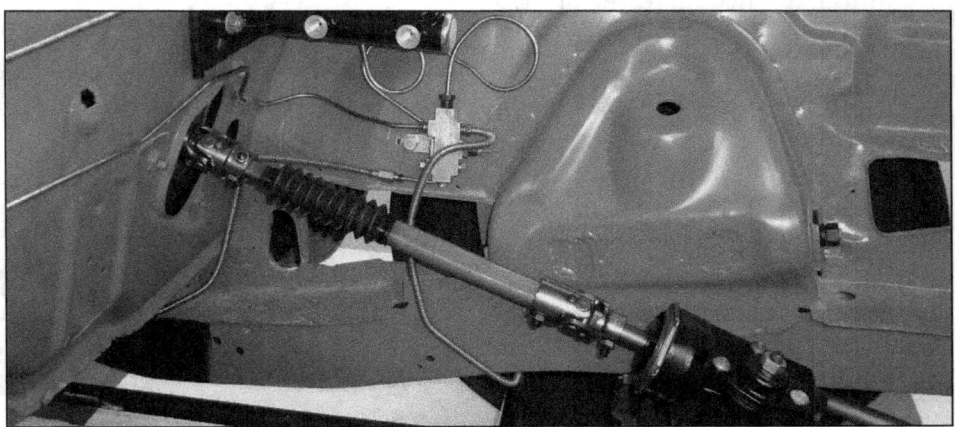

This 1971 Charger is equipped with a custom steering shaft assembly and uses two U-joints instead of the original coupler design. (Photo Courtesy Gary Beineke)

Using C-Body tie rod ends to replace the stock B-Body ones has been a popular upgrade for many years. The C-Body tie rod end (bottom) has an 11/16-inch-diameter shank, which is twice as rigid as the B-Body tie rod end's 9/16-inch-diameter shank (top).

Firm Feel offers complete tie rod assemblies with the upgraded C-Body ends. These billet adjuster kits come complete with double jam nuts.

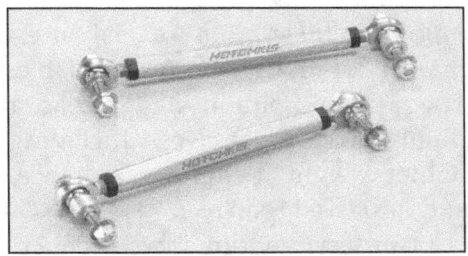

Hotchkis Performance went a different way with its tie rod kit. Hotchkis uses rod ends rather than tie rod ends, and then adds a spacer to change the bump steer. (Photo Courtesy Hotchkis Performance)

just replace a 1966 or 1967 K-member with a 1968-or-newer one. Unfortunately, there isn't an easy upgrade for the early B-Body cars due to the different location for the motor mounts.

Along the way, someone noticed that the 11/16-inch tie rod ends used on C-Body cars had the same taper as on the 9/16-inch B-Body tie rod ends. Because the taper is the same, the C-Body tie rod ends can simply be swapped into place without any modifications. The tie rod sleeve needs to be replaced at the same time in order to accommodate the 11/16-inch ends, but a standard C-Body sleeve works.

Although the increase of 1/8 inch in diameter does not seem like a lot, it is enough to more than double the bending resistance of the tie rod shank. This is a significant increase in bending strength for such a small weight penalty. To further improve this area, aftermarket vendors, such as Firm Feel, have created 11/16-inch upgrade kits with billet adjuster tubes. The cumulative effect of all of these upgrades is reduced deflection and increased preciseness.

Rack-and-Pinion Steering

Chrysler never installed rack-and-pinion steering on any of the B-Body vehicles, but several aftermarket solutions are now available. The rack-and-pinion design has a number of advantages, including lighter weight, better performance, and improved road feel.

Unisteer Performance Products sells a rack-and-pinion system that replaces the factory steering system on a production K-member. This type of conversion requires some steering column fabrication, as well as alterations to the exhaust system.

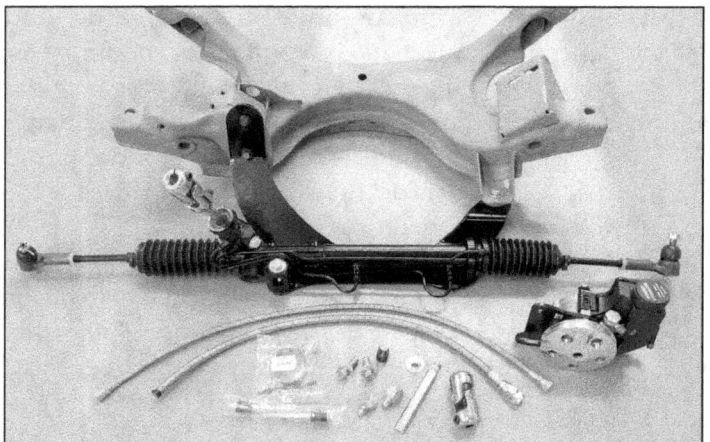

Unisteer has developed a bolt-in rack-and-pinion kit for the 1968 to 1972 B-Body vehicles that attaches to the stock K-member. This is a rear-steer design, so the original ball joints are still used.

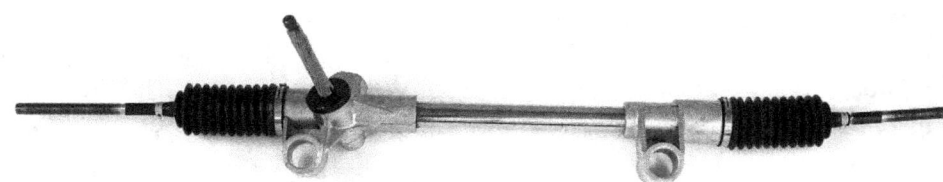

Most modern cars use a rack-and-pinion unit like this. Most of the coil-over-type suspensions currently offered for B-Body cars use a front-mounted rack-and-pinion unit.

Modern power steering pumps are much smaller and lighter than the original designs. One of these newer pumps can be retrofitted to a B-Body car with a little creative fabrication.

As discussed in Chapter 9, there are also vendors, such as Magnum Force and RMS, that provide a rack-and-pinion steering system integrated into complete front suspension kits.

Lightweight Power Steering Pumps

The original Mopar power steering pumps were quite heavy and bulky. Over the years, the factory engineers have figured out how to take weight out of these assemblies by replacing steel parts with aluminum and plastic parts. Several vendors have developed retrofit kits for Mopar applications using modern power steering components. Not only are these modern pumps lighter and more efficient, but some of them are quite attractive.

CHAPTER 12

UNIBODY CHASSIS UPGRADES

Mopar muscle cars built during the 1960s and 1970s were based on a frameless unibody chassis. The chassis is constructed of large stamped sheet-metal parts, with welded-in subframes holding the front and rear suspensions. The B-Body unibody construction becomes apparent once the fenders and doors have been removed. At that point, you can see how the front inner fenders are a key element in the strength of the entire assembly.

The unibody concept provides a stiff, lightweight structure, if all of the elements are properly attached. It can be thought of as a shell design in which the shell is quite strong, as long as it is intact. Once part of the shell has been removed, the stiffness is reduced significantly. The inner fender wells are often modified for header clearance or tire clearance, and these modifications can severely weaken the structural integrity of a Mopar unibody if other actions aren't taken.

The Mopar unibody chassis is more than adequate for the original design parameters of these vehicles, but it is not up to the task of transmitting huge amounts of torque to the rear wheels. A high-powered Mopar can crack the windshield when launching on slicks, and it is fairly common to find wrinkles in the rear quarter panels on dedicated drag race cars. Fortunately, there are some easy ways to solve most of these problems. Although road racing and drag racing are totally different types of racing, they both require a stiff and lightweight chassis. So in many ways, what applies for one type of racing also translates quite well to other forms of racing.

Frame Connectors

One of the easiest modifications to make to the unibody chassis is to tie the front and rear subframes together with additional sections of frame rail. The new frame rails can be made from either rectangular tubing or round tubing, but the tubing needs to be large enough to resist the bending loads that the chassis sees. A section of 2 x 3-inch tubing makes a natural connection between the front and rear subframes, but the floorpan in the rear seat area needs to

This Mopar is getting a full performance upgrade, including significant improvements to the chassis. Here are a pair of large subframe connections, which have been welded in place. Close inspection shows the subframe connectors running through the floor of the car. Sometimes, the car owner does not want to cut the floors, so smaller tubing is used.

CHAPTER 12

The front subframes on this car angle out toward the rocker panels, so they do not line up with the subframe connectors. To make the chassis stronger, the owner decided to continue the subframe connectors past the torsion bar crossmember and tie them into the front subframe.

A set of profiled subframe connectors is fitted to this Mopar. These subframe connectors are welded to the bottom of the floorpan and do not require any cutting of the floorpan. (Photo Courtesy US Car Tool)

be removed to provide straight-shot access between the two subframes. Some car owners are unwilling to cut into the floorpan of their vehicle, so they either use a smaller size of tubing or notch the tubing in this area to clear the floor.

Several vendors, such as US Car Tool, have introduced frame connector kits that are profiled to fit the floorpan. These connector kits are designed to provide a very clean-looking product when fully welded in and painted. This type of connec-

After the subframe connectors have been welded in place, the bottom of the car can be painted body color for a more original appearance. (Photo Courtesy US Car Tool)

tor might not be quite as strong as a section of 2 x 3-inch tubing, but strength isn't always the only objective. Bolt-in frame connectors are also available, although they are the least-effective design. A bolt-in frame connector is better than nothing, but it should only be used on street cars that just occasionally see the track.

The frame connectors should be installed with the car properly supported and square. If the chassis is twisted when the connectors are welded in place, the chassis will be permanently twisted. Remember when you were a kid and your mother would tell you that if you made a bad face it would stay that way? Same issue here; if the frame is twisted when you weld in the subframe connectors, the car will remain that way.

Torque Boxes

The factory installed sheet-metal braces between the frame and the rocker sills on selected models, such as the Hemi cars and convertibles. These sheet-metal braces are often called "torque boxes," which seems to be an apt description. Torque boxes can be installed at both the front and the rear of the unibody structure.

The front torque boxes sit just behind the front wheels and tie the front of the rocker sills to the rear of the front subframe. The rear torque boxes tie the front portion of the rear subframe to the rocker sills just ahead of the rear tires. The rear torque boxes need to have a window in them for access to the spring hanger bolts.

Various aftermarket vendors, such as US Car Tool, offer replacement torque boxes that can be welded in place. Adding a complete set of four torque boxes noticeably stiffens the chassis.

Bracing Systems

Carroll Shelby used a triangular "export brace" to connect the shock towers to the firewall on early Mustangs when setting them up for road racing. Those export braces added considerable stiffness to the front of the old Mustangs, and that concept is still a good idea today for a B-Body. XV Motorsports makes export braces for the 1968 to 1972 B-Body vehicles. The XV brace is a full triangle that ties the firewall to the inner fender wells. This type of design provides enough room for an open-element type of air cleaner, but there probably would not be enough room for the larger "shaker" hood type of air cleaners.

A straight bar running from fender to fender is called a "Monte Carlo" bar on a Ford, but nobody makes a part like this for Mopar vehicles. However, it wouldn't be too difficult to fabricate. A Monte Carlo bar should be removable, so the engine can be pulled. XV makes a pair of braces that fit on the bottom side of the inner fender wells. These braces

UNIBODY CHASSIS UPGRADES

tie the upper shock mounting portion of the inner fender well back to the stiffer corner sections of the firewall.

A similar idea can be fabricated for the tops of the inner fender wells, if you're willing to make visible modifications to your muscle car. For maximum effectiveness, the fender well braces should run the full distance from the firewall to the radiator support, and they should be fully welded at both ends. These two pieces of additional tubing add support to the inner fenders, and they are an excellent place to anchor a motor plate.

Additional Crossmembers

Installing additional crossmembers to the existing subframes is fairly easy and provides greater strength. If the additional crossmembers are positioned correctly, they can also add functionality to the frame. One excellent place to add a new crossmember is just ahead of the rear axle. A crossmember in this location adds stiffness to the frame near the leaf spring mounts, and it can also be used as a brace for the pinion snubber to contact.

Another good location for an extra crossmember is at the very rear of the car, just inside of the rear bumper. A crossmember made from rectangular tubing can easily be fabricated to tie the rear frame rails together to provide additional support for the rear leaf spring mounts. This crossmember helps stiffen the frame and supports side loading from high-speed cornering. This rear crossmember also protects the gas tank in the event of an accident, and it can provide a convenient location to hang the tail pipes. For drag racing, a rear crossmember can also be a good place to mount extra weight.

Installing a crossmember between the door posts in the dash area provides a great deal of strength to the chassis, but it is difficult to accomplish in a street-driven vehicle. A crossmember can be mounted behind the dash, but it causes interference issues with the heater, glove box, and other dash-mounted items. For a race car, this is not an issue, but most owners want to retain some of these creature comforts on the street.

Radiator Support

B-Body vehicles have a light-gauge crossmember under the radiator. The OEM design is very flimsy, so it does not add a lot of rigidity to the front of the vehicle. The K-member primarily holds the front frame rails in place, but it is only bolted in, so this section of the car can really use some additional stiffness. XV Motorsports offers a weld-in radiator support made from heavy-gauge tubing, and it is bent to provide clearance for the radiator. Welding such a radiator support into place provides increased chassis stiffness at the front of the vehicle.

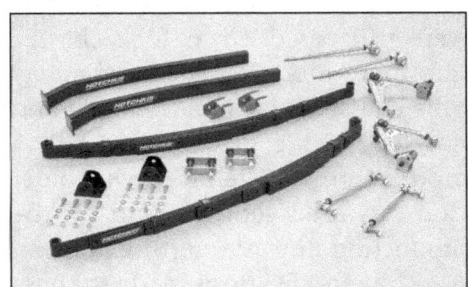

Hotchkis includes a set of subframe connectors in its B-Body suspension kits. The Hotchkis subframe connectors only attach at the ends, rather than being welded the entire length to the floor. (Photo Courtesy Hotchkis Performance)

An additional crossmember was added just behind the rear axle kick-up area on this car. The extra crossmember was added because this car is being converted to coil-over springs. An extra crossmember in this area is a good idea for any car, because it adds torsional rigidity to the chassis. But, on a leaf-spring car, the crossmember does not need to be this large.

CHAPTER 12

Second Floorpan

Installing a second floorpan is used on occasion to stiffen the unibody. Obviously, the vehicle needs to be stripped down almost completely in order to install a second floorpan, but the increase in stiffness can be significant.

A second floorpan is installed on top of the existing floor, and then the two pans are welded together. This effectively doubles the thickness of the floorpan. The additional material does add some weight, but the weight increase is low to the ground. The floor of a car is an excellent place to add material, because it provides rigidity, improved safety in the event of an accident, and reduced road noise.

Seam Welding

The factory unibody is held together with hundreds of spot welds that are located every few inches. Although this system works fine for a production vehicle, adding stitch welds or fully welding all of the seams between body panels makes the body stiffer. A small MIG welder makes quick work of this operation once all of the paint and seam sealer has been removed from the chassis. Of course, you are only going to have welding access to all of the panels if the car has been completely torn down. Having the car mounted on a rotisserie provides the best access for seam-welding all of the body panels.

Roll Cages

Installing a roll cage is the ultimate way to increase chassis stiffness. A well-designed roll cage not only protects the driver in the case of an accident, but it also keeps the chassis from twisting or bending during typical use. A close examination of a professionally constructed roll cage shows that bars in the cage are arranged to pick up the loads from the suspension mounting locations. On a leaf-spring car, a roll cage designer typically installs bars down to the spring hangers, and on a coil-spring car, the bars go to the point where the coil springs attach to the frame. Up front, the roll cage picks up the K-member and torsion bar mounts on a conventional suspension or goes to the shock towers in a coil-over car.

The XV radiator support can be welded to the factory sheet metal for a cleaner look. If the job is done correctly, the support appears stock, while providing extra stiffness for the front subframe.

A roll cage is a complicated design that requires careful consideration before construction. For a street-driven car, it is important that the roll cage allows ease of entry and exit, as well as functionality of items such as the heater and defroster.

Race Car Techniques

I am occasionally able to study older Mopar race cars to see how the chassis builders modified them for racing duty. The most interesting cars to look at are the older Grand National or Winston Cup race cars from the 1960s and 1970s, as they were still based on a stock chassis. The more modern cars have a steel tube chassis built on a frame jig and have very little in common with a production vehicle. But, the older Cup cars used vehicles right off the production line as a starting point.

The modifications made to these older Cup cars are more extensive than what most people would consider for a street car, but the ideas still provide some food for thought. A close examination of these older race cars shows the steps taken to stiffen the chassis and to improve

Seam-welding the front sheet metal together is a dirty and time-consuming task, but it does add some rigidity to the chassis. This B-Body car has had all of the sheet-metal panels stitch-welded in an effort to make the front end more rigid.

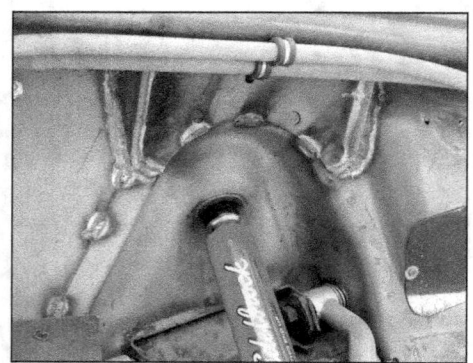

A close-up view of the shock tower area shows that factory sheet-metal supports have been boxed in. Adding small pieces of sheet metal to box in the existing structure is an easy way to increase chassis rigidity.

UNIBODY CHASSIS UPGRADES

A closer view of the firewall area on the track car shows how the down bars are welded to a plate, which is welded to the firewall. This type of attachment makes the whole area stiffer and prevents the bars from punching through the firewall.

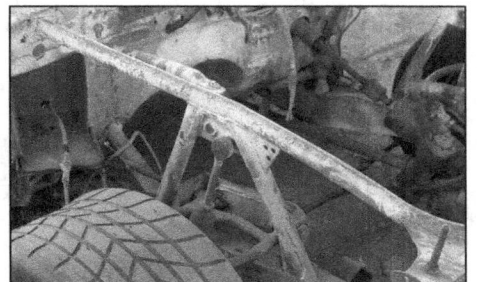

A close look at the upper shock mount on an early B-Body race car shows how seriously the chassis builder focused on this area. Along with the double upright bars, the tower area is gusseted and braced back to the firewall. The shock absorbers play a very important role in chassis tuning, so the chassis builder wanted this area to be very rigid.

This heavily modified Mopar also has a set of front down bars. These are tied into the shock towers and provide even more chassis stiffness. (Photo Courtesy Magnum Force Racing)

the weight distribution. Obvious modifications, such as full roll cages, are installed for stiffness as well as safety, but more subtle modifications were also made on these vehicles.

The suspension mounting points are heavily reinforced, as are the mounting points for the shock absorbers. It is obvious that the chassis designers were concerned about the amount of stress that would be passed to the chassis by the shock absorbers, both front and rear. The engine bay area is often heavily reinforced with additional braces and crossmembers, although you can see that the amount of bracing drops off significantly ahead of the front wheels. The structure ahead of the front wheels is only there to support the sheet metal and the radiator, and the area behind the wheels carries the weight of the vehicle.

On the underside of these older Cup cars, you can see a large X-brace welded beneath the passenger compartment. An X-brace is a very effective way to stiffen a large rectangular structure, such as a perimeter frame, by turning it into four triangles. A rectangle is rather weak, and can be easily pulled out of shape, but a triangle-shaped structure is very stiff. Of course, it is easier to add a big X-brace under the car when you do not need to worry about the exhaust system!

This older B-Body circle track car has a full roll cage. Some of this cage is designed for driver protection, and other parts are for chassis strength.

The backseat area of this 1971 Charger illustrates the type of roll cage bracing required in a serious track car. (Photo Courtesy Gary Beineke)

This old Mopar race car has a lot of rust damage, but some of the original modification ideas are still clear. One interesting item is the X-structure built from tubing beneath the floor. Obviously, a lot of things had to be moved around before the X-braces would clear the floor and the driveline.

CHAPTER 12

Another old Mopar race car shows how the chassis construction uses large-diameter tubing to the front wheels, and then, after that, only lightweight tubes are used. The idea here is to make the chassis very rigid for the suspension pickup points, but lighter in the areas where the frame is just holding up the sheet metal.

K-member Modifications

The K-member is a vitally important part of the Mopar vehicle. Not only does it hold the front subframe together, but it is the mounting location for the steering box, the engine, the lower control arms, torsion bars, and sway bar. Because the K-member is such a key part of the chassis, a lot of performance modifications for it have been developed over the years.

The original K-members were a fairly complex structure created by welding together various sheet-metal stampings. The factory's welding process produced very ugly welds, but the original K-members were a robust design. The factory design is fairly heavy and bulky, but these issues can be addressed with appropriate modifications. Original K-members usually show some signs of abuse and often need to be repaired before being put back into use.

A proper re-work process on a K-member requires removal from the vehicle as a first step. This is a rather complicated process because the engine has to be either removed or supported. The majority of the front suspension also needs to be removed, as well as the steering box and linkage. On a fully assembled vehicle, it can easily take an entire day of work before the K-member is lying on the shop floor ready for the next step.

An original K-member requires extensive cleaning before repairs and modifications can be made. Hot-tanking the K-member is probably the easiest way to remove several decades of grease and oil.

Once the frame is clean, a close inspection for damage is required. Besides the typical damage to the bottom side of the K-member, there are often cracked welds around the lower control arm pivot points. These pivot points are an extremely important part of the K-member because these two pivot pins support the entire weight carried by the front tires.

Oil Pan Clearance

The original K-member design has a wide flange of sheet metal surrounding the front portion of the oil pan. This flange is the result of the factory sheet-metal fabrication process. In order to gain room for a larger oil pan, the flange needs to be either cut down or cut away completely.

For a minor increase in space, the flange can be trimmed back, and the seam can be re-welded to retain the necessary strength. A more radical modification is to remove the flange area completely by filling in the resulting hole in the K-member with new vertical side pieces.

When re-working the K-member, it is often a good idea to carve out a rectangular area for the oil pan to provide maximum clearance around the sides of the pan.

Added Strength

The K-member plays such an important role in the rigidity of the front suspension and frame area of the vehicle that any modifications must be carefully thought out. If you are unfamiliar with modifications to this area, it is worth spending some time studying all of the functions that the K-member manages and thinking about how to best add strength and rigidity to the frame. Some areas present fairly easy modifications, such as adding reinforcement rings around the lower control arm pivot pins. The factory tubes sometimes crack after years of use (and abuse), but it is fairly simple to weld reinforcement around the tubes to add substantial strength.

Another area of the K-member that can benefit from some additional strength is the steering box mount. On an original frame, the steering box is mounted on a flat plate that is welded to the frame at several points. You can see this area slightly flex when the wheels are turned with the car sitting, which indicates that the bracket is not as rigid as it could be. Simply boxing in the factory mount with some additional material increases the rigidity of the steering box mount. If the space is available, a more substantial brace can be built that ties down to the frame, but this might get in the way of the motor mounts or headers.

Sway Bar Brackets

Chrysler engineers used a variety of methods over the years for attaching the sway bar to the K-member. Some of these methods were quite inconvenient, as they captured the bushing in a non-repairable bracket, or used bolt-on brackets, which were not very rigid. With the K-member on the welding bench, a good fabricator can easily fix some of these original design issues. A pair of sturdy mounts can be welded in place on the bottom side of the K-member to accept standard sway bar bushings. This makes it much easier to install different types of bars, and to accept a variety of bar diameters.

Lifting Points and Tow Hooks

Several modifications can be made to the K-member to add functionality to the front end of the vehicle. The K-member is a convenient point for lifting the car with a floor jack, or for supporting the vehicle with jack stands, but it wasn't really designed to handle those loads. The original sheet-metal construction is not designed to withstand a point load from a jack stand, so the metal dents or caves in. Welding in jack points fabricated from heavy-gauge steel plate, or tubing, easily fixes this.

Other modifications to make at the same time would be to add a couple of tow hooks for either towing the vehicle with a tow rope or for securing the vehicle to a trailer. These tow brackets can be simple plates with oval-shaped holes that are welded to each end of the frame. It is nice to have a feature like that built in, rather than have a tow truck operator wrap a chain around a lower control arm or bend a sway bar by hooking onto it.

Skid Plates

Chrysler engineers added skid plates to some of the original K-members to protect the stock-depth oil pan from damage. These skid plates were an excellent idea and are a fairly easy item to add to any K-member.

Several vendors produce skid plates, including reproductions of the original design, as well as heavy-duty skid plates, which are both deeper

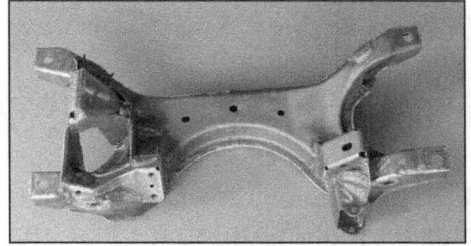

Firm Feel has given this K-member the full reinforcement treatment. Firm Feel offers this service for most B-Body cars. It also sells a kit of reinforcement plates for those who want to do the job themselves.

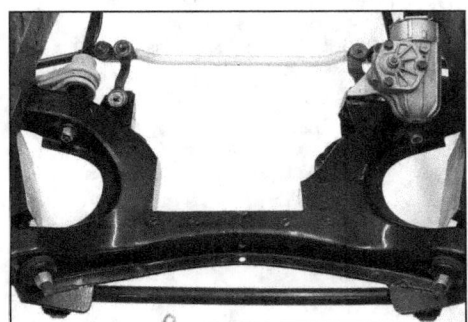

This K-member is modified for extra oil pan clearance. The normal U-shaped area has been cut and re-welded with square corners. The motor mounts have also been removed, because this car uses a motor plate.

After the modifications have been made to the K-member, there is plenty of clearance around the oil pan. With the K-member modified like this, there is enough room for a full front sump on the oil pan.

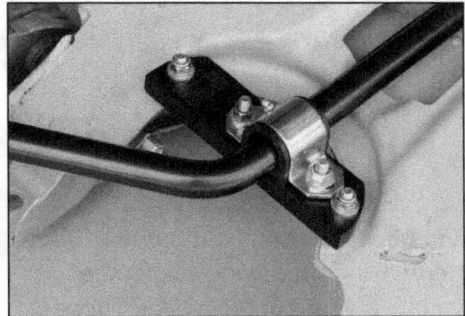

On the 1970 to 1972 cars, the sway bar attaches to the K-member with brackets that bolt to the bottom of the outer flange. This area would be even stronger if the brackets were welded to the K-member.

and thicker than the original. The reproduction designs are best used for restored vehicles with stock-type oil pans, and the heavy-duty skid plates can be used for vehicles that are lowered, or have deep oil pans.

Motor Mounts

B-Body vehicles used the rubber, sandwich type of motor mounts from 1962 to 1972, and then switched over to a spool-mount design in 1973. The primary disadvantage to the earlier pad-style mount is that the motor mounts do not last long. The combination of high heat and oil contamination causes the pad-style mount to deteriorate fairly quickly. Once the mounts deteriorate, a high-powered engine can pull the driver's-side mount apart fairly quickly.

It is possible to convert a pre-1973 K-member to the spool-mount design, but it does require significant fabrication. A more common modification is to strengthen the factory brackets on the K-member, and then add a torque strap to keep the engine from pulling the driver's-side mount apart.

The K-member in this older Mopar circle track car is extensively modified. Most of the original K-member material has been cut away and replaced with steel tubing. The K-member has also been moved up into the frame rails and welded in place.

It appears that the only portion left of the original K-member is the curved section holding the lower control arm pivots.

For serious drag race use, the stock motor mounts are usually cut off the frame, and the engine is installed solidly to the frame with a motor plate. Removing the factory motor mount brackets from the K-member reduces the weight slightly, and it also creates additional clearance for the exhaust system or an external oiling system.

Weight Reduction

The stock K-member is fairly heavy, especially for a drag race car. Vendors, such as Bob's Pro Fab and QA1, have developed methods for reducing the weight of the K-member. These race shops cut apart the K-member and use tubing to rebuild most of the center section. This rework process eliminates a significant amount of weight and also opens up the space for an oversize oil pan. Weight reductions like this have been proven to be safe for drag racing duty, but they are not designed for road racing or other applications with higher cornering loads.

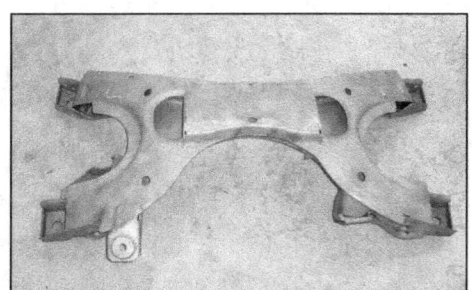

The underside of this original B-Body Hemi K-member shows what the factory skid plate looks like. These are often damaged after years of abuse, but this one appears to still be in good shape. Vendors, such as Firm Feel, sell aftermarket skid plates, which can be welded on your own K-member.

CAP Auto Products builds a lightweight K-member that works with the stock lower control arms and steering box. This type of K-member provides maximum weight reduction and plenty of clearance for an oil pan. (Photo Courtesy QA1 Performance Products)

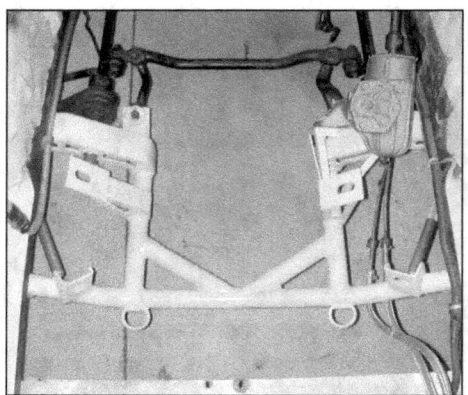

A slightly different version of the CAP K-member has motor mounts and triangular bracing. Also notice the tow loops, which are welded to the front crossbeam. (Photo Courtesy QA1 Performance Products)

CHAPTER 13

WEIGHT REDUCTION AND DISTRIBUTION

Weight reduction is one of the easiest and most cost-effective ways to improve the overall performance of your Mopar muscle car. A lighter-weight vehicle accelerates quicker, handles better, and stops sooner. Weight reduction can be accomplished for very little cost early in the project, but as the easy opportunities are exhausted, the price for further weight reduction increases dramatically.

Almost every part of the vehicle has opportunities for weight reduction, but that doesn't mean that weight should be reduced indiscriminately. Rather, a weight-reduction plan should be made and followed for the most cost-effective results. For almost all forms of high-performance driving, weight reduction should be focused on weight that is either ahead of the center of gravity or above the center of gravity. For most types of racing, you want the vehicle's center of gravity as low as possible.

It is also desirable to balance the weight distribution equally on all four wheels. Most Mopar muscle cars came from the factory with a very nose-heavy weight distribution. So, any weight that can be removed from the front of the vehicle lightens the vehicle and moves the center of gravity toward the rear at the same time. Any weight that can be removed from above and in front of the center of gravity provides a triple benefit. Not only is the overall weight reduced, but the center of gravity is shifted downward and rearward at the same time. Each of these changes has a cumulative effect, and eventually you will be rewarded with a car that handles noticeably better.

Front End Weight Reduction

Given the previous discussion, the best place to start with a weight-reduction program is at the very front of the vehicle. With a street-driven vehicle, you might not want to remove the bumper or any of its reinforcements, but the radiator is fairly far forward on the vehicle and is fair game.

Radiator and Battery

Replacing the factory copper-based radiator with an aluminum one can shed a few pounds and

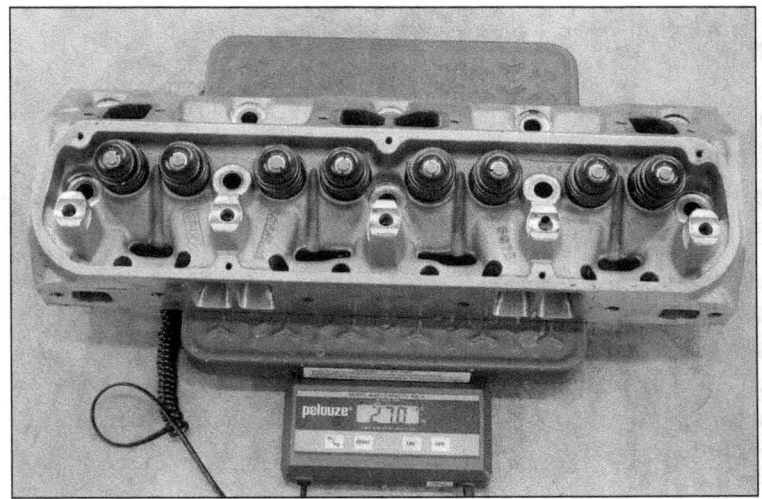

Installing a pair of aluminum cylinder heads is an excellent way to reduce weight. The fact that the weight savings comes off the front of the car is even better.

increase cooling capacity at the same time. The factory battery location is usually high in the engine compartment and ahead of the front wheels. Some owners may wish to maintain a front-mounted battery for convenience, but they replace the heavy OEM-style battery with a lighter aftermarket version.

Drag racers have been moving the battery back to the trunk for many years now. In fact, this is a trick that Chrysler used in the 1960s with some of the drag-race-package vehicles. Moving the battery to the rear of the trunk results in a shift of the vehicle's weight distribution, even if the overall weight remains the same.

External Engine Parts

The engine itself is a prime candidate for weight reduction. Not only is the engine in the front of the vehicle, but many of the weight-reduction possibilities such as the cylinder heads, intake manifold, and alternator, are located high on the engine.

Replacing cast-iron cylinder heads with aluminum heads saves roughly 50 pounds on either a small-block or a big-block Mopar engine. The original cast-iron intake manifold can be replaced with an aftermarket aluminum intake for an additional 20-pound savings. On big-block engines, the heavy cast-iron water pump and water pump housing can be replaced with aluminum versions for a 9-pound savings. The later-model Chrysler vehicles came with lightweight starters, which can replace the heavy factory versions. Not only are the late-model starters 7 pounds lighter, but they also require less space. The factory alternator can be replaced with a lighter and more efficient Denso unit from a late-model vehicle for a 4-pound reduction. The carburetor is also a good place to look for weight reduction. Edelbrock carburetors are significantly lighter than older Holley carburetors, although the newer Ultra HP Holley carbs with the billet-aluminum parts have shed a few pounds. Another place to save weight on the engine is the harmonic dampener. Original dampeners are quite heavy, but vendors such as ATI offer fairly lightweight parts.

Internal Engine Parts

Obviously, you need to open up the engine to install lightweight parts in the rotating assembly, so

Holley carbs usually weigh about 11 pounds, and Edelbrock carbs weigh about 7 pounds. ThermoQuads are the lightest 4-barrels at 6 pounds. Aftermarket carbs, such as this one from BLP, use aluminum parts, so they weigh several pounds less than the original Holley carbs.

The aluminum water pump and water pump housing combination saves 9 pounds off the front of any big-block or Hemi motor. This weight reduction comes off the very front of the engine.

Mopar starters are available in at least three sizes. The full-size starter on the left weighs 15 pounds. The mini starter on the right weighs only 8 pounds, and the one in the middle weighs 10 pounds.

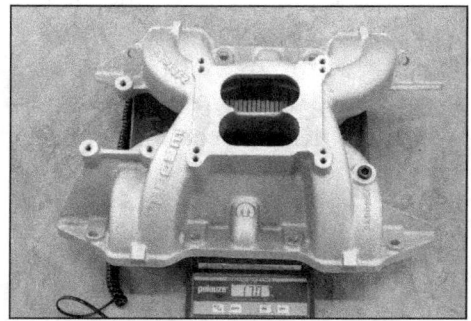

Aluminum intake manifolds are about 20 pounds lighter than factory cast-iron intakes. Single-plane intake manifolds tend to be a few pounds lighter than dual-plane intakes.

Original Mopar alternators weighed about 15 pounds. By contrast, this 60-amp racing alternator weighs only 6 pounds. The popular 60-amp Denso alternator that Mancini Racing sells weighs 10 pounds.

WEIGHT REDUCTION AND DISTRIBUTION

Aftermarket crankshafts are not always lighter than the factory cranks; some are significantly heavier, depending on the application. SCAT produces a variety of lightweight crankshafts for both small-block and big-block engines.

Aftermarket pistons are usually significantly lighter than production pistons, especially when combined with a smaller piston pin. These stroker pistons from JE weigh 454 grams each, which is several hundred grams lighter than stock pistons.

Aftermarket engine blocks are usually much heavier than the factory blocks, sometimes as much as 50 pounds heavier. An aluminum engine block can shave a significant amount of weight off the front of the car if the budget is big enough.

you might want to wait until it's time to rebuild the engine. The factory pistons and piston pins are much heavier than modern replacements, especially when building a stroker motor. It isn't uncommon for lightweight replacement piston-and-pin assemblies to be 1 pound lighter per cylinder. An 8-pound total reduction in piston weight requires additional weight to be removed from the crankshaft counterweights in order balance the new assembly, so the total weight reduction that results from using modern forged parts can be more than 10 pounds.

Several vendors, such as SCAT and Callies, offer special lightweight crankshafts. The SCAT super lightweight package can reduce the crankshaft by up to 15 pounds compared to an average aftermarket crankshaft. These lightweight cranks have specially scalloped counterweights, drilled journals, and profiled flywheel flanges.

Engines built exclusively for racing can use even more exotic parts, such as titanium connecting rods, super-lightweight pistons, thin-wall piston pins, titanium valves, and gun-drilled camshafts. Racers often machine away excess weight from heavy parts, such as the engine block and the cylinder heads. Up to 20 pounds of material can usually be removed from a cast-iron cylinder block without compromising strength, as long as the machine operator has a good understanding of how the block is stressed during competition.

Drivetrain Weight Reduction

There are many places in the drivetrain where weight can be reduced. The weight-reduction program can start at the flywheel and continue all the way to the rear wheels and tires. Drivetrain weight reduction is beneficial from the standpoint

This big-block drag race engine weighs only 490 pounds. Aluminum heads, a single-plane intake, lightweight internals, and a remote water pump all help to reduce the weight.

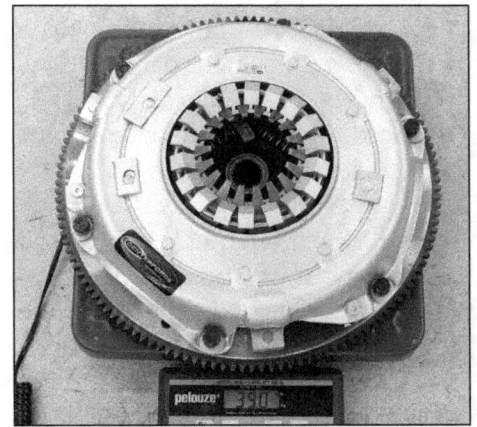

This lightweight clutch and light steel flywheel assembly weighs a total of 39 pounds. A factory-replacement-type assembly typically weighs about 55 pounds. An aluminum flywheel would have reduced the weight another 8 pounds.

CHAPTER 13

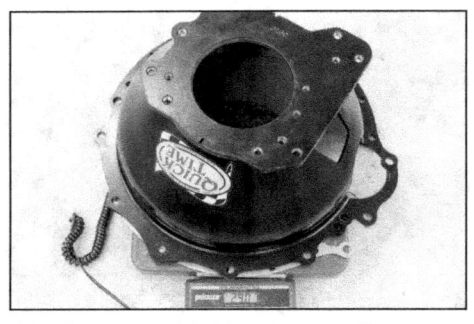

Steel scattershields are usually very heavy, but QuickTime has developed a process that produces bellhousings in the 30-pound range.

Passon Performance has tooled up to produce aluminum cases for the Mopar 4-speed transmission. This example was built with a complete set of the Passon aluminum parts. Total weight is just 81 pounds.

of a reduction in total vehicle weight and rotating weight. Some parts of the drivetrain, such as the rear axle, are also unsprung weight, so a weight reduction of these parts has additional handling benefits.

Flywheel

The flywheel is an excellent place to look for weight reduction, especially when combined with a high-torque stroker motor.

OEM-installed flywheels are constructed from a cast-iron material and often weigh more than 30 pounds. These original-equipment flywheels do not meet the SFI standard required by racing bodies, such as NHRA, so they need to be replaced when racing the vehicle in certain classes.

SFI-rated steel flywheels are available for Mopar engines in weights as low as 18 pounds, and aluminum flywheels are available in the 12-pound range.

The weight of the flywheel influences how smooth the engine idles, the speed at which the engine accelerates, and how much stored energy is available at launch. A heavy vehicle with a smaller engine requires a heavy flywheel to launch properly, and a lightweight car with a powerful engine can use a lighter flywheel.

Clutch

A variety of lightweight clutches are available for high-performance use. CenterForce has the LMC series clutch, which uses an aluminum pressure disc. Circle track cars use small-diameter clutches, which are very lightweight, but those clutches tend to be too "grabby" for a street-driven car. Dual-disc clutches required for high-powered vehicles are fairly heavy, but when combined with a lightweight flywheel, the total weight is roughly the same as a factory setup.

Bellhousing

Mopar V-8 bellhousings were typically cast from aluminum and are quite light. Unfortunately, these lightweight bellhousings are not SFI-rated and, therefore, must be replaced with a steel scattershield for racing. The traditional Lakewood or Ansen scattershields weigh about 35 pounds, due to hydro-formed steel plate construction.

Recently, QuickTime has developed a new spinning method for fabricating SFI-rated bellhousings, which results in a substantial weight savings. QuickTime bellhousings for small-block and big-block engines only weigh 22 pounds. As a further benefit, QuickTime bellhousings are available with multiple transmission bolt patterns.

Transmission

Original B-Body A833 4-speed transmissions used a heavy cast-iron case. Aluminum cases were available from the factory for a few years, but those part numbers were discontinued many years ago. Fortunately, Passon Performance re-created the tooling necessary to produce the 4-speed case in aluminum. Using the Passon aluminum case and tailshaft saves about 30 pounds. The transmission is usually located slightly ahead of the vehicle's center of gravity, so this weight reduction improves weight distribution.

Driveshaft

Factory driveshafts were made from steel tubing. Although they were not excessively heavy, switching to an aluminum or carbon-fiber driveshaft reduces weight. In an attempt to decrease vehicle weight, many modern vehicles are factory-equipped with aluminum driveshafts. Carbon-fiber driveshafts are extremely expensive and typically are not found on street-driven vehicles, but they are commonly used on dedicated race cars.

Differential Components

Mopar Performance currently offers an aluminum center section for the 8¾-inch rear end. This aluminum center section is PN P4876445 and uses a "742"-style large stem ring and pinion. Total weight reduction with this aluminum center section is about 12 pounds. The aluminum center section can be used on the street, although it is quite expensive.

WEIGHT REDUCTION AND DISTRIBUTION

For drag race use, a heavy limited-slip package can be replaced with a lightweight spool. A spool provides a solid connection between the rear axles, as well as a substantial weight reduction. A spool is only recommended for drag racing because the locked differential greatly increases the stress on the rear axles when cornering. Lightweight axles are also an option for a race vehicle, although such exotic items are rarely installed on a street-driven car.

The 8¾-inch rear end housing is lighter than the Dana 60 housing, but it also is not quite as robust, so a compromise has to be made. The aftermarket has put a lot of support behind the Ford 9-inch design, including fully fabricated housings and numerous types of aluminum center sections. So, if ultimate weight reduction is your goal, you might need to look outside of the traditional Mopar solutions.

Interior Weight Reduction

The interior has a lot of potential for weight reduction, including lightweight bucket seats, the removal of the backseat, and the removal of carpeting and pads. The dash area can shed a lot of weight, if you are willing to get rid of the heater, radio, air conditioning, and other such creature comforts. You wouldn't want to remove too much for a daily driver, but lightweight carpet and racing seats can be tolerated in a weekend warrior.

A heater and defroster aren't required for a car that only goes out in nice weather, although you would want to keep them for anything that is driven in the rain or cold. A high-performance motor usually makes enough heat to keep the firewall warm on a cool summer night, but it won't keep the driver warm on a really cold winter day.

Weight Distribution

Weight distribution is a very important aspect of vehicle design. High-performance vehicles tend toward a 50/50 weight distribution, with a slight rearward bias preferred for very high performance vehicles. Having a slight rearward bias works out best for a rear-wheel-drive vehicle, as it allows the most weight on the rear tires for acceleration. Having a slight rearward bias also helps during heavy braking by keeping the weight more evenly distributed. A nose-heavy vehicle has problems transferring weight to the rear tires under acceleration, and it overloads the front tires during braking and hard cornering. Maximum-performance vehicles, such as those designed by Ferrari, Porsche, and Lamborghini, have the engine located behind the driver in order to shift the weight bias to the rear wheels.

Mopar muscle cars are fairly nose-heavy by design, and without radical surgery, they stay nose-heavy, but that doesn't mean that some weight can't be moved around. Earlier, I discussed ways to reduce weight. If those weight reductions are focused at the front of the vehicle, the overall weight distribution shifts rearward.

Four Corner Weights

The first step to take before making any changes to the weight distribution is to record the corner

Gutting the interior saves a lot of weight. This street-legal track car gets by without any carpet or sound deadening, but of course, removing all of these items makes the ride a bit noisy. It has lightweight race seats, and the heater has been removed.

Keeping track of the total weight, as well as the weight distribution, is a good idea when building a car. It is easier to move items around when the car is under construction than it is to move them after it's built.

CHAPTER 13

Racing scales should provide corner weights and the total weight. This scale from Longacre shows the weight at each tire, as well as the sum of the four weights. The cross weight is the sum of the right front and left rear corner weights.

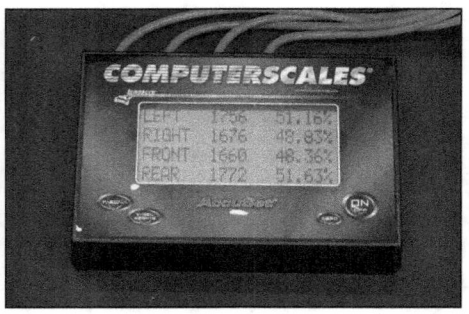

It is also nice to be able to toggle to a screen that shows the weight distribution front to rear and side to side. This B-Body car shows a slight rearward weight bias, but the car was still missing some of the front sheet metal when this picture was taken.

weights of the vehicle. Several vendors, such as Longacre, sell scale systems that are designed for race car setups. These scale systems contain a set of four individual scales and a control box, which calculates and displays the corner weights.

When scaling a car, it is important to look at front-to-rear weight distribution as well as side-to-side weight distribution. Production vehicles are usually fairly well balanced from side to side, but they often have up to 55 percent of the total vehicle weight on the front tires. With 55 percent on the front tires, the rear tires are obviously left with only 45 percent. A heavy front weight bias such as this limits the amount of traction that the rear tires have under both acceleration and braking.

Weight Distribution Math

It is advantageous to be able to calculate how the weight distribution changes when planning to make changes to the car. If you are fortunate to have a set of scales, the car can be weighed before and after each modification. Otherwise, you need to weigh the parts and calculate what the effect will be.

The car needs to be scaled first, and the four corner weights recorded as the starting point. You also need to know the wheelbase of the car so that you can calculate where the center of gravity is located between the wheels. For example, given a car with 3,200 pounds total weight that has 55 percent of the weight on the front wheels, you can calculate that the front weighs 1,760 pounds, with 1,440 pounds at the rear. In this case, you would need to move 160 pounds from the front wheels to the rear wheels to achieve a 50/50 weight distribution.

The center-of-gravity location can be found by multiplying the wheelbase length by the weight distribution percentage. For our 3,200-pound car: If the wheelbase is 108 inches, the center of gravity is located 45 percent of the wheelbase behind the front wheels, or 48.6 inches. (If this seems confusing, it might help to remember that the center of gravity has to be closer to the end of the car that is carrying the most weight.) In this case, the front wheels are carrying 55 percent of the weight, so the center of gravity has to be closer to the front wheels than to the rear wheels.

If the car had a 50/50 weight distribution, the center of gravity would be at the exact middle of the wheelbase. As the center of gravity moves forward, the weight on the front wheels increases, and the weight on the rear wheels decreases.

Drag Racing

A vehicle that is optimized for drag racing wants at least 50 percent of the weight on the rear axle in order to maximize traction of the rear tires. If there is too much weight on the rear axle, the car wheelstands; if there is too little weight on the rear tires, the car has trouble launching.

The side-to-side weight distribution of a drag car is also important because the car accelerates faster if both rear tires are equally loaded. For a drag race car, the engine torque has to be considered in addition to the vehicle weight because the engine torque working through the rear axle tries to lift the right rear corner of the car during acceleration. Drag racers often locate heavy items, such as the battery, in the right rear corner of the trunk as a way to shift the weight distribution of the car.

Road Racing and High Performance

A vehicle that is designed to turn corners instead of just accelerate in a straight line has a different set of requirements in terms of weight distribution. For circle track racing, where the car only turns left, the car works best if weight is shifted slightly to the left side of the car. The extra weight on the inner side of the car helps to balance the weight on the tires during high-speed cornering.

For a car that road races with

WEIGHT REDUCTION AND DISTRIBUTION

Moving the battery to the trunk is an excellent way to change the weight distribution. The battery is quite heavy and usually mounted close to the nose of the car, so the total distance moved is quite large.

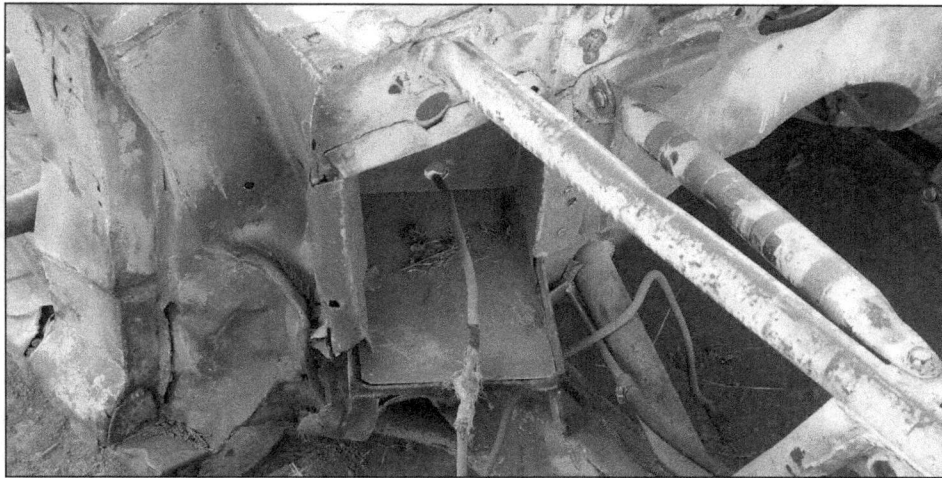

This older NASCAR B-Body has the battery tucked in behind the right front tire. This is a good location if the battery has to stay up front. Modern NASCAR chassis builders now put the battery in front of the left rear wheel.

an equal number of right- and left-hand corners, the weight distribution is set up with equal distribution side to side. Road race cars also want a slight rearward bias, if possible, in order to maximize the traction to the rear tires during heavy braking and acceleration.

Polar Moment of Inertia

One interesting concept to think about when setting up a car for high-performance use is the idea of weight location versus weight distribution. Compare the effort required to spin a 20-pound barbell to the effort required to spin a 20-pound bowling ball. Even though both items weigh the same amount, the bowling ball is much easier to spin than the barbell because the weight is located at the center of the object.

Applying this same principle to a car shows us that if the vehicle's weight is concentrated in the center of the body, it is easier to change directions. Conversely, if the same weight is distributed at the ends of the car, that weight must be swung through a long distance when the car changes directions. Engineers describe this concept as the polar moment of inertia, and it is a very important concept. A drag race car works great when weight is moved to the rear bumper, but having all the weight located at one end increases the polar moment of inertia and makes the car difficult to turn. This doesn't matter for drag racing, of course, but it can be very detrimental when road racing.

With the weight concentrated at one end, the vehicle is difficult to turn into a corner, and if it starts to spin, it's very difficult to stop spinning. Because of this behavior, road race vehicles are typically designed with as much weight as possible concentrated toward the center of the vehicle.

Indy cars are an excellent example of low polar moment of inertia. The typical Indy car design has the driver and the engine located in the center of the car, and very little weight is allowed at either end of the car.

The aluminum master cylinder from late-model cars only weighs 2 pounds. The original cast-iron master cylinders typically weigh about 7 pounds. The master cylinder is located up high, and in the nose of the car, so weight savings in this area is a double bonus.

Modern high-performance brake systems not only work better than original B-Body brake systems, but they are also significantly lighter. This setup from Baer includes a two-piece rotor and an aluminum six-piston caliper.

CHAPTER 14

RIDE HEIGHT, WHEELS AND TIRES

The performance of your B-Body car can be dramatically impacted by adjustments to ride height, the type of wheels, and the size of tires you choose.

Ride Height

Lowering a vehicle's ride height is one of the easier ways to improve handling. With a lower center of gravity, the car leans over less during hard cornering. Excessive body lean during cornering increases camber, which narrows the tire's contact patch with the road. Muscle cars were often described as "cornering on the door handles," due to the body lean observed during hard cornering. Some of this was due to the typical Detroit practice of using soft springs and the lack of sway bars, but some of the corning lean came from having a tall ride height.

The factory engineers specified a fairly generous ride height as a compromise among ride comfort, load capacity, and road clearance. The taller ride height allows for more suspension travel, which in turn provides a smoother ride. Also, a taller ride height allows for more load capacity before the suspension bottoms on the frame. And, of course, the higher the ride height, the less chance there is that the oil pan or frame contacts the road while going over bumps or entering driveways.

For a high-performance vehicle, you can afford to make some compromises in load-carrying capacity, ride comfort, and road clearance in

Wheels, tires, and ride height all work together to give Gary Beineke's B-Body a killer stance. It takes a lot of work to fit everything together this well, so be prepared for some trial and error. (Photo Courtesy Gary Beineke)

It can be tough to make large-diameter wheels look right on a B-Body, but this 1971 Charger looks great with custom 17-inch rims. (Photo Courtesy Gary Beineke)

order to improve the handling capability. There is a limit to how far you want to lower a vehicle, though, depending on the intended application. A race car that is only driven on a specially designed road race course can be lowered extensively, but a muscle car that is going to be driven on the street can't go quite that low. There are a variety of changes that can be made to a B-Body to reduce the ride height, so it is just a choice as to which of these methods you use.

Jack Screw Adjustment

Adjusting the ride height at the front end of a B-Body is very simple due to the torsion bar design. The ride height can be changed simply by turning the torsion bar adjustment lever located inside the lower control arm. The adjustment lever contains a small jacking screw, which applies the load from the suspension to the torsion bar. As the jack screw is turned out, the ride height decreases until the car is sitting on the bump stops. Obviously, you don't want the car sitting on the bump stops if it is going to be driven, but if you are willing to accept the occasional instance when the car frame bottoms on the bump stop, then it can be okay to lower the ride height a significant amount.

Dropping the ride height by unwinding the torsion bars most likely changes the alignment of the front end. So, once you find a ride height that works for you, the car needs to have the front end aligned. In some cases, the alignment shop might not be able to get the suspension back into alignment if the car has been lowered too much. If that is the case, a change needs to be made to the upper control arms or the steering knuckles. Adjusting the jack screw to lower the ride height is easy, and it doesn't cost anything, but it does change the alignment settings, and it reduces the suspension travel. Another possible approach is to leave the ride height adjustment in the stock location, but lower the vehicle by using dropped knuckles.

Dropped Knuckle

The idea behind the dropped knuckle is to move the spindle location up on the knuckle in order to lower the vehicle. If the dropped knuckle is designed correctly, the vehicle is lowered without changing the alignment or the suspension travel. Magnum Force sells a disc brake steering knuckle for Mopar front ends that has a 2-inch drop. This knuckle is based on the 1973-and-newer big-bearing spindle, so the factory 11¾-inch brake system, as well as many aftermarket brake systems, fit.

A dropped knuckle is one of the best ways to lower the ride height on a vehicle, because it still provides for full suspension travel. However, there can be issues with a dropped knuckle installation that need to be looked into before a decision is made.

One potential problem with moving the spindle up is that wheels with a lot of backspacing can interfere with the lower ball joint. With the stock spindle, a wheel with a lot of backspacing usually interferes with

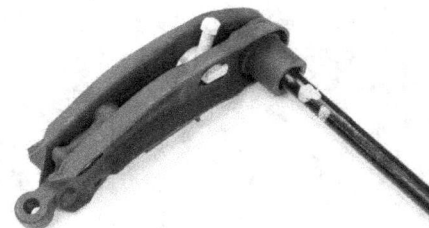

Ride height is easy to adjust with the stock torsion bar suspension. The adjustment bolt mounted in the lower control arm can be backed out to lower the car. Although this is a quick-and-easy way to change the ride height, going too far with this method can cause some problems.

A shorter shock absorber is required when running a Mopar at a lower ride height. This track car uses custom Bilstein shocks because replacement shocks would bottom out and prevent full suspension travel.

Magnum Force Racing has tooled up to produce knuckles with a 2-inch drop. These knuckles use the large inner wheel bearing from the 1973-and-newer cars. Factory brakes, as well as most aftermarket brake kits, should bolt on these knuckles.

CHAPTER 14

One possible problem with a dropped knuckle is that the lower ball joint is moved into a location where it can interfere with the rim. This 17-inch wheel has been mounted on the Magnum Force dropped knuckle, and the outer tie rod end is very close to the lip of the rim.

A view from the side shows how close the rim on this 17-inch wheel comes to the outer tie rod end when using the dropped knuckle. This wheel has 5 inches of backspacing, which is fairly typical for a performance application.

the upper ball joint, while there is ample room for the lower ball joint. But when the spindle is moved up, the wheel is also moved up relative to the suspension, and now the wheel can hit the lower ball joint. The ball joint is mounted in a fixed location, so the larger the diameter of the rim, the more clearance there is around the ball joint. A 17-inch rim provides more clearance than a 15-inch rim, but a really deep rim might require an 18-inch-diameter (or even larger) wheel to gain clearance for the lower ball joint.

There is one other issue with the use of an aftermarket knuckle. Although all of the aftermarket brake kits are designed to fit an OE knuckle, there might be slight design differences with the aftermarket knuckle that cause some interference issues. Experienced car builders know that as more aftermarket parts are used, the odds of some parts not fitting increase.

As discussed in Chapter 9, the shock absorbers need to be shorter to work with the suspension on a lowered car. Several vendors, such as Firm Feel, are offering shock absorbers designed to work with lowered vehicles. The advantage of using a dropped knuckle is that the shock absorber installed length does not change when the vehicle is lowered. The suspension travel is still the same as on a stock vehicle, but the nose of the vehicle is lowered.

Lowering Blocks

The classic way to lower the rear end on any leaf spring suspension is to install spacers between the axle and the leaf springs. Lowering blocks were all the rage in the 1950s, and they are still around today. Using lowering blocks for the rear suspension is roughly equivalent to using the torsion bars to lower the front suspension. That is, it is cheap and easy, but it has some negative side effects. Lowering blocks reduce the suspension travel, as the frame is brought down closer to the axle. Lowering the vehicle this way reduces the load-carrying ability, as well as the ground clearance.

Another negative effect of lowering blocks is that the axle is spaced farther away from the leaf springs, which means the axle has more leverage on the springs. For a higher-powered car, the rotating force on the axle during acceleration can more easily twist the leaf spring out of shape, due to the extra leverage. Twisting the spring like this can cause wheel hop and other traction issues.

Spring Hangers

Another easy way to lower the rear suspension is to use dropped spring hangers. A dropped hanger is a spring hanger that has been drilled with an additional hole above the stock ride height eye bolt hole. Moving the spring up to the upper

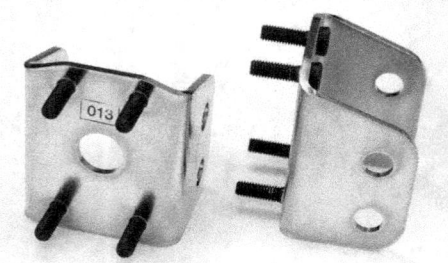

These dual-ride-height spring hangers are available from both Firm Feel and Mancini Racing. They are available for almost all of the B-Body applications. Dodge hangers are different than Plymouth hangers for most years.

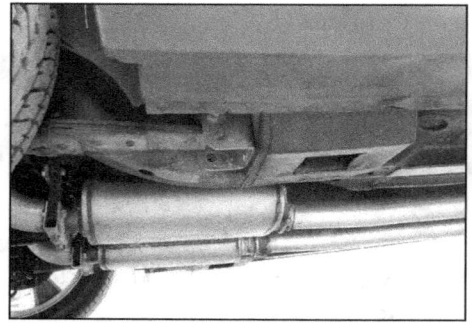

To lower the rear of the car, just install the leaf spring eye bolt into the upper hole in the hanger. The dents in the torque box and the scrapes on the mufflers are typical for a car that has been lowered significantly.

mounting location lowers the car an inch or two, depending on the specific hanger.

Although suspension travel is reduced by this design, the relationship between the axle and the leaf springs is not changed, and therefore, there is less chance of wheel hop during acceleration. One item that does change slightly is the pinion angle, so that must be checked and brought back into specification if it changes.

Leaf Spring De-Arch

To lower the rear suspension, a spring shop can de-arch the rear springs. The spring shop uses a heavy press to flatten the spring and remove some of the original arch. Flattening the spring like this reduces the load capacity of the spring, but that may not matter for a high-performance vehicle. Vehicles that are modified for high performance are often lighter than stock vehicles, and they usually are not carrying heavy loads or towing trailers. Therefore, the original load capacity can be compromised to some extent to get the correct stance.

A leaf spring, made up of multiple leaves, can also have several leaves removed to reduce the spring rate and to lower the ride height. Some of the heavy-duty rear leaf springs came with five or six leaves, and these can be reconfigured with only three or four leaves. Some experimentation might be required before the best combination of ride height and spring rate is achieved.

Race Car Techniques

An examination of older Grand National or Winston Cup cars shows some innovative methods for lowering a Mopar muscle car. These older race cars were built from production vehicles, and therefore, the chassis builders needed to work with the same basic structure that today's muscle car enthusiasts are working with. Of course, the Winston Cup chassis builders didn't need to worry too much about ride comfort or ride height, so we can't copy all of their tricks!

The Grand National and Winston Cup cars were lowered extensively in order to improve handling and aerodynamics. Kicking up the frame rails lowered these cars by dropping the entire body over the tires and suspension. Some of the older race cars still had a bolt-on K-member that was installed in the stock location, while other cars had the K-member moved up between the frame rails and welded into place. A modification like this would be very extensive for a street-driven vehicle and most likely wouldn't be attempted by anyone other than a professional chassis builder, but the idea is interesting.

Early NASCAR race cars used a leaf spring rear suspension with a modified frame to lower the back of the vehicle. The transmission tunnel in these race cars was enlarged and moved up in order to provide clearance so the body could be dropped lower to the ground.

Wheels

B-Body cars came from the factory with either 14- or 15-inch-diameter wheels. These wheels were available in a variety of widths ranging from 5 to 7 inches, with most wheels being in the middle of that range. Factory muscle cars typically rode on 14- or 15-inch wheels until 1984, when the C4 Corvette was introduced with special Goodyear tires mounted on 16-inch wheels. After the C4 came to market, wheel diameters across the industry increased to 17 inches, and then they moved on up to 18 and 19 inches as tires became available.

Some of the push for larger wheel sizes came from the design department, but the bigger wheels also provided functionality. These

This B-Body race car was lowered by moving the K-member up into the frame. The K-member was cut down and then welded to the inside of the front subframe. Most Mopar owners are not willing to perform such a severe modification, but this was a common practice when building factory-based circle track cars.

Rear leaf springs are available with different arch heights. The springs in the rear with the large arch heights are Mopar Performance Super Stock springs. The springs in the front are Mopar Performance oval track springs. Flat rear springs are better for handling, and the highly arched design works better for drag racing.

CHAPTER 14

Larger wheels look great on B-Body cars, as long as the tire size is correct. Lowering the car slightly helps improve the proportions if the tires are a little shorter than stock. This Road Runner looks tough with 17 x 8-inch wheels up front and 18 x 10-inch wheels in the rear. Tire size is 245/45 in front and 285/40 in the rear. (Photo Courtesy Stu Harmon)

Gary Beineke's SRT71 Charger has an elegant look with polished 17 x 8-inch wheels at all four corners. (Photo Courtesy Gary Beineke)

This Charger uses 295/45-18 tires on 18 x 9½-inch wheels to fill up the rear wheel wells. A 295/45 tire is a little over 28 inches tall and has a little more than 5 inches of sidewall height. Front tire size is 255/45-17 on a 17 x 8-inch wheel. (Photo Courtesy Kevin Norman)

large-diameter wheels worked together with low-profile tires and large-diameter brakes to provide handling capability that was vastly superior to anything available during the muscle car era. Having been exposed to the ride and handling of modern vehicles, many Mopar owners would now like to install larger wheels and tires onto their classic muscle car.

There is a fairly long list of requirements that a wheel must meet in order to be a "proper" fit. Some of these dimensions are obvious, but others seem to be overlooked on a regular basis. Some people choose a wheel just on looks, but the wheels are a very important part of the vehicle, and all of the requirements should be considered.

Bolt Pattern

All B-Body vehicles came from the factory with five-lug wheels, with the lug bolts arranged on a 4.500-inch-diameter bolt circle. This type of mounting is called a 5 x 4.50 wheel and is common with most Ford vehicles, as well as a variety of vehicles from other manufacturers. The metric equivalent of the 4.500-inch bolt pattern is 114.3 mm. There are a few modern wheels that are advertised with the metric dimension rather than the inch callout, so be sure to research both measurements when looking for wheels.

Hub Center Diameter

A close examination of the center of a Mopar axle, or hub, shows that there is a small lip to locate the brake drum (or rotor) and slightly smaller lip to center the wheel. The smaller lip is called the wheel register. Chrysler engineers used a common dimension for the register for many years in an effort to provide maximum interchangeability. The wheel register on Mopar brake drums and disc rotors is 2.813 inches for the 5 x 4.50 rims. Mopar factory rims are designed with a small amount of clearance to properly sit on this register and be centered.

A wheel with a center diameter properly sized to slip-fit onto the hub is called hub-centric because the hub centers the wheel. The wheel-to-hub clearance on a hub-centric wheel is usually a small amount, such as .005 inch. This means that if you order custom wheels for a Mopar, you would most likely specify a nominal center bore size of 2.818 inches. Of course, measuring your own hubs before placing an order is the best approach.

If the center hole in the wheel is smaller than the register lip, the wheel does not properly mount onto the vehicle. This is a dangerous situation, as the wheel hangs up on the face of the hub rather than be centered onto the register.

The opposite situation, where the wheel center is larger than the mounting register, can also be a problem, but it is not nearly as dangerous. In this situation, the lug nuts hold the wheel in place, and the cone on each lug nut centers it. Although using the five lug nuts to center the wheel seems to work, it is always better to use a wheel with a center hole that properly fits onto the hub.

Some aftermarket wheels are made with oversize center holes, and the manufacturer includes a set of centering rings. The centering rings are thin rings that slip over the hub and provide a register that centers the wheel. The use of centering rings is a compromise design that seems to work okay, but it isn't nearly as clean of a solution as having properly designed wheels.

Wheel Offset

The topic of wheel directly offset often confuses people, because it is a calculated number rather than something that can be measured directly. Simply speaking, wheel offset is the distance from the centerline of the rim to the face of the wheel mounting pad. A wheel with 0 offset has a pad that bolts to the brake hub exactly in the center of the tire; a wheel with positive offset has the center of the tire moved back behind the hub face.

Modern suspension design calls for long control arms and big brakes, which in turn requires large-diameter wheels with the mounting surface pushed out toward the face of the wheel. When viewed in cross section, it is easy to see how a wheel with a lot of positive offset allows more room for the suspension and brake components with the wheel "folded" back over these parts.

Negative offset is when the center of the tire is outboard of the hub mounting pad. Wheels with a lot of negative offset are sometimes used on the rear of a drag race car in order to make the rear axle as short as possible. Wheels with negative offset used to be called "deep-dish" wheels, but that term isn't quite as common now as it used to be. The deep-dish look has faded away, and it is now quite rare to see negative offset wheels used in any high-performance handling application.

B-Body wheels typically have 1/2 inch of positive offset, which places the center of the tire slightly behind the surface of the brake hub. Modern wheels, for a Viper, a Corvette, or other high-performance vehicle, can have positive offset of up to 2 inches. This big change in offset numbers over the years is one reason it is so difficult to retrofit wheels from a modern car to a B-Body.

Backspacing

Wheel backspacing is an easier concept to grasp than offset, because the backspace measurement can be made directly with a tape measure

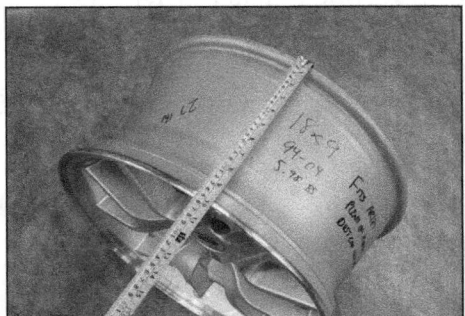

Wheel width is measured from bead mounting surface to bead mounting surface, but the overall width shown here is needed when working with backspacing dimensions. The overall width on an aluminum rim is usually 1 inch wider than the rated width. This 18 x 9-inch rim has an overall width of about 10 inches.

Backspacing is easily measured by using a tape measure and a straightedge across the wheel lip. Generally speaking, B-Body cars work best when the backspacing is in the range of 4.0 to 5.0 inches. Excessive backspacing can cause interference with the leaf springs, ball joints, or tie rod ends.

and a straightedge. The backspace dimension is the distance from the wheel mounting pad to the back edge of the rim. There is a direct relationship between backspacing and offset, but offset can only be calculated if the actual wheel width is known. For example, an 8-inch-wide rim typically measures about 9 inches across the outside of the rim, due to the extra thickness of the lip on the rim. If the mounting pad of this wheel is on center, the backspacing is 4.5 inches, and the offset is 0.

As stated earlier, the wheels on most B-Body cars came from the factory with 1/2 inch of positive offset. For a 6-inch-wide rim, this equates to a backspacing of 4 inches. (7 inches across the rim, so 0 offset would have a backspacing of 3.5 inches. Adding 1/2 inch of offset results in 4 inches of backspacing.) It is unclear why the Chrysler engineers chose a positive offset of 1/2 inch, but that was their design choice, and it has implications when picking aftermarket wheels.

The wheel offset dictates the location of the rim's center in relationship to the mounting surface on the brake drum. The location of the center of the rim is important because this determines where the weight of the vehicle is applied to the wheel bearings. If the wheel offset is changed significantly from the original design specification, the wheel bearings can become overloaded and fail. If you ever see a car going down the road with high-offset wheels sticking out of the wheel wells, you can be sure that the outer wheel bearings are being asked to do something that they weren't designed to handle.

Caliper Clearance

The area between the wheel mounting face and the wheel spokes is usually dished out on a modern wheel to provide clearance for the brake caliper. Original Mopar wheels were not designed to clear large disc brake calipers, as such a need didn't exist in the 1960s. Often, there isn't enough caliper clearance to use factory steel rims on cars that have disc brake conversions. Chrysler changed the stamping dies eventually in order to clear the factory disc brake fitments, but many of the OEM disc brake calipers were fairly small, so the caliper clearance in even the disc brake wheels isn't overly generous.

Some of the factory rims now available have clearance built in for use with large, multi-piston disc brake calipers. These wheels have spokes that sweep out from the center before curving back in to connect to the rim. You may or may not like this style of wheel, but if you are planning on running a big-brake system, a wheel with curved spokes might be the only style that fits.

Scrub Radius

The scrub radius is the distance between the center of the wheel (center of the tire's contact patch, to be more precise) and where the steering inclination angle intersects the road surface. This concept is more easily illustrated by thinking of a king pin angle in a solid axle, but it's the same concept for an independent front suspension. The importance of the scrub radius is that the design of the steering system is connected to where the center of the tire is in relationship to the load. The location of this contact patch determines the loads that the steering system sees, as well as the wheel bearings.

If the installation of wheels with a different offset changes the scrub radius, the reaction of the vehicle changes during turning and braking. A conservative approach is to not change the scrub radius when adding aftermarket rims, but that basically means that the center of the rim needs to stay in the stock location. This can be accomplished, but only if the replacement wheels are not too wide.

Width

The width of the wheel has obvious implications in terms of tire size,

Late-model rims, such as this Mustang F500 wheel, usually are designed with plenty of caliper clearance. The F500 rims are 18 x 9 inches, and the spokes curve outward to clear large aftermarket calipers.

A massive Baer 6S caliper mounted on a 13-inch rotor barely tucks inside this 17-inch Fikse rim. Fikse rims are famous for their strength and nice, clean machine work.

Ford Racing wheels are fairly light, even though they are mass-produced and budget-priced. This 18 x 9-inch wheel weighs 27 pounds. Vendors, such as Fikse or Forgeline, offer three-piece rims that save a few pounds, but they are also significantly more expensive.

but the width is also very important because it's a factor that determines what size physically fits in the wheel well. If the wheel offset is kept at 1/2 inch in order to keep the loads on the wheel bearings properly centered, as the wheel width is increased, the inner rim moves in toward the inner fender the same amount that the outer lip moves out toward the fender. It is usually much easier to modify the outer fenders than the inner fenders, which is why people often install wide wheels that have less offset (less backspacing) than the stock wheels. Although it is better to keep the center of the wheel in the designed location, sometimes that isn't possible if a really wide tire is required.

Adding extra-wide tires onto a Mopar with a stock suspension means that the wheel offset needs to be decreased. The back side of the rim stays in the same location (backspacing stays the same), but the front of the rim is moved out. The outer fender can then be modified with fender flares or cut away for clearance of the wider tire. Moving the center of the wheel out away from the car increases the loads on the outer wheel bearing and increases the scrub radius. The extra scrub radius means that the load from the tire patch is acting on a longer lever arm against the suspension components, such as the tie rods. This results in extra toe-out as the vehicle is driven in a straight line.

Given these terms, you can now start to shop for different rims. What is desired is a rim with the correct bolt pattern, the correct offset, and, hopefully, the right size of center hole. The diameter and width of the wheel are also important, obviously, but those dimensions are limited by what fits.

Weight

The weight of the wheel has a direct impact on handling performance, due to the dynamic forces of a large spinning mass hanging off the end of the suspension. The lighter the wheel, the easier it is for the suspension to keep it under control. Unfortunately for the performance enthusiast on a budget, wheel weight is almost always directly correlated to the price. Bargain-basement rims available at lower-end tire stores are usually very heavy, due to the use of low-quality materials and inferior manufacturing processes. Cast rims are cheaper and heavier than forged rims. High-end, three-piece rims made from high-quality materials are the lightest option, but they are also the most expensive.

Retrofitting Modern Wheels

Modern muscle cars, such as the Mustang, Camaro, and Challenger, are equipped with at least a 17-inch rim, if not larger. The base-level Challenger comes equipped with a 17 x 7.0-inch rim and has optional wheels up to 20 inches in diameter. A fairly common concern has to do with the possibility of retrofitting these modern rims to older muscle cars.

The Mustang Special Edition GT wheel, also known as the "Bullitt" rim, is a popular choice for retrofitting onto Mopars. Both the 1968 Valiant (right) and the 1965 Coronet (left) are equipped with the Special Edition rims. The Valiant uses stock Mustang 245/45 tires to fit into the smaller A-Body wheel wells, while the Coronet uses the slightly taller 235/55-17 tires.

CHAPTER 14

Bolt Pattern and Backspacing

Bolt pattern and backspacing are the two primary issues with retrofitting modern OEM wheels to the older muscle cars. In some cases, the bolt patterns have shifted from the old 5 x 4.50 inches to a metric pattern of 5 x 115 mm. The 115-mm bolt pattern is only .0300 inch larger than the 4.500-inch bolt pattern, but that is a significant mismatch when using lug nuts with a tapered nose.

The taper forces the lug nut sideways into the wheel when being torqued in place. The side force results in a false torque being applied, which in turn can lead to the wheel loosening up during use. A slight mismatch in bolt patterns could be tolerated if the wheel were hub-centric and the lugs used a flat washer type of attachment, but there aren't many wheels like that.

The newer Challenger rims use an offset of 20 mm, which is slightly larger than the 1/2 inch of offset usually recommended for muscle car fitments, but that is within an acceptable range if the wheels fit all of the other criteria. It is possible that the extra width combined with the extra offset would push the rim too far back into the wheel well to properly fit, so test-fitting the rims before buying them would be a good idea.

Center Hole

The diameter of the mounting hole in the center of the rim is going to be different on any modern rim than on an older Mopar rim. In a few cases, the newer rims have a larger center hole that allows for the use of centering rings, but more often than not, the hole in the wheel is too small. If the center hole in the rim is only slightly smaller than stock, the register on the hub can be turned down in a lathe. Turning down the hub provides an excellent register for mounting the wheels, but when it comes time to buy new brake rotors or axles, the work has to be done all over again.

Mustang Rims

Unlike Chrysler, Ford kept the same 5 x 4.50-inch bolt pattern for the highly popular Mustang over the years, so the modern wheels still share the same bolt pattern as the older muscle car wheels. The SN-95 chassis was produced in very large numbers from 1994 to 2004.

Starting in 2005, the backspacing on the Mustang wheels increased. This 2005 wheel is 18 x 8½ inches with 6.820 inches of backspacing. The extra backspacing of the 2005-and-newer wheels makes them difficult to retrofit to a Mopar. A thick spacer was required to mount this rim.

The 2003 Mustang Mach 1 rim has a classic-looking design that is somewhat similar to that of a Mopar Magnum wheel. These rims are 17 x 8 inches with the 5.720-inch backspacing that was common to the SN-95 cars.

Ford Performance offered many aftermarket parts, including multiple wheel options, during this period. Although Mustang wheels do have the correct bolt pattern to fit on any Mopar muscle car, they have a lot of offset, and the center hole diameter is only 2.780 inches, which is just slightly smaller than the Mopar hub dimensions.

Most of the SN-95 rims are cast, but a few are forged, which is a huge bonus. Ford racing rims are fairly light compared to other aftermarket rims, and they are manufactured to rigorous OEM quality standards. The SN-95 rims are most commonly available as a 17 x 8-inch rim with 5.720 inches of backspacing and 32 mm of offset, but there are a variety of other sizes available. Cobra rims are available in a 17 x 9-inch size with 6.120 inches of backspacing, as well as an 18 x 9-inch size.

When the SN-95 platform came to an end in 2004, Ford changed the chassis design in a number of ways, which included adding some offset to the wheels. While the SN-95 rims typically have 5.720 inches of backspacing, the newer wheels have 6.250 inches of backspacing. The bolt pattern is still 5 x 4.50 inches, and the center hole has the same diameter of 2.780 inches, but the additional backspacing makes it fairly difficult to use these late-model Mustang rims on a Mopar muscle car.

Wheel Spacers

Sometimes the only issue with a set of wheels is that the correct offset just isn't available. In these cases, it is tempting to space the wheel away from the brake hub a certain amount in order to provide additional clearance. Many sources advise against using wheel spacers, but there are some situations in which a wheel spacer is a well-engineered solution.

A simple flat piece of material can be used to space the wheel away from the brake hub. This is an effective solution, as long as the spacer is thin enough for the wheel to still register on the center of the hub and the lug nuts are fully engaged with the wheel studs. However, if the spacer is thicker than about 1/4 inch, positioning on the axle register is often lost. If the wheel is spaced out away from the register on the hub, the weight of the vehicle is cantilevered on the wheel studs. If the spacer is thick enough, the lug nuts may not fully engage with the wheel studs, which further compounds the situation. Wheel studs that are overstressed like this can easily fail, leading to a loss of control and possible vehicle damage.

A good spacer design is one in which the spacer is machined with steps that properly register to the hub and the wheel. This type of spacer is usually going to require custom fabrication, but the fabrication is fairly easy on a large lathe. With the step type of spacer, a set of aftermarket rims can be adapted to an older muscle car in a safe manner. The spacer requires longer wheel studs in order to provide a full thread engagement into the lug nuts, but that shouldn't be an issue.

It is also possible to find custom hubs and axles that are designed for flat spacers. If an axle is made with an extra-long wheel register, you are able to easily swap different wheels and spacers on the axle and move the wheel in and out as required.

Typically, only road racers go to these lengths because different wheels are required for different tracks. But, this could also be a great idea for a street-performance vehicle owner who wants to run several different rims. If the wheel registers are made properly, they would not add much weight, and the convenience of being able to quickly change wheels without the need for step-type spacers would be nice.

Wheel Studs

Wheel studs are rarely the focus of any performance upgrade, but they can cause problems if ignored. The factory wheel studs were designed to be just long enough to secure stamped-steel wheels, and they work perfectly fine for that application. However, many aftermarket wheels, especially those made from aluminum, have a thick center section. The factory-installed wheel studs are sometimes too short to reach

Using custom hubs up front and 3/4-inch-thick spacers in the rear, SN-95 Mustang rims can be mounted on a B-Body. Longer wheel studs need to be used with the spacers for the rear wheels.

Many of the commercially available wheel spacers are poorly designed and should not be used. This pair of spacers, used to mount a set of Mustang rims on the rear axle of a B-Body car, is an example of correctly designed spacers. The counterbore on the backside fits snugly over the center boss on the axle, and the nose of the spacer is a slip-fit into the backside of a Mustang rim.

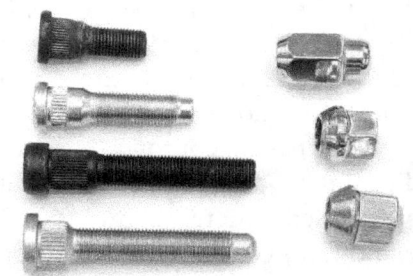

Extra-long wheel studs are required when using spacers. Take careful measurements of the shank diameter before purchasing wheel studs for your Mopar. Many of the aftermarket studs have large shanks and do not fit properly. The silver wheel stud near the top is a Dorman 610-290. This is available at most auto parts stores and is an excellent replacement for the original wheel studs. Various types of lug nuts are also available; look for ones with oversize cones and 13/16-inch wrenching.

CHAPTER 14

Extra-long wheel studs are often required with thick aluminum wheels and/or wheel spacers. But watch out when the shanks extend through the axle flange. The lug holes in the rear disc brake rotors had to be reamed out to clear the shanks of these wheel studs.

through the thicker center section on these aftermarket wheels, so the factory studs need to be pressed out and replaced with longer wheel studs.

Although a variety of wheel studs are available in the aftermarket, only a few of them properly fit a Mopar B-Body vehicle. The Mopar vehicles used a unique knurl size, which must be duplicated, or else the replaced wheel studs do not fit properly.

To further complicate matters, disc brake and drum brake hubs often used different knurl sizes, so you often need to purchase different wheel studs for the front wheels than for the rear wheels. The correct wheel studs should be available for any B-Body configuration, but you need to carefully measure the original studs before ordering replacements. If replacement studs cannot be found, the existing holes in the axle or hub can be reamed out to a larger size where long wheel studs are available.

Custom Wheels

Sometimes a custom wheel is the only solution when there are many design requirements to meet. If you are trying to maximize the tire size while also trying to be hub-centric, lightweight, and have plenty of caliper clearance, the task can quickly become impossible. Fortunately, a variety of aftermarket vendors have the capability of machining custom wheel centers and attaching them to standard rims. A custom wheel center can provide the correct hub diameter, bolt pattern, and caliper clearance. These two- or three-piece rims can be fairly lightweight because they are fabricated from high-quality materials.

Vendors, such as Fikse, are capable of building wheels with a variety of widths, diameters, and backspacing. Custom wheels are several times more expensive than standard wheels, but sometimes they are required.

Tire Considerations

As you would assume, high-performance tires are more available for the popular wheel sizes. A tire mold is expensive to create, so it makes sense to only produce tires in sizes that sell in higher volumes. For this reason, it makes sense when modifying a Mopar muscle car to stick with wheel sizes that are common and that fit rather easily. Although replacement tires can be found for 14- and 15-inch wheels, few high-performance tires are available anymore for wheels this small. High-performance tires are readily available for 17-, 18-, and 19-inch rims, because these larger wheel sizes are used on almost every high-performance vehicle sold.

Diameter

The overall diameter of the tire needs to be matched to the size of the wheel well for clearance reasons and aesthetic reasons. In general, it's a good idea to keep the tire diameter about the same as the original size unless the vehicle is being heavily modified. Keeping the overall diameter the same as the wheel size increases requires the use of lower-profile tires. The tire industry usually speaks about this as +1 or +2 tire changes when the wheel size increases by 1 inch or 2 inches.

For example, a B-Body car that came with 15-inch rims from the factory can be given a +2 wheel-and-tire package to end up with a 17-inch wheel. An original GR70-15 tire was 27.400 inches tall and 8.600 inches wide. With a 17-inch wheel, a similar tire size would be 215/60-17. The 215/60-17 tire is 27.200 inches tall and 8.500 inches wide, but the sidewall profile is lower. The GR70-15 tire had a sidewall height of 6.200 inches, and the 215/60-17 tire has a sidewall height of only 5.100 inches.

When the wheel size increases, the overall tire size does not necessarily need to increase. The outside dimensions for a 17- or 18-inch tire

The backside of a Fikse rim shows the intricate machine work that goes into a custom three-piece wheel. Notice the high-strength bolts that hold the wheel together and how the center of the wheel is drilled and tapped for a bolt-on spacer. Little touches, like this, make Fikse rims so desirable, as well as so expensive.

can be just the same as a 14-inch tire if the proper tire size is selected. What does change when going with a larger-diameter wheel is the profile of the tire. As the wheel diameter increases, the sidewall needs to become shorter to keep the overall diameter the same. As the sidewall becomes shorter, it becomes much stiffer, and is, therefore, able to better retain its shape during cornering. One negative feature of a stiffer sidewall is that the vehicle becomes harsher and louder because the stiff sidewall transmits more noise and vibration.

There should not be any issue with tire clearance inside the wheel well as the wheel size increases, as long as the overall tire size remains the same. The overall width of the tire can be increased slightly from the factory size without any problems because the wheel well clearance was originally generous enough to allow space for tire chains. If the tire diameter is kept close to the OEM tire diameter, the overall gear ratio remains the same, and the speedometer does not need to be recalibrated.

Style and Looks

One issue that is frequently debated is the looks of larger-diameter wheels on older muscle cars. There are plenty of cases where people have made unfortunate wheel choices and ended up with cars that do not look very good. But that doesn't mean that larger-diameter wheels always look bad on a muscle car. One of the key elements is overall tire diameter because the lines of the vehicle were originally styled around a certain tire size.

Most of the cases where a muscle car looks funny with aftermarket wheels are the result of people installing a larger-diameter rim with

A classic combination of spokes and Centerlines, although, in this case, the spokes are Mustang Bullitt rims wearing 235/55-17 tires. The 235/55 tire is a perfect fit for most B-Body cars; it is tall enough to fill the wheel well, and it is wide enough to handle the weight of a heavy car.

a super-low-profile tire. These low-profile tires have a smaller diameter than the original tires and, therefore, get lost in the wheel wells. If there is a lot of space around the tires, the car can look like a roller skate. The easiest way to solve this issue is to stick with tires that are close to the original diameter. For a B-Body or E-Body, use a 50 or 55 series tire, which is 27 inches tall, rather than a 40 series tire, which is only 24 inches in diameter. B-Body cars came with tires in the 27-inch-diameter range, so you need to stay with taller tires of that size, unless other modifications are planned.

Shorter tires can be used if the entire vehicle is lowered over the tires to eliminate the space in the wheel wells, but lowering the vehicle leads to other issues, such as reduced ground clearance and reduced suspension travel. You need to take a careful look at the total package and design intent of the vehicle before picking the tire size.

The Perfect Size

An argument can be made that the modern 235/55-17 tire is the perfect size for B-Body muscle cars. This tire size is currently quite common because it is an OEM fitment on several modern vehicles. This popularity keeps the cost down, and it's easy to find a replacement when traveling. The 235/55-17 tire is a little over 9 inches wide and is 27.2 inches tall. This size is fairly similar to that of older performance tires, such as the GR70-15 tire, which was a common fitment on B-Body cars during the muscle car era. The slightly wider 235 tire typically fits in any of the stock wheel wells without modification, but it provides noticeably better handling, due to the shorter and stiffer sidewall.

The use of a 17-inch rim rather than a 15-inch rim opens up the space for a 13-inch brake rotor. Using larger brake rotors provides significantly better braking capacity than the factory 11-inch rotor and improves the overall performance of the car.

CHAPTER 15

DRIVETRAIN UPGRADES

The stock driveline components were designed for the stock engine package. So when an owner builds a modified street or a race engine, most often the driveline cannot withstand the added engine torque. And if suspension upgrades are made and stickier tires are used, they place greater stress on the driveline, and the result is often component failure, such as broken axles, shattered clutches, and wrecked transmissions. Therefore, you need to select aftermarket high-performance flywheels, clutches, axles, and other driveline components that will withstand the increased power output from the engine.

Flywheels

Mopar engines were generally equipped with either a 130- or a 143-tooth flywheel. The larger 143-tooth flywheel allows the use of 11- or 12-inch clutches to handle higher torque loads, but the weight (and rotating inertia) of the assembly increases with the larger diameter. Performance flywheels are available for both sizes of flywheels, for either six- or eight-bolt crank flanges. Aftermarket flywheels are usually neutral-balanced, but some flywheels are available for externally balanced engines, such as the 360 and the later-model big-blocks.

Flywheels are available in several materials, including cast iron, steel, and aluminum. The original cast-iron factory flywheels were an excellent choice for lower-performance applications. Flywheels made from

A wide variety of flywheels are available from aftermarket vendors. This eight-bolt Hemi flywheel from PRW has 130 teeth, weighs 27 pounds, and is drilled with a dual clutch pattern.

This steel McLeod flywheel weighs only 20 pounds. This view of the backside shows how material was removed to reduce the weight. This flywheel has 130 teeth and a six-bolt crankshaft pattern.

Aluminum flywheels can be significantly lighter than their steel counterparts. This 130-tooth McLeod flywheel weighs only 12 pounds. The eight-bolt crankshaft pattern is used on many aftermarket crankshafts.

billet steel are used for higher engine speeds or when required by a sanctioning body. Aluminum flywheels are used when a lightweight rotating assembly is needed.

The weight of the flywheel can be a factor in overall vehicle performance. The rotating inertia of a heavy flywheel is beneficial in getting a heavy car to accelerate from a stop, and a road race car usually works best with a lighter flywheel.

Direct Connection used to have steel flywheels in its catalog with weights ranging from 21 to 58 pounds. It also had six- and eight-bolt aluminum flywheels available, which weighed only 11 pounds. These parts were discontinued many years ago, but similar parts are still available from aftermarket suppliers.

The factory bellhousing works just fine for moderate-performance street cars, but as engine speeds increase, so does the need for a safety bellhousing. Not all bellhousings accept the larger 143-tooth flywheels, and of course, the bellhousing bolt pattern needs to match the transmission. QuickTime offers a wide variety of SFI-rated bellhousings for both small-block and big-block engines.

There are a number of flywheel bolts available for Mopar engines, but many of them are too long. ARP has flywheel bolts that are the correct length. The eight-bolt flywheels use 1/2-20 bolts, and the 6-bolt design uses smaller 7/16-20 bolts.

Clutches

Original Mopar pressure plates used the Borg & Beck design, but that type of clutch is rarely used anymore. Aftermarket racing clutches are usually a Borg & Beck/Long plate for high-powered racing engines, and less-powerful applications use the diaphragm design. The diaphragm-style pressure plate has become very popular as an OEM fitment, due to its low cost and moderate pedal pressure. The diaphragm clutch was originally avoided for high-performance applications because of concerns about high-speed operation, but design changes over the past 20

The CenterForce Light Metal Clutch is a low-inertia performance clutch system. When combined with a PRW steel flywheel, the total assembly is 20 pounds lighter than the factory clutch and flywheel assembly. The system uses a dual-friction-style clutch disc with carbon-composite lining.

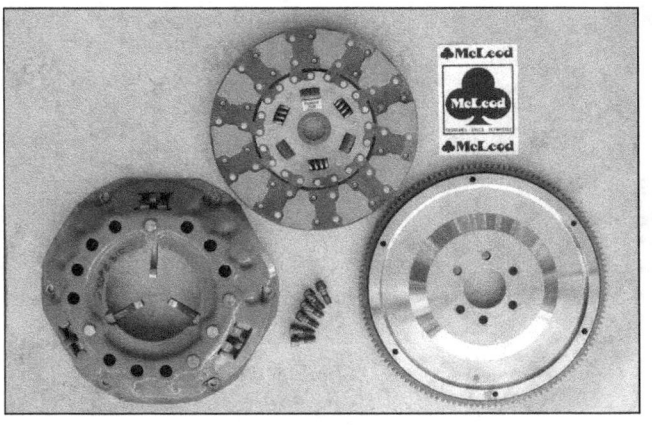

years have fixed those issues. These days, a number of vendors, including CenterForce and McLeod, offer high-performance clutches using the diaphragm design.

There are a lot of factors at work when choosing a pressure plate, including size, mounting bolt pattern, required load, and shifting speed. Typically, the pressure plate is larger on cars with more horsepower. Hemi cars were equipped with an 11-inch-diameter pressure plate, and Vipers have a 12¼-inch-diameter pressure plate.

The clutch can be designed with centrifugal assist, which increases pressure plate force as the engine speed increases. Centrifugal assist

Be sure to use the correct pressure-plate bolts for your clutch assembly. These bolts have a properly sized shank to locate the pressure plate, as well as a smaller head for additional wrenching clearance.

McLeod offers a variety of clutch packages that fit B-Body vehicles, including this Borg & Beck/Long–style pressure plate with a dual-friction-style clutch disc. This disc uses organic facing on the pressure-plate side and Kevlar facing on the flywheel side.

CHAPTER 15

Excessive clutch slippage overheats the flywheel and can lead to damage, such as warping or cracking.

rollers were used by Chrysler on some performance clutches, such as those behind the 340 and Hemi engines. These roller-assisted clutches that Chrysler used are not very popular anymore, but the aftermarket does offer a variety of centrifugal-assist designs. Centrifugal assist is not necessarily the hot setup if you're going to be shifting at high speeds, so you need to carefully understand the pros and cons of adding centrifugal assist to your clutch.

Both RAM and McLeod also offer sophisticated "slipper" clutches that allow a car to be launched at the drag strip on limited-traction tires. Clutch technology is one reason why you see those stock-appearing cars run deep into the 11s on street tires. But, these special clutches are expensive, and they require constant maintenance, so they are not suitable for most applications.

Just as with flywheels, the choices for a pressure plate get rather complicated, so once again, talk to the clutch manufacturer's tech line and follow their guidance. Remember, your pressure plate choices are limited to what bolts onto your flywheel, and you also need to select a pressure plate that works with the clutch disc that you intend to use.

Clutch Discs

A typical street-performance application requires a clutch disc with organic facing material and an inner spring called a marcel that provides some cushioning during engagement. In addition to the marcel, the hub on most street discs has springs built in to further cushion the shock loads. As the power levels go up, the organic clutch disc material is often replaced with materials that are capable of withstanding the higher temperatures caused by performance usage. These high-temperature materials, such as bronze, Kevlar, or sintered iron, are sometimes used on just the flywheel side of the disc in an attempt to make a compromise between performance and smoothness. As you move further toward a racing-type disc, you can specify bronze or sintered-iron facings on both sides of the disc.

For racing applications that require fast gear changes, the marcel is often deleted, and sometimes, the center hub is solid rather than being sprung. As you can imagine, the elimination of the marcel and the hub springs makes the clutch operation much harsher than in a production car. This increased harshness brings with it more noise and vibration, as well as more shock loads to the drivetrain.

The spline count on the clutch disc obviously needs to match the spline count on the transmission input shaft. Most Mopar transmissions used the 1 x 23 spline; a beefier 1 3/16 x 18 spline was used on the Hemi and other high-performance transmissions. Performance clutch discs might not be available in both spline configurations, so double-check this. As I discuss in Chapter 16, some of the aftermarket transmissions use a General Motors or Ford input shaft rather than a Mopar configuration.

Clutch Design

A number of years back, Tom Monroe wrote *Clutch and Flywheel Handbook*. That book has been out of print for a number of years, and some

Vendors, such as McLeod, offer a full range of clutch discs, including ones for specialized applications.

Sintered-iron discs are used in high-torque, high-temperature applications. The iron disc is fairly "grabby," which increases the torque capacity of the clutch, but it also makes it fairly temperamental for street driving. This particular disc was destroyed when my car was caught in a traffic jam on a long uphill stretch of road.

DRIVETRAIN UPGRADES

The standard bronze pilot bushing on the right was used for small-block and big-block engines. The roller bearing on the left is from a Magnum engine. The roller bearing can be retrofitted to earlier engines, if desired.

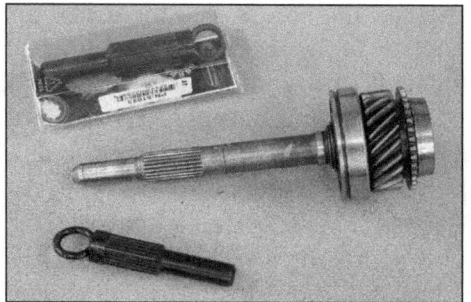

An alignment tool is required to hold the clutch disc in position while installing the pressure plate. Plastic tools are available for both 18- and 23-spline clutches, but an actual input shaft works better, if you have one.

The LMC assembly from CenterForce was installed behind this 427-ci small-block stroker motor. An input shaft is being used to locate the clutch disc while the pressure-plate bolts are being installed with a torque wrench. Proper assembly technique is critical on these high-powered combinations.

of the material is obsolete, but it is still a good reference manual if you can find a copy. There are currently not many books about clutches available, so the best sources of information are vendors' tech lines and websites.

The most common clutch diameters available for small-block and big-block Mopars are 10½ and 11 inches. Both the 10½- and 11-inch scalloped clutches use an 11⅝-inch bolt pattern and fit on the smaller 130-tooth flywheel. The 11-inch clutch used on the 1966 to 1969 Hemi and the 1967 to 1969 440 engine requires the larger 143-tooth flywheel.

For general street-performance applications, the pressure plates have between 2,200 and 3,000 pounds of force. A 2,200-pound pressure-plate load with a 60:1 pedal ratio provides a comfortable pedal force of 37 pounds. A 3,000-pound pressure-plate load requires a pedal force of about 50 pounds, which most people consider stiff or even excessive.

Once you know the pressure-plate loads and the clutch sizes, you can calculate the torque capacity by assuming a 20-percent margin of safety standard and a friction value of .30. Given those assumptions, a 10½-inch clutch with 2,200 pounds of pressure-plate force provides 380 ft-lbs of torque capacity. The 11-inch clutch at the same load handles 400 ft-lbs of torque, and the big 12-inch clutch, used in the Viper, can hold 450 ft-lbs of torque.

If you go ahead and crank the pressure-plate load up to 3,000 pounds, the 10½-inch clutch now handles 520 ft-lbs of torque, the 11-inch clutch handles 550 ft-lbs, and the 12-inch clutch is good for 610 ft-lbs. As you can see, size matters, and so do the pressure-plate load and the friction factor. The amount of torque that the 12-inch clutch can handle is pretty impressive when you look at these numbers. Aftermarket clutches of this size were not always available, but now McLeod is selling a 12-inch diaphragm pressure plate that bolts to a Mopar 143-tooth flywheel. A large-diameter clutch can handle a lot of torque without heavy pedal force, which makes it an excellent choice for a daily driven street car. The drawback to a large-diameter clutch is the weight, so it wouldn't be the best choice for drag racing.

The Street Twin

Most passenger car clutch assemblies use a single disc to transmit the engine torque from the flywheel to the transmission input. But, there are limitations to the single-disc clutch in terms of torque capacity because the overall diameter can't be any larger than the bellhousing. Also, the pedal force that can be generated by an average driver limits the spring pressure. Sintered-iron clutches try to get around these limitations by using a surface with higher friction, but the extra friction can make these clutches "grabby," which compromises the drivability.

Multiple-disc clutches are capable of having an extremely high torque capacity because the addition of a second disc effectively doubles the capacity of the clutch. As calculated earlier, a single-disc, 10½-inch clutch with 2,200 pounds of force can only hold 380 ft-lbs of torque. Doubling those numbers means that a Street Twin (from McLeod) with the small 10½-inch discs and a light pedal force of 37 pounds can handle twice that amount (2 x 380), or 760 ft-lbs of torque! 760 ft-lbs is plenty of capacity for most cars, and the drivability is excellent with low pedal force and the smooth engagement of the organic discs. Of course, a twin-disc setup means more parts and some extra rotating weight, so a tradeoff has to be made.

Although the Street Twin is an impressive clutch, it is fairly expensive, due to the associated hardware and custom flywheel. To reduce costs, McLeod developed the RST twin-disc clutch, which can be installed on a factory-style flywheel. The RST clutch is rated at 800 hp and uses organic discs for smooth operation on the street. A more aggressive version of the RST, called the RXT, uses ceramic material on the discs and is rated at 1,000 hp.

Driveshafts

B-Body vehicles were fitted with a steel driveshaft using either 7260 or 7290 U-joints. This combination works fine up to about 500 hp, and then an upgrade is recommended for engines producing more than 500 hp. Spicer U-joints are available in several sizes, including 1310, 1330, and 1350. The Spicer 1350 U-joint has become the de facto standard used for heavy-duty street use, as well as many forms of drag racing. The 1350 U-joints are rated at 1,200 ft-lbs of torque capacity, which should handle everything except super-high-powered vehicles. The 7290 U-joint is roughly equivalent to a Spicer 1330 U-joint, so it has decent load capacity, but it isn't quite as popular in the aftermarket as the 1350 Spicer design.

Aluminum driveshafts have become popular on newer vehicles, due to their reduced weight. A number of vendors offer aluminum driveshafts for muscle car applications, as well as replacement steel shafts and the more exotic carbon-fiber shafts. A high-quality steel driveshaft with Spicer 1350 U-joints should work fine for the majority of B-Body vehicles, but aluminum is an option for the weight-conscious.

The critical speed of the driveshaft can be a consideration with cars that

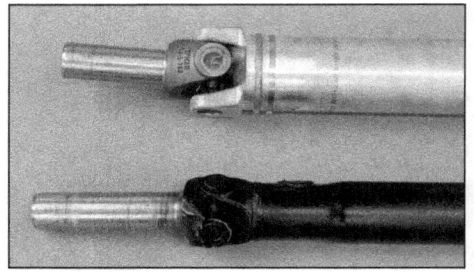

A larger-diameter aluminum driveshaft with bigger U-joints can replace a stock driveshaft without incurring a weight penalty. The larger U-joints increase the torque capacity of the driveline, and the larger-diameter driveshaft raises the critical speed.

operate at higher speeds. The critical speed is the speed at which the driveshaft becomes unstable. The critical speed for a 3-inch steel B-Body driveshaft is roughly 6,500 rpm, depending on the exact length. This speed can be reached on faster drag cars or vehicles used for road racing. If your combination is close to the critical speed, you need to either use a larger-diameter driveshaft or change to a stiffer material, such as carbon fiber.

Aluminum driveshafts are useful in resolving critical-speed issues, because the larger-diameter aluminum shaft increases the critical speed

Using a large-diameter aluminum driveshaft under this 1971 Charger makes a tight fit for the X-type exhaust system. A driveshaft loop is required by most race sanctioning bodies. (Photo Courtesy Gary Beineke)

The required length needs to be carefully determined before ordering a custom driveshaft. The driveshaft should be long enough to provide full engagement of the yoke into the back of the transmission, but the yoke cannot be allowed to bottom on the output shaft. (Photo Courtesy Gary Beineke)

Several U-joints have been used under B-Body cars over the years. From left to right are the 7260, 7290, Spicer 1330, and Spicer 1350. The Spicer 1330 U-joint was used behind Hemi motors in 1966 and 1967. Over the years, the large 1350 has become the standard for performance use.

without adding weight. A 3½-inch aluminum driveshaft has a critical speed of 7,400 rpm, and a 3-inch steel driveshaft of the same length has as a critical speed of only 6,300 rpm.

Be very careful when using an overdrive transmission because the driveshaft speed is higher than the engine speed in overdrive. With a .50:1 overdrive ratio, the driveshaft turns at twice the speed of the engine. With this sort of arrangement, a high-performance engine can easily spin the driveshaft into the critical-speed zone during high-speed driving, and it could eventually fail.

Rear Ends

B-Body vehicles were available from the factory with a variety of rear end housings, but for performance applications, I focus on the 8¾ unit and the Dana 60. The 8¾ has a slight weight advantage over the Dana 60, as well as a wider selection of gears. There is also an aluminum center section available for the 8¾ rear end for additional weight savings. Starting in 1966, Chrysler engineering specified the light-truck Dana 60 as a heavy-duty option behind the Hemi and other high-horsepower engines. More than 45 years later, it is still a viable option for high-performance street cars and serious drag race cars. The Dana 60 is currently available as a brand-new assembly from several vendors, which makes it easy to source a complete rear end ready to drop into a project vehicle. Either rear end can be fitted with a variety of limited-slip differentials, as well as modern disc brake kits and a variety of gear ratios.

Both the 8¾ and the Dana 60 were available in several widths from the factory. Narrowing the rear axle housing is usually required when using wide rear wheels, but in some cases, it makes sense to use a wider rear end housing in order to work with modern wheels that have a lot of backspacing. New housings are available for both the Dana 60 and the 8¾, so, these days, it might be easier to just order a new housing that is the correct width rather than modify an original housing.

The classic Dana 60 passenger car rear end is now available new from vendors, such as Strange Engineering and Moser. This new Dana 60 assembly is outfitted with a DoctorDiff disc brake kit and a beefy aluminum cover. (Photo Courtesy DoctorDiff)

Moser Engineering is now producing new 8¾-inch housings. By using a new housing, you have the freedom to build the correct-width rear end without having to modify original parts. (Photo Courtesy Moser Engineering)

This 1971 Charger is equipped with one of the new Moser 8¾-inch housings. The housing is oval, rather than round, because Moser uses a common stamping for both the 8¾-inch and its Ford 9-inch housing. (Photo Courtesy Gary Beineke)

The 8¾-inch rear end uses a drop-out center section, which allows for quick gear changes. Several center section castings were used in B-Body vehicles over the years. The different housings require different ring-and-pinion sets, so take note of the casting number before ordering parts. (Photo Courtesy Gary Beineke)

A spool is the lightest and most direct way to connect the rear axles to the ring gear. Spools are widely used in drag racing, but the lack of differential action makes them a poor choice for street use.

CHAPTER 16

AUTOMATIC AND MANUAL TRANSMISSION SWAPS

The 5-speed technology was still a decade or more in the future when the muscle car era ended. Starting in 1983, the Mustang GT came from the factory with a 5-speed transmission. Shortly thereafter, General Motors began to use the same basic transmission in the Camaro and Firebird vehicles, further increasing the supply of 5-speed transmissions. As the modern muscle cars grew more powerful, the new T5 transmission was modified and improved until it became capable of handling a significant amount of power.

And with increased production volumes, the T5 transmission and its successors became fairly inexpensive to find. As the prices for these 5-speed transmissions dropped, a number of them began to find their way into various B-Body applications. Eventually, aftermarket vendors noticed the opportunity and began to produce transmission swap kits.

Mopar vehicles were blessed with one of the best 4-speed transmissions ever designed, but the addition of a fifth gear allows the engine speed to be dropped significantly for highway driving. Most performance vehicles have lower rear end ratios for improved acceleration, but the low gearing keeps the engine speed higher than desired for freeway cruising. The use of an overdrive ratio on the freeway drops the engine speed, which reduces noise and improves gas mileage. Fifth-gear ratio varies by the type of transmission, but an overdrive ratio of .60:1 is fairly common. Installing a .60:1-ratio fifth gear turns a 4.10:1 rear end gear into a freeway-friendly 2.50:1 ratio.

5-Speed Options

There was never a 5-speed option from the factory for B-Body vehicles, so there aren't any "bolt-in" setups available from a wrecking yard. Due to the many changes made over the years, transmissions sourced from

Hurst Driveline Conversions offers several complete kits for B-Body cars, including this one, which features a Tremec TKO transmission. The complete kits include the clutch, bellhousing, driveshaft, transmission mount, and related hardware. (Photo Courtesy Hurst Driveline Conversions)

newer vehicles do not have the correct dimensions to drop into a B-Body. Clever shade-tree mechanics can overcome some of the swap issues, but most people are going to need help swapping in a "foreign" transmission. Fortunately, the aftermarket has created several options that allow the average person to install a 5-speed transmission into a B-Body.

Tremec

Tremec, a major transmission vendor within the automotive sector, has developed a line of 5-speed transmissions for the aftermarket. The Tremec lineup includes the light-duty T5, as well as two versions of the heavier-duty TKO. The TKO-500 is rated at 500 ft-lbs, and the TKO-600 is rated at 600 ft-lbs. The TKO-500 has gear ratios of 3.27, 1.98, 1.34, 1.00, and .68:1, and the TKO-600 uses ratios of 2.87, 1.89, 1.28, 1.00, and .82:1. These TKO transmissions weigh 99 pounds and are roughly similar in size to the original Mopar 4-speed. The Tremec transmissions are currently only available in Ford and GM configurations, so certain modifications have to be made before they can be used behind a Mopar engine.

Several vendors, such as Hurst Driveline Conversions and Keisler Engineering, have focused their business around the mission of adapting Tremec transmissions to older muscle cars. These vendors have a very broad range of options for Mopar vehicles, including the 1962 to 1974 B-Body cars. Kits are available for both the Tremec TKO-500 and the Tremec TKO-600 transmissions. These kits include modifications to the transmissions, which make them easier to swap into Mopar vehicles. For example, the shifter is relocated, and the transmission case is modified to improve the fit. Most of the Mopar kits are designed to work without any sheet-metal fabrication, but in some cases, the floor needs to be modified to get the correct drivetrain alignment.

Various vendors offer a complete line of parts, such as bellhousings, clutch linkages, crossmembers, shifter handles, pedal kits, and sheet-metal tunnels, to further facilitate Tremec transmission swaps.

Passon Performance

As this book was going to press, Passon Performance was in the process of introducing a new 5-speed transmission. The Passon A855 is designed to be a 5-speed version of the A833 and should, therefore, bolt right into any B-Body vehicle. The A855 transmission uses the larger Hemi input shaft, so an 18-spline clutch disc and matching throw-out bearing need to be installed. The A855 is designed to bolt directly to a stock bellhousing, as well as to the factory crossmember. Gear ratios for the A855 are 2.64, 1.92, 1.40, 1.00, and .70:1. Passon is planning to produce an extension housing for the 1969-and-earlier B-Body cars, as well as the 1970-and-later cars. Early B-Body cars need to convert to a slip-yoke-style driveshaft to use the A855.

Richmond Gear

Another vendor that manufactures aftermarket 5-speed transmissions is Richmond Gear, which offers a Street 5-speed, as well as a Road Race 5-speed and a Super Street 5-speed with overdrive. The Street and the Road Race units are rated at

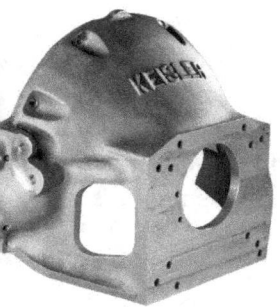

Keisler has tooled up to produce a big-block bellhousing designed to fit various Tremec transmissions. Starting with a transmission-swap bellhousing reduces the need for expensive custom fabrication. (Photo Courtesy Keisler Engineering)

Keisler Engineering also offers various 5-speed kits, including several based on the Tremec TKO transmission. Keisler offers 5-speed kits for 1962 to 1974 B-Body cars. (Photo Courtesy Keisler Engineering)

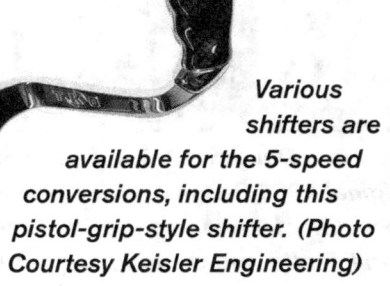

Various shifters are available for the 5-speed conversions, including this pistol-grip-style shifter. (Photo Courtesy Keisler Engineering)

CHAPTER 16

A number of vendors currently manufacture transmission humps designed to fit 5-speed transmissions. (Photo Courtesy Keisler Engineering)

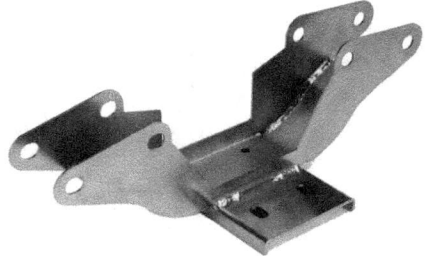

Transmission crossmembers are also available from vendors, such as Hurst and Keisler. Crossmembers vary according to the vehicle's make and model, as well as the specific transmission being installed. (Photo Courtesy Keisler Engineering)

Complete pedal assemblies are available for some B-Body models, if you wish to convert from an automatic to a 5-speed. (Photo Courtesy Keisler Engineering)

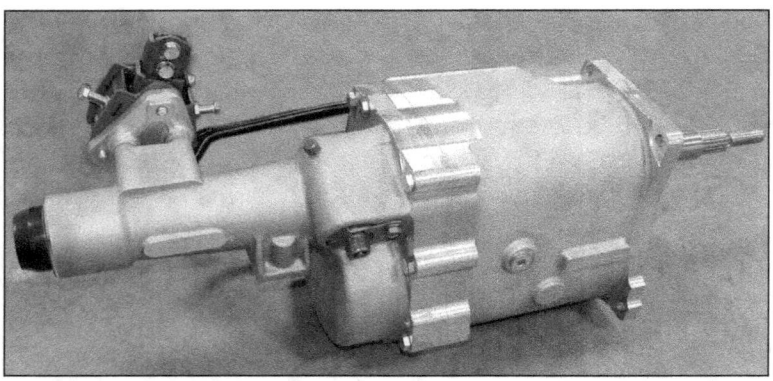

This prototype 5-speed transmission from Passon Performance is almost ready to go into production. The Passon 5-speed is designed to be a direct swap for any factory 4-speed transmission. The new Passon transmission uses the original shifter location, transmission mount, and bellhousing. (Photo Courtesy Richard Ehrenberg)

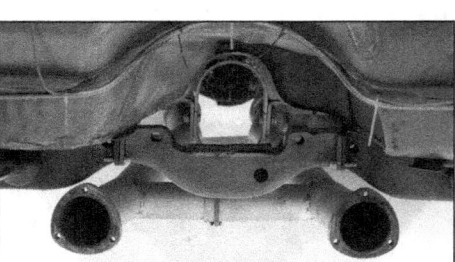

Installation of the Doug Nash (or a Richmond 5-speed) into a B-Body vehicle requires the removal of the top of the torsion bar crossmember. A new bolt-in transmission crossmember was constructed for this 1965 B-Body.

Placing a Doug Nash 5-speed transmission next to an original 1965 B-Body 4-speed highlights the differences. The shifter location on the Doug Nash is moved back significantly, and the main case is both wider and longer.

Considering the size and strength of this transmission, the Doug Nash 5-speed is fairly lightweight at 113 pounds.

This Lakewood bellhousing has been modified to mate to the Doug Nash transmission. One of the mounting holes needed to be relocated, and the pivot ball mount was altered. This swap was originally designed for a drag race car, so a heavy-duty Z-bar was custom-built for it.

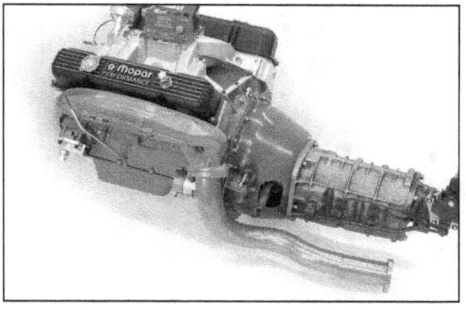

The Doug Nash (now Richmond) transmission is a good match for a high-powered stroker motor, such as this 512-ci big-block. It is a big strong transmission designed for drag racing.

QuickTime has a number of transmission-swap bellhousings for both small-block and big-block engines. The modular design of the QuickTime bellhousing allows the company to produce many variations of each design.

QuickTime bellhousing #6072 allowed us to bolt a Doug Nash transmission directly to a Mopar R3 block. This assembly was being trial fitted to a Mopar road race car when this picture was taken.

450 ft-lbs of torque capacity, and the Super Street version is rated at 600 ft-lbs.

The Street 5-speed transmission is not an overdrive; rather, it uses a deep 3.28:1 first gear and a 1.0:1 fifth gear. Typically, this transmission is coupled with a high rear end ratio, such as a 3.23:1, for best overall performance. One potential problem with the 1:1 fifth gear is that high-ratio rear end gears are not available for the Dana 60 rear end. With no way to go higher than a 3.54:1 final drive ratio, engine speeds might stay higher than desired.

The Super Street version is an overdrive with a fifth-gear ratio of .77:1. Having the overdrive allows you to use a commonly available 3.91 or 4.10:1 rear end ratio for performance, while still dropping the engine speed on the highway.

Richmond transmissions are available with the Hemi 18-spline input shaft, so commonly available Mopar clutches, pilot bushings, and throw-out bearings can be used. The Richmond transmissions do use a GM-style 1⅜ x 32 spline output shaft, so a GM transmission yoke is required. A stock bellhousing can be modified to accept the Richmond transmission, or an SFI-legal bellhousing can be purchased from QuickTime.

The Richmond transmissions are physically larger than an A833, so significant modifications are required to the tunnel area. In addition to the larger size, the shifter location is rearward of the stock location, resulting in interference with the torsion bar crossmember.

6-Speed Options

If five speeds aren't enough, there are several 6-speed transmissions that can be installed in a B-Body. The 6-speed transmissions are physically larger than the factory A833, and therefore, extensive modifications to the transmission tunnel, crossmember, and driveshaft are required.

Tremec

The T56 is a popular OEM unit that is fitted into a variety of performance rear-wheel-drive vehicles, including the Viper, Corvette Z06, and Mustang Cobra. It is a fairly large transmission with a dry weight of 122 pounds and a shifter location about 28 inches behind the back of the engine block. This location puts the shifter into the torsion bar crossmember on most Mopar vehicles. Removing the torsion bar crossmember is a very significant modification on a Mopar, because the unit is such a key structural part of the frame. This type of modification becomes much easier if the front suspension is converted to a coil-over suspension.

Due to the popularity of the T56 in OEM vehicles, many of these transmissions are available from salvage yards. However, most of the OEM versions of this transmission are difficult to swap into a B-Body, due to an integrated bellhousing and the non-Mopar input shaft. Another issue with the OEM versions of the T56 is that many of them are rated for less than 450 ft-lbs of torque capacity.

CHAPTER 16

The T56 transmission (top) is roughly the same length as the Mopar A833 (bottom), but it is wider and deeper. The T56 weighs 145 pounds, and the Mopar aluminum-case 4-speed weighs only 81 pounds.

The tailshaft on the A833 (left) is very slender when compared to the same general area on the T56 (right). The shifter is in the same general area on both transmissions, but the transmission mount needs to be moved.

Tremec recently introduced an aftermarket version of its T56 6-speed transmission. The T56 Magnum is rated at 700 ft-lbs of torque capacity and is a substantial upgrade from older-production T56 transmissions. Installing a T56 into a B-Body isn't an easy task, but several vendors offer parts that can help with the project. (Photo Courtesy Hurst Driveline Conversions)

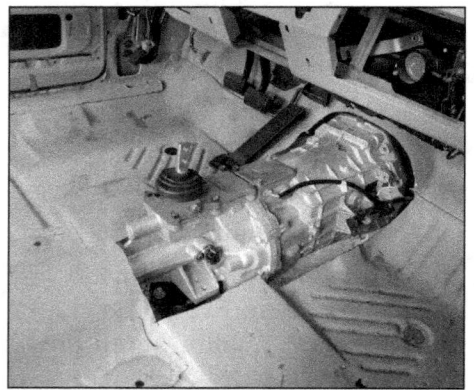

Mopar enthusiast Darren Beale was in the process of installing a T56 Magnum into his B-Body car when he took this picture. The factory transmission tunnel had to be cut away to provide room for the T56. (Photo Courtesy Darren Beale)

The Dodge Viper used a version of the T56 that was rated at 550 ft-lbs of torque capacity. Quick-Time sells bellhousings to mate the Viper T56 to either a small-block or a big-block, but the clutch linkage, transmission tunnel, and mounting crossmember would all need to be fabricated.

Tremec recently introduced the T56 Magnum, which is rated at 700 ft-lbs of torque capacity. It has a number of improvements over the regular T56, including wider gears, a stronger input shaft, a mechanical speedometer pickup, and triple-cone synchronizers. Tremec currently only offers GM and Ford versions of the T56 Magnum, but parts are available to adopt these to Mopar engines.

Hurst Driveline recommends PN TUET-11009, which is the Chevy LS version. The TUET-11009 is a double-overdrive unit with gear ratios of 2.66, 1.78, 1.30, 1.00, .80, and .62:1. With the double overdrive, a rear end ratio of 4.56 or 4.88:1 can be selected for excellent acceleration, while still having the equivalent of a 2.94:1 rear gear for freeway operation. When using a super-low rear end ratio, you would most likely only use gears second through fifth on the street, with first gear reserved for drag racing and sixth used only on the freeway.

Richmond Gear

Richmond Gear offers a 6-speed version of its Street 5-speed transmission. It is 24 inches long and has a dry weight of 108 pounds. The transmission mount is located 18 inches behind the face of the transmission. Just like the 5-speed, the 6-speed transmission can be ordered with a Hemi input shaft. The Hemi input shaft allows the transmission to be used with a standard Hemi

Once the transmission had been properly located in Darren's car, a new transmission tunnel was fabricated from sheet metal. (Photo Courtesy Darren Beale)

A new transmission crossmember had to be fabricated for Darren's B-Body. Also notice that the upper portion of the original crossmember has been replaced with one fabricated from thick steel plate. (Photo Courtesy Darren Beale)

The GV overdrive unit bolts to the back of the transmission and hangs behind the transmission mount. Typically, only minor clearancing of the transmission tunnel is required. An X-style exhaust system still fits with the GV unit, but the cross-over may need to be moved back a small amount.

clutch package, as well as the stock throw-out bearing and pilot bushing. The front of the Richmond 6-speed is drilled with the same bolt pattern that's on its 5-speed, so either a QuickTime bellhousing is required or the factory bellhousing needs to be modified.

Summit Racing has an excellent article on its website showing the swap of a Richmond 6-speed transmission into a 1969 Dodge Charger. The Summit article illustrates how much of the floor needed to be cut and how the shifter box was relocated.

The Richmond 6-speed is a single-overdrive unit with a deep-ratio first gear, so it is best matched to a medium rear end ratio, such as a 3.73:1. With a 3.73:1 rear end ratio, the drive ratios in the first four gears are similar to those of a 4-speed with a 4.56:1 rear end. The .80:1 sixth gear turns the 3.73:1 rear end ratio into an effective final drive ratio of 2.98:1 for highway cruising.

Gear Vendors Overdrive

Gear Vendors (GV) offers an overdrive unit that bolts onto the back of the transmission. It has kits for the Mopar 727 automatic and the A833 4-speed. There are several advantages to a bolt-on overdrive, especially when compared to the extensive modifications that need to be made for some of the 5- and 6-speed conversions. The GV overdrive provides a .78:1 ratio reduction, which drops a 4.10:1 rear end ratio to the equivalent of a 3.20:1 final drive.

Another interesting option with the GV unit is that it can double the number of transmission gears by splitting gears. A wide-ratio transmission can be "smoothed out" by using the GV unit to create a first low and a first high gear. It probably isn't worth the extra effort to split all four gears, but there are situations where adding one or two splits can really make a noticeable improvement in performance.

There are a number of photos posted on the Gear Vendors website showing the installation of the unit into second-generation B-Body vehicles without any sheet-metal modifications. Someone else posted pictures at www.moparts.com of a Gear Vendors installation into a 1973 B-Body. This late-B-Body application did require some cutting and welding of the tunnel sheet metal.

Gear Vendors offers a bolt-on overdrive for either the A833 4-speed or the 727 automatic. The overdrive has a .78:1 ratio and is capable of handling more than 1,000 hp. (Photo Courtesy Gear Vendors)

CHAPTER 16

Automatic Overdrives

Chrysler added an overdrive to both the 904 and 727 transmissions in the late 1980s in an effort to improve fuel economy. The nomenclature was changed, with the 904 becoming the A500 and the 727 becoming the A518. The big-block engines were long gone by the time these transmissions were developed, so big-block versions of these transmissions were not developed. But either of these overdrives can be used behind a small-block stroker motor for improved fuel economy at highway speeds.

The overdrive ratio for both the A500 and A518 transmissions is .69:1, which drops a 4.10:1 rear end ratio to an effective final ratio of only 2.84:1. Shifting into overdrive results in a 30-percent drop in engine speed at cruise, which improves fuel economy and reduces noise. Multiple variations of these overdrive automatic transmissions exist, so you need to conduct some research before just grabbing a transmission from a late-model car in the salvage yard.

These transmissions have electronic controls for the overdrive that need to be switched, and some versions also have a lockup convertor that needs to be switched. The lockup converter improves fuel economy, but performance may suffer because the stall speed of the stock lockup converters is usually quite low.

Both the A500 and the A518 transmissions can be physically bolted to a small-block engine, but they do not fit in a B-Body until some modifications are made to the transmission crossmember and the tunnel floor. The transmission mount on the overdrive automatics is located slightly lower and to the rear of the mount on a 904 or 727, so the transmission mount needs to be modified. The overdrive automatics are also slightly longer, so the driveshaft needs to be shortened several inches to fit.

Richard Ehrenberg of Mopar Action covered the A518 swap in an early issue of the Mopar Tech Special. (These Mopar Tech Special pieces are available on CD from Mopar Action, if you don't have the original printed versions.) A member on the Moparts forum posted a thread showing the installation of an A518 into his A-Body car. He had to cut the torsion bar crossmember and modify the tunnel sheet metal for clearance. A B-Body vehicle should have more clearance in the tunnel area than an A-Body, but it is likely that some modifications to either the floor or the transmission case would be required.

QuickTime Bellhousings

QuickTime, Inc., sells bellhousings to adapt the GM 4L60E to either a Mopar small-block or big-block engine. It also sells a 4L80E bellhousing that fits big-block and Hemi engines. The 4L60E and 4L80E are 4-speed automatic transmissions widely used in GM rear-wheel-drive cars and light trucks. Multiple aftermarket vendors provide ample support for these transmissions, selling transmission parts as well as complete units. Installation of either of these transmissions into a Mopar B-Body vehicle requires some modifications, including the fabrication of a new transmission mount and the creation of some sort of shift controller.

Keisler Engineering A41

Keisler offers an overdrive automatic transmission for big-block and Hemi engines called the A41. The Keisler A41 is based on the 4L60E, with internal modifications that improve torque capacity up to 650 ft-lbs. The Keisler kit includes a transmission controller, conversion flexplate, and a complete wiring harness. Keisler also modifies the transmission so that it accepts a standard speedometer cable, and it offers a selection of transmission mounts for B-Body vehicles. The Keisler A41 transmission has gear ratios of 3.01, 1.63, 1.0, and .70:1. This wide spread provides a deep first gear for better acceleration and the 30-percent overdrive to reduce engine speed for highway driving.

TCI Automotive 6X Six-Speed

TCI has recently introduced a new 6-speed automatic transmission called the 6X Six-Speed. The TCI 6X is based on the GM 4L80E, but it has been modified to handle 850 hp. The 6X transmission is a fairly large transmission, so tunnel modifications are likely. Gear ratios are 2.97, 2.23, 1.57, 1.18, and 1.0:1, with a .75:1 overdrive ratio. Rear end ratio with a 6-speed transmission depends on tire size as well as intended use, but the 6X gear splits look like they would work well with a 3.54 or 3.73:1 rear gear.

Keisler Engineering has developed an overdrive automatic transmission that bolts to any big-block or Hemi engine. Based on the General Motors 4L60E, the Keisler A41 has a torque capacity of 650 ft-lbs and a .70:1 overdrive ratio.

SOURCE GUIDE

440Source
Lancaster, CA 93534
661-951-3700
www.440source.com

AEM Electronics
Hawthorne, CA 90250
310-484-2322
www.aemelectronics.com

AR Engineering
Wilsonville, OR 97070
www.arengineering.com

ARP, Inc.
Ventura, CA 93003
800-826-3045
www.arp-bolts.com

ATI Performance Products
Baltimore, MD 21207
410-298-4343
www.atiracing.com

Auto Metal Direct
Buford, GA 30518
866-591-8309
www.autometaldirect.com

Baer Brake Systems
Phoenix, AZ 85029
602-233-1411
www.baer.com

BLP Products, Inc.
Orlando, FL 32805
407-422-0394
www.blp.com

Callies Performance Products
Fostoria, OH 44830
419-435-2711
www.callies.com

Calvert Racing Suspensions
Lancaster, CA 93536
661-728-9600
www.calvertracing.com

CAP Auto Products
Detroit, MI 48207
248-757-0367
www.capautoproducts.com

Carbotech Performance Brakes
Concord, NC 28027
877-899-5024
www.ctbrakes.com

CenterForce Clutch
Prescott, AZ 86301
928-771-8422
www.centerforce.com

Cometic Gaskets
Concord, OH 44077
800-752-9850
www.cometic.com

Comp Cams
Memphis, TN 38118
800-999-0853
www.compcams.com

Custom Wire Sets
North Ridgeville, OH 44039
866-973-9473
www.customwiresets.com

Diamond Racing Products
Clinton Twp., MI 48035
877-552-2112
www.diamondracing.net

DoctorDiff
Polson, MT 59860
406-883-4772
www.doctordiff.com

Earl's Performance Plumbing
Rancho Dominquez, CA 90220
310-609-1602
www.earlsplumbing.com

Edelbrock Corp.
Torrance, CA 90503
310-781-2222
www.edelbrock.com

Firm Feel, Inc.
Vancouver, WA 98685
360-546-3633
www.firmfeel.com

Flaming River Industries
Berea, OH 44017
800-648-8022
www.flamingriver.com

G-Force Transmissions
Cleona, PA 17042
717-202-8367
www.gforcetransmissions.com

Gear Vendors, Inc.
El Cajon, CA 92020
800-999-9555
www.gearvendors.com

Griffin Thermal Products
Piedmont, SC 29673
800-722-3723
www.griffinrad.com

Hellwig Products
Visalia, CA 93292
800-435-5944
www.hellwigproducts.com

Holley Performance Products
Bowling Green, KY 42102
270-782-2900
www.holley.com

Hotchkis Performance
Santa Fe Springs, CA 90670
888-735-6425
www.hotchkis.net

Hughes Engines
Washington, IL 61571
309-745-9558
www.hughesengines.com

Hurst Driveline Conversions
Vista, CA 92081
760-598-2244
www.hurst-drivelines.com

Indy Cylinder Heads
Indianapolis, IN 46239
317-862-3724
www.indyheads.com

Imperial Services
Frankenmuth, MI 48734
989-652-6309
www.imperialservices.net

K1 Technologies
Byron Center, MI 49315
616-583-9700
www.k1technologies.com

Keisler Engineering
Rockford, TN 37853
888-609-0094
www.keislerauto.com

Keith Black Racing Engines
South Gate, CA 90280
562-869-1518
www.keithblack.com

Koffel's Place
Huron, OH 44839
419-433-4410
www.b1heads.com

SOURCE GUIDE

JE Pistons
Huntington Beach, CA 92649
714-898-9764
www.jepistons.com

Koleno Performance
Griffith, IN 46319
219-924-9247
www.kolenoperformance.com

Longacre Racing Products
Monroe, WA 98272
360-453-2030
www.longacreracing.com

Magnum Force Race Car Fabrication
Campbell, CA 95008
408-559-6633
www.magnumforce.com

Mancini Racing
Clinton Twp., MI 48035
586-790-4100
www.manciniracing.com

McLeod Racing
Placentia, CA 92870
714-630-2764
www.mcleodracing.com

Mega Parts
Coon Valley, WI 54623
608-452-2045
www.megapartsusa.com

Meziere Enterprises
Escondido, CA 92029
800-208-1755
www.meziere.com

Milodon, Inc.
Chatsworth, CA 91311
818-407-1211
www.milodon.com

Modern Cylinder Head
Clinton Twp., MI 48036
586-468-7914
www.moderncylinderhead.com

MSD Ignition
El Paso, TX 79936
915-857-5200
www.msdignition.com

Oil Filter Service Co.
Portland, OR 97214
888-232-5126
www.oilfilterserviceco.com

Passon Performance
Sugarloaf, PA 18249
570-401-8949
www.passonperformance.com

Pertronix Performance Products
San Dimas, CA 91773
909-599-5955
www.pertronix.com

PRW Industries
Orange, CA 92867
714-792-1000
www.prwindustries.com

QuickTime, Inc.
Oskaloosa, IA 52577
641-673-4468
www.quicktimeinc.com

Race Car Dynamics
El Cajon, CA 92020
619-588-4723
www.racecardynamics.com

RedLine Oil
Benicia, CA 94510
707-745-6100
www.redlineoil.com

Reilly Motorsports
White Have, PA 18661
570-443-7440
www.reillymotorsports.com

Richmond Gear
Liberty, SC 29657
864-843-9231
www.richmondgear.com

Rocker Arm Specialist
Anderson, CA 96007
530-378-1075
www.rockerarms.com

SCAT Enterprises, Inc.
Redondo Beach, CA 90278
310-370-5501
www.scatcrankshafts.com

Schumacher Creative Services
Seattle, WA 98125
206-364-7151
www.engine-swaps.com

Shady Dell Speed Shop
Port Matilda, PA 16870
814-692-4232
www.shadydellspeedshop.com

Smith Bros. Pushrods
Bend, OR 97701
800-367-1533
www.pushrods.net

SSBC Performance Brake Systems
800-448-7722
www.ssbrakes.com

Superformance Products
Akron, OH 44319
866-925-7855
www.superformanceproducts.com

TCI Automotive
Ashland, MS 38603
888-776-9824
www.tciauto.com

TTi Performance Exhaust
Corona, CA 92880
951-371-4878
www.ttiexhaust.com

Wilwood Engineering
Camarillo, CA
805-388-1188
www.wilwood.com

World Products
Ronkonkoma, NY 11779
631-981-1918
www.worldcastings.com

XV Motorsports
Irvington, NY 10533
914-693-1122
www.xvmotorsports.com

www.ingramcontent.com/pod-product-compliance
Lightning Source LLC
Chambersburg PA
CBHW051414070526
44584CB00023B/3422